Money

Mohammad Ashraf

Money

Understandings and Misunderstandings

palgrave
macmillan

Mohammad Ashraf
Department of Economics and Decision Sciences
The University of North Carolina at Pembroke
Pembroke, NC, USA

ISBN 978-3-030-50377-2 ISBN 978-3-030-50378-9 (eBook)
https://doi.org/10.1007/978-3-030-50378-9

This Palgrave Macmillan imprint is published by the registered company Springer Nature Switzerland AG
The registered company address is: Gewerbestrasse 11, 6330 Cham, Switzerland

To those who set out for Ithaka.

Preface

I wrote this book to clarify the *concept* of money and how money facilitates a smooth functioning of the economy. Depending upon one's lack of understanding, often the conduct of monetary policy—changes in money supply by the Federal Reserve System (the Fed), central bank of the United States—is considered shady if not outright illegal. In the aftermath of the 2007–2009 financial crisis and the Great Recession that followed, the Fed significantly increased money supply. The terms "quantitative easing" became ubiquitous in the media and everyday discourse. Critiques of the Fed's actions followed.

Movements that call for the Fed to close its door resurfaced. Ron Paul, former Congressman from Texas, wrote a book in 2009 titled *End the Fed*. Mr. Paul dedicated his book to "the young people who … are at the heart of the anti-Fed movement."[1] Rick Perry, who was governor of Texas at the time, was seeking the Republican nomination for the 2012 presidential election. He called the actions of the Chairman of the Fed at the time, Mr. Ben Bernanke, "treasonous." In a campaign stop in Iowa on August 16, 2011, he reiterated his opposition to the Fed's stance. "I don't know what y'all would do to him in Iowa, but we would treat him pretty ugly

[1] Ron Paul's book dedication. Ron Paul. *End the Fed*. New York, NY: Grand Central Publishing, 2009. Print.

down in Texas," said Mr. Perry referring to Mr. Bernanke.[2] Even some professional economists, academics, and financial market players urged the Fed to reconsider its stance. They feared that the Fed's actions would lead to "currency debasement and inflation."[3]

The concept of money remains elusive to many. Worse still, misinformation abounds. From financial TV pundits, to self-help gurus, to hucksters of the Prosperity Gospel,[4] and everyone in between, stand ready to impart words of wisdom. Lack of expertise in economic matters is not an impediment. All telling those seeking advice that they can get wealthy without having to work. Or some version of it.

Jim Cramer's CNBC Website states that, "Mad Money with Jim Cramer takes viewers inside the mind of one of Wall Street's most respected and successful money managers. Cramer is your personal guide through the confusing jungle of Wall Street investing, navigating through opportunities and pitfalls with one goal in mind—to help you make money."[5]

Tony Robbins is a self-help guru who purports to teach you how to be happy and realize your full potential. In his sold-out seminars, among other acts, he teaches the attendees how to walk on fire. He also sells physical training videos and supplements on his Website.[6] The magazine, *Money*, had a cover story on Tony Robbins in its May 2017 issue. John "Jack" Bogle, the founder of Vanguard Fund interviewed Mr. Robbins. "TONY ROBBINS WANTS TO MAKE YOU RICH," was imprinted in bold letters on the cover with Robbins's picture showing him with a huge smile, his teeth on full display.

Perhaps the lack of knowledge about money and monetary policy is not exactly the fault of public either. Keeping the actions of central banks

[2] Rick Perry on Ben Bernanke. https://www.nytimes.com/2011/08/17/us/politics/17perry.html. (Accessed: May 17, 2020)

[3] Open letter to Ben Bernanke. https://www.hoover.org/research/open-letter-ben-bernanke. (Accessed: May 17, 2020)

[4] Prosperity Gospel. Kate Bowler. *Blessed: A History of the American Prosperity Gospel.* New York: Oxford University Press, 2013. Print.

[5] Jim Cramer, TV pundit. https://www.cnbc.com/mad-money/. (Accessed: June 5, 2019)

[6] Tony Robbins. https://www.tonyrobbins.com/. (Accessed: June 5, 2019)

secret was considered a valued tool in the conduct of monetary policy, and "mumbling with great incoherence" was a skill much valued in a central banker.[7] It was the understanding of monetary economists that for monetary policy to take effect it has to have an unanticipated component. It is relatively recently that this understanding in the discipline has changed.[8] Nowadays transparency is considered imperative for the conduct of monetary policy and the smooth functioning of the economy.

A lot changed over the course of writing this book. The Fed increased and decreased money supply, and then increased it again. When the manuscript was in its final stages, the Coronavirus (COVID-19) engulfed the globe. Due to the COVID-19 the world economy practically shut down. To provide support to the US economy the Fed had to increase money supply. This world event renewed public's interest in the Fed's and other central banks' actions, making the topic of this book ever more relevant.

In this book I use the terms "pecunia" and its plural "pecunae" to represent money. This is as opposed to using dollar, pound, the euro, or any other name for currency. The purpose behind coining these terms was to start the reader afresh and baggage-free. During the spring semester of 2020 one of the classes I taught was International Trade. I used the Krugman, Obstfeld, and Melitz textbook for this course.[9] I was reviewing this textbook during the fall semester of 2019 and over the Holidays before the spring 2020 semester. To my surprise Krugman *et al.* had already used pecunia, as in the "Bank of Pecunia" in Chapter 18. And I thought I was an original in coining these terms.

Finally, to all my friends and colleagues, please know that I remain ever grateful for your help and encouragement throughout the process of writing this book. Usually authors provide a list of names of individuals

[7] Alan Greenspan quote. Alan S. Blinder, et al. "Central Bank Communication and Monetary Policy: A Survey of Theory and Evidence." *Journal of Economic Literature* 46.4 (2008): 910–945. *JSTOR*. Web.

[8] Secrecy in central banks. Alan S. Blinder, et al. "Central Bank Communication and Monetary Policy: A Survey of Theory and Evidence." *Journal of Economic Literature* 46.4 (2008): 910–945. *JSTOR*. Web., Alan S. Blinder. *The Quiet Revolution: Central Banking Goes Modern*. New Haven, Conn.; London: Yale University Press, 2004, 2004. Web.

[9] Krugman, et al. textbook. Paul R. Krugman, Maurice Obstfeld, and Marc J. Melitz. *International Economics: Theory and Policy*. 11th ed. New York, NY: Pearson, 2018. Print.

who have been helpful during the writing of a manuscript. I will avoid providing such a list for fear of leaving someone out.

Sincerely,

Mohammad Ashraf
May 2020

Contents

List of Figures

List of Tables

CHAPTER 1

Why Another Book About Money?

In 1787, John Adams, who later served as the 2nd President of the United States, wrote in a letter to Thomas Jefferson, who later served as the 3rd President of the United States:

> All the Perplexities, Confusions and Distresses in America arise not from defects in their Constitutions or Confederation, not from a want of Honour [*sic*] or Virtue, So much as from downright Ignorance of the Nature of Coin, Credit and Circulation.[1]

Why another book about money? Because misunderstandings remain. While the *phenomenon* of money is ubiquitous and has been for tens of thousands of years—we all use money to buy and sell goods and services, as did our ancestors in one form or another—for many, however, the *concept* of money remains elusive. These misunderstandings are not benign. On the one hand, this lack of understanding unfairly treats the professionals who deal with money, underestimates the value of their services, and undermines the institutional setup that a modern economy needs. On the other hand, this misunderstanding leaves us all exposed to

[1] Letter of John Adams to Thomas Jefferson. John Adams and Lester J. Cappon. *The Adams-Jefferson Letters: The Complete Correspondence Between Thomas Jefferson and Abigail and John Adams*. Chapel Hill, NC: Published for the Omohundro Institute of Early American History and Culture, Williamsburg, VA, by the University of North Carolina Press, 1987. Web.

M. Ashraf, *Money*,
https://doi.org/10.1007/978-3-030-50378-9_1

frauds by those who see room for exploitation. Lured by the promises of getting rich overnight, the uninitiated are robbed of their savings by the likes of Bernie Madoff to Jim Cramer of the TV show "Mad Money" on CNBC, to the purveyors of the Prosperity Gospel, to the self-help gurus like Tony Robbins. The list goes on. This introductory chapter provides an overview of the topics covered in the rest of the book.

1.1 From Bands of Hunter-Gatherers to Farmers

Researchers have found artifacts in the Chinese Loess Plateau that date back to about 2.12 million years ago. These findings were reported in an article published on July 11, 2018, in the journal *Nature*.[2] The authors of the article reported that an earlier branch of human ancestors that separated from those of modern-day chimpanzees from our common ancestor, called *Hominin*, used stone tools. These findings indicate that these ancestors of modern-day humans knew how to make flint blades, attach them to wooden handles to hunt, and knew how to make fire. These ancestors of modern humans lived in bands of hunter-gatherers and ventured out for miles in search of food. It is not too much of a stretch of imagination to suggest that while they shared food and exchanged favors with their band members, they probably also exchanged food and favors with other bands. Banding together against a common enemy is certainly a good survival strategy, and exchanging food and favors is a good strategy to form bonds.

Our human ancestors domesticated maize and other varieties of cereals and became sedentary around 70,000 years ago. They learned to farm around 10,000 years ago. Farming "emerged in seven or eight regions across the world, almost simultaneously at the beginning of the Holocene: in the Levant, in North and South China, in New Guinea and Ethiopia, and in eastern North America, Mesoamerica, and South America, all during the chronological window from 11,500 to 3500 years ago," writes Jean-Pierre Bocquet-Appel. With this agricultural revolution, known as the Neolithic Revolution, population density also increased and "the number of potential mouths it was possible to feed," from "0.05 people

[2] Use of tools by human ancestors. Zhaoyu Zhu, et al. "Hominin Occupation of the Chinese Loess Plateau Since About 2.1 Million Years Ago." *Nature* 559.7715 (2018): 608–12. Web.

per [kilometer] with the foraging system as against 54 today."[3] Farming provided relatively safer environment better suited for survival. Group sizes increased. With the advent of farming, the need for exchanging food and favors increased further.

In order to take advantage of a larger group size, and the social complexities that accompany, our ancestors needed larger brains. There is evidence of a positive correlation between the brain-sizes (especially the size of neocortex) of primates and group sizes.[4] Evidence further suggests that as the group size increases, time constraint puts a limit on social activities an individual can partake. Along with grooming, which creates social bonding, other social activities may include "play, courtship and mating, agonistic interactions, territorial behaviour [*sic*]."[5] Studies show that once group size reaches about 40, complexities of social life reach to the point where social cohesion suffers and fission takes place.[6] One band is divided into two, or more.

Division, however, has costs as well—fewer bodies to lend a hand. A larger band is better suited, not only to hunt and find food but also to fend against attacks by rival bands as well. A way to deal with the chaos resulting from a larger group size is to come up with rules.

> Among one group of social animals—the human species—social interaction advanced far beyond that possible among any other animal groups. This occurred through the rise of *culture*, which permitted coordinated behavior more varied and precise than anything previously known. Through the

[3] Emergence of farming. Jean Bocquet-Appel. "When the World's Population Took Off: The Springboard of the Neolithic Demographic Transition." *Science* 333.6042 (2011): 560–61. *JSTOR*. Web.

[4] Brian size and group size. Robin Dunbar. "Neocortex Size as a Constraint on Group Size in Primates." *Journal of Human Evolution* 22.6 (1992). Print, H. Kudo and Robin Dunbar. "Neocortex Size and Social Network Size in Primates." *Animal Behaviour* 62.4 (2001): 711–22. Print, J. Lehmann, A. H. Korstjens, and Robin Dunbar. "Groups Size, Grooming and Social Cohesion in Primates." *Animal Behaviour* 74.6 (2007): 1617–29. Print, Robert L. Carneiro. "The Evolution of Complexity in Human Societies and Its Mathematical Expression." *International Journal of Comparative Sociology (Brill Academic Publishers)* 28.3 (1987): 111–28. Web.

[5] Social activities. Lehmann, Korstjens, and Dunbar: 1617–29.

[6] Social cohesion suffers. J. Lehmann, A. H. Korstjens, and Robin Dunbar. "Groups Size, Grooming and Social Cohesion in Primates." *Animal Behaviour* 74.6 (2007): 1617–29. Print.

cohesiveness of social structure that culture made possible, the genus *Homo* grew, spread, and prospered as no other. [italics original] (p. 112)

Writes Robert Carneiro.[7] "[W]e might say that social evolution is largely the struggle to increase *structure* in proportion to *size*," [italics original] argues Carneiro (p. 115).[8] He goes on to write that, "[W]e might say that autonomous villages ... become increasingly unstable as they grow larger but fail to develop their structure accordingly" (p. 122). Because larger group sizes offer economic and survival benefits at the cost of social cohesion, the cost-benefit analysis has to have been the source of decision that led to the invention of some means of remembering favors received and rendered.

1.2 The Need to Invent a Numeraire: The Functional Limits of Barter Exchange

It is not a fanciful speculation to suggest that as the band members increased in number, and the number of favors rendered and received, inter-band and intra-band, increased, they had to come up with some way to keep track of transactions; they had to use a numeraire. The reason? Barter—exchanging goods and services for other goods and services—can become infeasible in a short order. Let me give an example.

Suppose that there are two goods. Call them Good A and Good B. To make things simple, suppose also that both Good A and Good B are of only one kind and quality. How much is Good A worth in terms of Good B? Simple. Compare Good A with Good B and one gets the value of Good A in terms of Good B, and vice versa. If the producer of Good A wants to exchange Good A for Good B, all she has to do is to offer a quantity of equivalent value of Good A to the producer of Good B and the exchange can take place. Of course, I am assuming here that the producer of Good B wants to make the exchange. This is what economists call "double co-incidence of wants." That is, for this exchange to take place, the producer of Good A has to want Good B, and the producer of

[7] Increase in numbers and the complexity of society. Carneiro: 111–28.

[8] Structure and group size. Robert L. Carneiro. "The Evolution of Complexity in Human Societies and Its Mathematical Expression." *International Journal of Comparative Sociology (Brill Academic Publishers)* 28.3 (1987): 111–28. Web.

Good B has to want Good A. This is important. If either of them does not want what the other has to offer, the exchange does not take place.

Make the situation just a bit more complicated. Suppose that there are four goods—Good A, Good B, Good C, and Good D. Continue supposing that each good is produced only in one kind and quality. If one wants to exchange one good for the other one has to come up with a value of one good in terms of the other good or goods. Add another little wrinkle. Suppose that the producer of Good A wants Good B, but the producer of Good B wants Good C. The producer of Good C, however, wants Good D, and not Good B. But the producer of Good D does not want Good B. She wants Good A. The coincidence of wants does not exist—each wants what the other does not have to offer.

All is not lost, however. The producer of Good A can exchange Good A with the producer of Good D. Take Good D to the producer of Good C. Get Good C, take it to the producer to Good B, and exchange Good C for Good B. Notice that we are supposing away the possibility that the producer of each good want the other good in a whole unit, and not a part of one good and a part of another good or goods. We are assuming away the possibility that the vintner wants stake for dinner and not the whole cow. Even with this extreme simplification, the level of complication seems head spinning. We need to know how much is Good A in terms of Good D. We also need to know how much is Good B in terms of Good C, and we need to know how much is Good C in terms of Good D. The number of evaluations is three. When we add a bit realistic condition that the producer of, say, Good A may want part of Good B, part of Good C, and part of Good D, assuming, of course, that goods are divisible. Same goes for the producers of Good B, Good C, and Good D. How many evaluations does one need to perform? The answer is six evaluations. How much is Good A worth in terms of Good B? How much is Good A worth in terms of Good C? How much is Good A worth in terms of Good D? How much is Good B worth in terms of Good C? And so on. The formula for the number of evaluations needed is $\left[\frac{n \times (n-1)}{2}\right]$, where n is the number of goods.

Of course, in a modern economy, there are far more than four goods and services that are exchanged, and each usually comes in numerous kinds and qualities. Looking at the various products produced in the United States gives an idea about the complexity of the issue. The United States Census Bureau, in partnership with its Canadian and Mexican

Table 1.1 The North American Product Classification System (NAPCS) codes of fresh vegetables

[1]	*[2]*
NAPCS Code	Category
1110112	Fresh vegetables
111011201	Leafy or stem vegetables
11101120101	Asparagus
11101120102	Cabbages
11101120103	Cauliflowers and broccoli
11101120104	Lettuce and chicory
11101120105	Spinach
11101120106	Artichokes
11101120107	Other leafy or stem vegetables

Source Table prepared by the author. *Data Source* https://www.census.gov/eos/www/napcs/index.html (Accessed: May 21, 2018)

counterparts, classifies various products produced in the three-country region in what is called the North American Product Classification System (NAPCS).[9] It is a hierarchical classification system. That is, it starts with a main category of products. Then each category is subdivided into more detailed categories. There are over 2100 main categories in NAPCS. For instance, various edible products fall under the classification: "Food, beverage, and tobacco products, except raw farm products." The NAPCS code for this category is 11. Fresh vegetables are part of food. Their NAPCS code is 1110112. Fresh vegetables, however, can be of numerous sub-categories. In Table 1.1, I provide sub-categories of fresh vegetables and their NAPCS codes.

Products in each sub-category may have varying quality; asparagus may vary by color, size, freshness, etc. It is easy to see that without a numeraire life becomes complicated rather quickly. So come up with a numeraire humans did. Today, we call this numeraire money. For something to function as money, it has to have three characteristic. It is something that people want to accept in exchange for their goods and services—a medium of exchange; they can use it to evaluate those goods and services—a unit of account; and they can transfer the value of these goods and services from the present to the future—a store of value. Nothing more, nothing less.

[9] North American Product Classification System. https://www.census.gov/eos/www/napcs/index.html (Accessed: May 21, 2018).

1.3 Overcoming Brain Limitations

How could a limited-sized brain that could not remember the favors rendered and received come up with such a device—a numeraire—you may ask? This is not as strange as it may sound. Humans have overcome brain-size limitations imposed upon by the evolutionary process through work-arounds. Think of four and higher dimensions. Our brains evolved in a three-dimensional space, and while not able to visualize higher dimensions, are able to come up with (perhaps more appropriately stated, discovered)[10] tools, i.e., mathematics, that allow us to overcome this limitation.

Let us walk through an example. Start with a two-dimensional space, say, height and width. We can all visualize height and width. Let us represent height by letter y, and width by letter x. We may represent this two-dimensional space, S_2, mathematically as follows.

$$S_2 = f_2(x, y)$$

The subscripts on S and f represent the number of dimensions. When students learn how to draw and interpret a two-dimensional diagram, they learn how to graphically represent such an idea. They learn how to plot one variable along the vertical axis, often referred to as the y-axis, and the other variable along the horizontal axis, often called the x-axis. For instance, one may plot time along the horizontal axis and income along the vertical axis. In Fig. 1.1, I have plotted the overall output of the US economy (along the vertical axis) from the first quarter of 1947 to the first quarter of 2017 (along the horizontal axis). The data are in inflation-adjusted billions of US dollars. I will go into more details about the concept of real output versus nominal output in Chapter 7.

Add depth to these two dimensions to make the space three-dimensional. This is the space in which our "neural architecture" evolved, as the physicist Leonard Susskind of the Stanford Institute of Theoretical Physics put it.[11] We can represent these three dimensions mathematically and visualize them. Let us represent height by letter y, width by letter x,

[10] Discovery of tools of mathematics. See Mohammad Ashraf. *Formal and Informal Social Safety Nets: Growth and Development in the Modern Economy*. New York, NY: Palgrave Macmillan, 2014. Print, Chapter 4, and the references cited therein.

[11] Leonard Susskind explains higher dimensions. https://www.youtube.com/watch?v=2bgZmBAnhdg&list=WL&index=49&t=0s (Accessed: June 16, 2019).

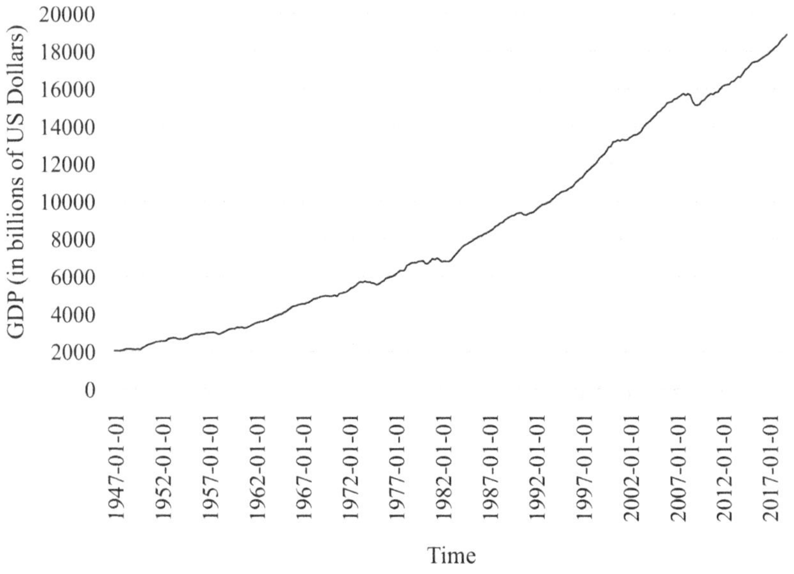

Fig. 1.1 Real gross domestic product of the United States (*Source* Figure prepared by the author. *Data Source* US Bureau of Economic Analysis. www.bea.gov [Accessed: June 16, 2019])

and depth by letter z. We may write this space, S_3, as follows.

$$S_3 = f_3(x, y, z)$$

A two-dimensional analog of this three-dimensional function is presented in Fig. 1.2. Note that the object is drawn on a two-dimensional page. Because of the shading, which gives the illusion of depth, however, our brain interprets it as a three-dimensional object.

This is as far as our visualization abilities go. Tools of mathematics, however, allow us to overcome this limitation. Suppose that we want to talk about a four-dimensional space. All we have to do is to add another letter, say, v. We may write this as follows.

$$S_4 = f_4(x, y, z, v)$$

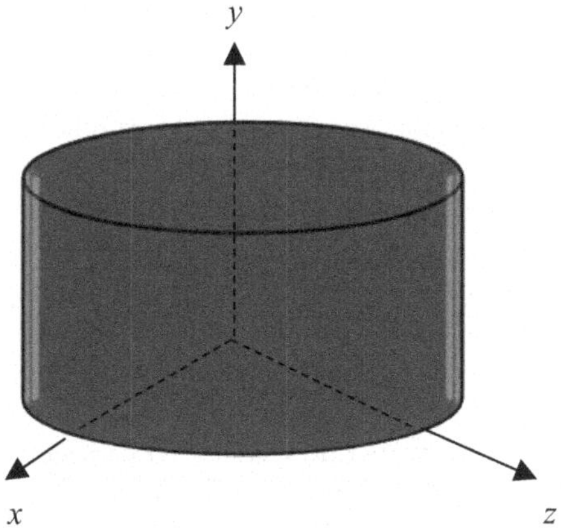

Fig. 1.2 A three-dimensional representation (*Source* Figure prepared by the author)

In fact, we can represent any number of dimensions this way. Say we want to represent an eleven-dimensional space. We may do so as follows.

$$S_{11} = f_{11}(x_1, x_2, x_3, x_4, x_5, x_6, x_7, x_8, x_9, x_{10}, x_{11})$$

Here, the subscripts of *x*s each represent a different dimension. Your imagination and mathematical skills are the only limits.

1.4 Misunderstandings Run Deep

We saw earlier that money was something that could be used as a medium of exchanges, as a unit of account, and as a store of value. Misunderstanding, however, about what money is, and what it is not, run deep and have a long history. In one form or another, misunderstandings about money are probably as old as money. For many, money is considered the root cause of all evil. In the New Testament, stories of Jesus cleansing the Temple of money changers and merchants appear in Gospels of Mathew (21: 12–17), Mark (11: 15–19), Luke (19: 45–48), and John (2: 13–14). In *Hamlet* Polonius advises Laertes to stay away from lending and borrowing as Laertes embarks on a journey.[12] Franklin Delano Roosevelt, the 32nd President of the United States, in his inaugural address on

[12] *Hamlet*, Act 1, Scene 3.

March 4, 1933, made reference to the "unscrupulous money changers."[13] Even before that, such had been the mistrust of banks that in 1840 the Congress passed the Independent Treasury Act. The Act dictated that the US Treasury, as opposed to commercial banks, would handle government receipts and payments.[14]

Usury, i.e., charging and paying interest, is considered one of the major sins in the Old Testament, the New Testament, and the Quran. Religious texts warn believers to stay away from interest. Interest, however, is nothing more than the rent for the use of money. Somehow it is considered perfectly fine when someone builds a house with one's saving and rents the house to someone who is looking for an abode. However, when someone rents one's saving to someone who wants an abode and charges rent for the saving, it is considered a sin. In the eyes of believers, the former is fine while the latter is an abomination.

While the complexity of human societies has increased tremendously since our hunter-gatherer bands, our instincts, our "gut-feelings," which evolved over millions of years prior to the advent of a modern complex society, have not kept up; we need formal education to stay abreast. Few among us can master all the knowledge that we, as humans, possess as a whole. While relying on our gut-feelings was enough in our early evolutionary history, it no longer is.

According to Steven Pinker[15]:

> Evolution left us with another burden: our cognitive, emotional, and moral faculties are adapted to individual survival and reproduction in an archaic environment, not to universal thriving in a modern one. To appreciate this burden, one doesn't have to believe that we are cavemen out of time, only that evolution, with its speed limit measured in generations, could not possibly have adapted our brains to modern technology and institutions. Humans today rely on cognitive faculties that worked well

[13] F. D. Roosevelt. *Inaugural Address*. New York: Modern Eloquence Corporation, 1933.

[14] Independent Treasury Act. https://fraser.stlouisfed.org/files/docs/bankunitedstates/bankoftheunitedstates_house_floyd_18400611.pdf (Accessed: July 12, 2019), https://fraser.stlouisfed.org/files/docs/historical/nmc/nmc_587_1910.pdf (Accessed: July 12, 2019). See also James N. Primm. *A Foregone Conclusion: The Founding of the Federal Reserve Bank of St. Louis*. Federal Reserve Bank of St. Louis, 1989. Print.

[15] The burden of evolution. Steven Pinker. *Enlightenment Now: The Case for Reason, Science, Humanism, and Progress*. New York: Penguin Books, 2018. Print.

enough in traditional societies, but which we now see are infested with bugs. (p. 25)

These "bugs" in our cognitive faculties also affect our understanding of how an economy works, what money is, and what role money plays in the functioning of the economy. One has to actively learn how to overcome these constraints imposed by our evolutionary past. After all, we have been able to overcome the limitations of a brain that evolved in a three-dimensional space. Formal education and concerted effort are the keys.

But that was then. We have learned an awful lot since those "dark ages," one may argue.

True, we have learned a lot through experience and formal education. Confusions still remain.

On July 13, 2011, there was a memorable and telling moment on the Capitol Hill. Ben Bernanke, the Federal Reserve Chair at the time, was testifying in front of the Committee on Financial Services. The following is an excerpt from the exchange that took place between Ron Paul, Congressman from Texas, and Ben Bernanke. Congressman Paul asked Chairman Bernanke.[16]

I am curious about the price of gold today is $1,580. The dollar during these last 3 years was devalued almost 50 percent. When you wake up in the morning, do you care about the price of gold?

Mr. BERNANKE. I pay attention to the price of gold, but I think it reflects a lot of things. It reflects global uncertainties. I think the reason people hold gold is as a protection against what we call tail risk, really, really bad outcomes. To the extent that the last few years have made people more worried about the potential of a major crisis, then they have gold as a protection.

Dr. PAUL. Do you think gold is money?

Mr. BERNANKE. No, it is not money; it is a precious metal.

[16] Ron Paul exchange with Ben Bernanke. https://www.gpo.gov/fdsys/pkg/CHRG-112hhrg67941/pdf/CHRG-112hhrg67941.pdf (Accessed: June 3, 2018). See also https://www.youtube.com/watch?v=iKYKLgzyF9o (Accessed: March 19, 2018).

Dr. PAUL. Even if it has been money for 6,000 years, somebody reversed that and eliminated that economic law?

Mr. BERNANKE. It is an asset. Would you say Treasury bills are money? I do not think they are money either, but they are a financial asset.

Dr. PAUL. Why do central banks hold it?

Mr. BERNANKE. It is a form of reserves.

Dr. PAUL. Why do not they hold diamonds?

Mr. BERNANKE. It is tradition, a long-term tradition.

Dr. PAUL. Some people still think it is money. I yield back. My time is up.

But that was in 2011, some may argue. Let me give two more recent examples. Senator Ted Cruz showed support for a gold standard in 2016.[17] As recently as May 7, 2019, Congressman Alexander Mooney of West Virginia introduced a bill (H.R. 2558) in the House that would fix the US dollar to gold.[18] According to the Bill,

Effective 30 months after the date of enactment of this Act—

(1) the Secretary of the Treasury (in this Act referred to as the "Secretary") shall define the dollar in terms of a fixed weight of gold, based on that day's closing market price of gold; and
(2) Federal Reserve Banks shall make Federal Reserve notes exchangeable with gold at the statutory gold definition of the dollar.

As of this writing, the Bill has not progressed any further.

The arguments between hard money (i.e., specie money or specie-backed paper money) versus fiat money are nothing new, of course. Indeed, at times the arguments have turned bloody. Here is an example

[17] Ted Cruz support for gold standard. https://www.washingtonpost.com/news/wonk/wp/2016/02/23/this-might-be-ted-cruzs-worst-idea/?utm_term=.b6e50d10fb75 (Accessed: July 12, 2019).

[18] Congressman Mooney's House Bill to fix dollar's value in terms of gold. https://www.congress.gov/bill/116th-congress/house-bill/2558/text?r=19&s=1 (Accessed: July 12, 2019).

of an event that took place in 1831. Nicholas Biddle was the President of the Second Bank of the United States. His brother, Major Thomas Biddle, who had fought in the War of 1812, was a director of the St. Louis branch of the Bank, got into an argument about money with Congressman Spencer Pettis of Missouri. Pettis was an ardent hard-money supporter. Thomas Biddle's brother, the President of the Second Bank of the United States, was a supporter of "bank money." At one point, the argument between Thomas Biddle and Spencer Pettis heated to the point that Pettis questioned Biddle's honor. A duel ensued. Both suffered injuries, which led to the death of both participants.[19]

1.5 Our Reptilian Brains

At some level, it is not surprising that the concept of money is confusing to so many. After all, we are trying to understand a modern concept with a rather primitive brain that evolved in very simple environments to perform simple tasks. In that environment, there was no distinction between a tree trunk and what it represented—a tree trunk was a tree trunk. There was no difference between a stone and what it represented—a stone was a stone. There was no difference between the concept and the phenomenon. The world today is much too complicated for the primitive mind to comprehend using simple rules of thumb. A piece of paper is not necessarily just a piece of paper. It represents one thing with certain markings on it and it represents a completely different thing with different markings on it. Reason is needed to make sense of it all. And while we are living in a time period in recorded history, which by all measurable accounts is the safest and most advanced,[20] scientific way to thinking—primacy of reason and evidence—is lacking.

Here is an example. At the start of the current millennium, the United Nations established a set of goals to be achieved by 2015 and beyond. The list included eradication of extreme poverty, achieving universal primary education, promotion of gender equality, reduction in child mortality, improved maternal health, combating HIV/AIDs and other diseases,

[19] Thomas Biddle's death in duel. Bray Hammond. "Jackson, Biddle, and the Bank of the United States." *The Journal of Economic History* 7.1 (1947): 1–23. *JSTOR*. Web.

[20] Safest time in history. Steven Pinker. *The Better Angels of Our Nature: Why Violence Has Declined*. New York: Penguin Books, 2011. Print, Pinker.

environmental sustainability, and global cooperation.[21] We have made progress on all these goals and we have data to show it, the impression of the public, however, is that the world is in a downward slide. Yes, there are ups and downs along the way the trend nevertheless is positive.

Why this pessimistic view of the world? One reason is that we confuse *now*—a moment in time—with the *trend*. As Steven Pinker points out, in the *now* there are news stories of hurricanes, droughts, wars, strongmen (almost all of them are men) gaining power and forming illiberal governments. It does not make the news when life is moving in a smooth fashion. The absence of death, absence of illiteracy, absence of droughts and famines, a female walking safely on a street alone at night, do not make the news. As a result, these events do not stick in our memory.[22] Only shocking events make the news and catch our attention. "It is the nature of the grotesque things that you cannot look away," said Pete Buttigieg, the mayor of South Bend, Indiana, in an interview with Chris Wallace of the *Fox News* on March 17, 2019.[23]

Given our evolutionary past, it is no wonder that a large majority of us falls prey to superstitions. This majority is beholden to magical thinking, as opposed to scientific thinking. It believes in miracles, angles, and relies on gut-feelings. "*I could just feel it*," they say. Above all, a majority among us shows a deference, indeed reverence, to the purveyors of such unscientific beliefs—rabbis, priests, pastors, imams, gurus, and their ilk.

Take the example of the United States. A large majority still believes in someone or something named "God," according to the Pew Research Center surveys.[24] Sixty-three percent believe in the existence of God with absolute certainty, and another 20 percent are "fairly certain." God answers our calls for intervention when we are distressed. Fifty-five percent of us pray "[a]t least daily" and another 16 percent pray weekly.[25]

[21] United Nations, Millennium Development Goals. https://www.un.org/millenniumgoals/stats.shtml (Accessed: June 6, 2019).

[22] Smoothly moving life events do not stick our memory. Pinker.

[23] Pete Buttigieg interview with Chris Wallace. https://www.reddit.com/r/Pete_Buttigieg/comments/b2613w/full_pete_interview_on_fox_news_sunday_with_chris/. See also https://www.youtube.com/watch?v=y97QknIG-Eo (Accessed: June 6, 2019).

[24] Belief in God. https://www.pewforum.org/religious-landscape-study/belief-in-god/ (Accessed: May 28, 2019).

[25] Frequency of Prayer. https://www.pewforum.org/religious-landscape-study/frequency-of-prayer/ (Accessed: May 28, 2019).

Seventy-two percent of us believe in a place called Heaven, 21 percent do not, and the rest seven percent fall under "Other/don't know." Fifty-eight percent among us here in the US believe in Hell, 34 percent do not, and the rest 8 percent fall under "Other/don't know." There are differences between religions though. These figures are according to the 2014 survey data.

To appease God, some of us starve ourselves and deny basic necessities of life. The faithful and their allies give numerous rationalizations, from detoxification to spiritual cleansing.[26] Some go even further; they engage in self-flagellation and sacrifice animals to show their devotion at least on an annual basis if not more frequently. Some of us pay financial tributes weekly and/or annually to solicit favors from God or to avoid God's anger, depending upon one's perspective. We pray to alleviate ailments.

But why? Because we, with our primitive brains, think that "words and thoughts can impinge on the physical world in prayers and curses." But why do we keep on doing this? Why do we not stop praying? Steven Pinker[27] argues that because laypersons "underestimate the prevalence of coincidence." And that they "are not so much intuitive scientists as intuitive lawyers and politicians, marshalling evidence that confirms their convictions while dismissing evidence that contradicts them. They overestimate their own knowledge, understanding, rectitude, competence, and luck" (p. 26).

Some of us believe in demons and exorcise them. The Catholic Church has a department devoted to exorcism and holds annual meetings to share new techniques. It teaches a course titled "Exorcism and Prayer of Liberation Course" especially geared to exorcism. Last year was the 14th such course offered, and it was open to all major Christian faiths for the first time, I might add.[28] At the time of this writing, the 15th course of this series was being offered. It is scheduled to run from May 11, 2020, to May 16, 2020, will cost €400.00 (about $450.00). The course will

[26] Fasting as spiritual cleansing. https://www.nytimes.com/2019/05/21/style/self-care/how-the-deprivation-of-ramadan-helps-care-for-the-spirit.html?searchResultPosition=1 (Accessed: May 28, 2019).

[27] Why do we pray? Steven Pinker. *Enlightenment Now: The Case for Reason, Science, Humanism, and Progress*. New York: Penguin Books, 2018. Print.

[28] Course in exorcism, *The Telegraph* link. https://www.telegraph.co.uk/news/2019/05/06/exorcists-different-denominations-gather-first-time-trade-tips/ (Accessed: May 28, 2019).

be taught in Italian. It will cost an extra €300.00 (about $335.00) for an attendee who wants simultaneous translation in English or Spanish. According to the course description, this is

> [t]he first course in the world on the ministry of the exorcism and prayer of liberation, it is organised in collaboration with the Group for Socio-religious Research and Information (GRIS) of Bologna and proposes an academic and interdisciplinary research on the ministry of exorcism and prayer of liberation. The course covers a wide range of issues: anthropological, phenomenological, social, theological, liturgical, canonical, pastoral, spiritual, medical, neuroscientific, pharmacological, symbolic, criminological, legal and juridical ones.[29]

When it comes to evolution and our existence on this planet, according to the Pew Research Center, 33 percent believe that humans evolved "due to natural processes," 25 percent believe that human evolved "due to God's design," and 34 percent believe that human "Always existed in present form."[30]

Perhaps not surprisingly there are differences on these views depending upon one's religious tradition. The Pew Center divides religious traditions into thirteen main categories. These include Buddhist, Catholic, Evangelical Protestant, Hindu, Historically Black Protestant, Jehovah's Witness, Jewish, Mainline Protestant, Mormon, Muslim, Orthodox Christian, Unaffiliated (religious "nones").[31] Differences also exist based on age, gender, race, education level, income, marital status, immigration status, and so on. Rather interestingly belief in God with absolute certainty increases depending upon whether one is a recent immigrant (56 percent), second-generation immigrant (55 percent), or third- or higher-generation immigrant (65 percent). By this measure by the third generation, we have fully assimilated ourselves into the larger US society—the overall society's belief in God with absolute certainty is 63 percent.

Then, there are "New Age" belief systems. According to the Pew Research Center data, about 62 percent of the US adult population

[29] Course in exorcism. https://sacerdos.org/en/exorcism-and-prayer-of-liberation/ (Accessed: May 28, 2019).

[30] Evolution and human existence. https://www.pewforum.org/religious-landscape-study/views-about-human-evolution/ (Accessed: June 3, 2019).

[31] Religion traditions in the US. https://www.pewforum.org/religious-landscape-study/ (Accessed: June 3, 2019).

adheres to at least one of these schools of thought—"belief in reincarnation, astrology, psychics and the presence of spiritual energy in physical objects like mountains or trees."[32] Roughly 41 percent believe in psychics and about 29 percent believe in astrology. Interestingly, about 22 percent of those who consider themselves atheists also hold at least one of these beliefs.

When it comes to political affiliations, Democrats and Democrat-leaning voters are more likely to hold these beliefs as compared with Republican and Republican-leaning voters. Representative Alexandria Ocasio-Cortez shared her birth time with psychic and astrologer Arthur Lipp-Bonewits. He created and publically shared her "birth chart/star chart." Tara Isabella Burton of *The American Interest* writes that, "Ocasio-Cortez's decision to share her birth-time with Lipp-Bonewits might be an unprecedented move for a political figure—Hillary Clinton famously avoided the question, sparking years of debate among astrologers. But it was also a canny one," given that Democrats and Democrat-leaning voters are more likely than Republican and Republican-leaning voters to adhere to the New Age belief systems.[33] According to the Pew Research Center data, 34 percent Republican and Republican-leaning voters "Believe spiritual energy can be located in physical things," whereas 47 percent of Democrats and Democrat-leaning voters hold such beliefs. Thirty-nine percent of Republican and Republican-leaning voters believe in psychics. This is as compared with 41 percent of Democrats and Democrat-leaning voters. Twenty-six percent of Republican and Republican-leaning voters believe in reincarnation, whereas 38 percent of Democrat and Democrat-leaning voters hold this belief. Twenty-four percent of Republican and Republican-leaning voters believe

[32] New Age beliefs. https://www.pewresearch.org/fact-tank/2018/10/01/new-age-beliefs-common-among-both-religious-and-nonreligious-americans/ (Accessed: June 3, 2019).

[33] Alexandria Ocasio-Cortes shares her birth time. https://www.the-american-interest.com/2019/06/07/the-rise-of-progressive-occultism/ (Accessed: June 11, 2019).

in astrology. Compare this with 32 percent of Democrat and Democrat-leaning voters who believe in astrology. Overall 56 percent of Republican and Republican-leaning voters and 67 percent of Democrat and Democrat-leaning voters hold at least one such belief.[34]

Our reptilian brains have a hard time comprehending the wonders of a modern world. Formal training is needed to fix the "bugs" that evolution left behind. To properly understand the concept of money one needs to rely on reason. One needs to understand the relationship between the goods and services sector of the economy and the financial sector of the economy. Money is what is used to exchange goods and services. Money is what is used to evaluate goods and services. Money is what is used to transfer purchasing power from now to the future. One aught not confuse the thing used as money with the goods and services that one exchanges with it. Congressman Ron Paul, Senator Ted Cruz, and Congressman Alexander Mooney (Sect. 1.4) and others who favor a gold standard seem to be confusing one with the other. They seem to be confusing the thing used as money with what it represents. They seem to be having a hard time understanding the relationship between the goods and services sector of the economy and the financial sector of the economy.

1.6 The Desire to Hold onto Something Solid

People, at least some if not most, prefer hard currency—gold, silver, and lately paper currency, etc. This is especially so in times of perceived or actual crises. The reason? People want to hold their financial assets in forms that they deem more reliable. This is another application of Gresham's Law: Bad money drives out good money. Read "bad money" as overvalued money and "good money" as undervalued.

Some clarification about the "Gresham's Law" is in order here.

First, while this insight is attributed to Sir Thomas Gresham, there is no record, as far as I can find, of Gresham being the first observer of this phenomenon. True, Gresham no doubt had a distinguished career—he was a successful merchant, a financial advisor to the English monarchs in the mid-1500s, represented the English Crown in Antwerp under King Edward VI, Queen Mary, and Queen Elizabeth I, founded the London

[34] New-Age belief systems by party affiliation. https://www.pewresearch.org/fact-tank/2018/10/01/new-age-beliefs-common-among-both-religious-and-nonreligious-americans/ (Accessed: June 11, 2019).

Royal Exchange, served as "English Ambassador to the Court of the Regent of the Low Countries," according to Frank Whitson Fetter (1932, p. 480),[35] and upon his death left enough wealth so that the eponymous Gresham College in London could be founded—he was not the one who coined the phrase that "bad money drives out good money." Nor was he the first one to have this insight. Some researchers argue that the Greek philosopher, Aristophanes, understood this phenomenon about half a century BCE,[36] and so did Nicole Oresme and Nicolaus Copernicus after him.[37] Raymond de Roover writes in his book, *Gresham on Foreign Exchange*, that, "Gresham's law was not the invention of Sir Thomas Gresham, but of Henry D. MacLeod, a nineteenth-century economist." He goes on to write that, "Nowhere does Gresham state either explicitly or implicitly that bad money drives out the good" (p. 91).[38]

How did this misattribution come to be? Frank Whitson Fetter[39] traces this misattribution to a letter that Gresham wrote to Queen Elizabeth when she ascended the throne in 1558. "At the time of Gresham's original appointment as financial agent in Antwerp in 1551 or 1552, the English coinage, composed principally of silver, was in a particularly bad state," writes Fetter. Sir Gresham was "commissioned to negotiate a loan in Antwerp." He wrote a letter to Queen Elizabeth before he embarked on his journey to Antwerp. It was titled "Information of Sir Thomas Gresham, Mercer, towching [sic] the fall of the exchaunge [sic], MDLVIII" (p. 482). The text of the letter, as quoted by Fetter on page 482, is worth presenting here, if for no other reason than to show how language—spelling, syntax, style—changes over time.

[35] Career of Sir Thomas Gresham. Frank Whitson Fetter. "Some Neglected Aspects of Gresham's Law." *The Quarterly Journal of Economics* 46.3 (1932): 480–95. *JSTOR*. Web.

[36] Insight of Aristophanes about bad money driving good money out. Frank Whitson Fetter. "Some Neglected Aspects of Gresham's Law." *The Quarterly Journal of Economics* 46.3 (1932): 480–95. *JSTOR*. Web.

[37] Insights of Oresme and Copernicus about bad money driving good money out. John K. Galbraith. *Money: Whence It Came, Where It Went*. Boston: Houghton Mifflin, 1975. Print.

[38] Henry D. MacLeod as the inventor of Gresham's law. Raymond de Roover. *Gresham on Foreign Exchange: An Essay on Early English Mercantilism with the Text of Sir Thomas Gresham's Memorandum for the Understanding of the Exchange*. Cambridge: Harvard University Press, 1949. Web.

[39] Misattribution of the insight to Gresham. Fetter: 480–95.

> Ytt may pleasse your majesty to understand, thatt the firste occasion of the fall of exchainge did growe by the Kinges majesty, your latte father, in abasinge his quoyne ffrome vi ounces fine too iii ounces fine. Wheruppon the exchainge fell ffrome xxvis. viiid. to xiiis. ivd. which was the occasion thatt all your fine goold was convayd ought of this your realme.[40]

I wonder what the results would be if the school kids competing for the Scripps Spelling Bee award were to spell these words this way.

John Kenneth Galbraith, in his book titled *Money: Whence It Came, Where It Went*[41] writes,

> In the ancient and medieval world the coins of different jurisdictions converged at the major trading cities. If there were any disposition to accept coin on faith, it was inevitably the bad coins that were proffered, the good ones that were retained.... Human nature may be an infinitely variant thing. But it has constants. One is that, given a choice, people keep what is best for themselves, i.e., for those whom they love the most. (p. 10)

As I mentioned earlier, people want to hold their financial assets in forms that they think are more reliable. Reliable in the sense that the asset will be broadly acceptable and maintain its value. Take the example to two forms of money—a twenty-dollar bill and an electronic record of a bank stating that you have twenty dollars in the account and that you are authorized to write a check in that amount. While the value of the bill and the value of the check are equal, it is more likely that in times of crisis a twenty-dollar bill will be more readily acceptable than a check written of equal amount. As a consequence, when you are expecting a crisis on the horizon, you are more likely to hold the twenty-dollar bill than leave the amount in the bank or hold a check. Now compare holding a twenty-dollar bill versus a piece of gold of equivalent value. Assuming that people have more faith in gold than in a twenty-dollar bill, you are more likely to hold gold than a twenty-dollar bill.

In fact, there need not be any crisis on the horizon. You must have noticed (perhaps you have done it yourself) that when someone has two

[40] Text of the letter to Queen Elizabeth from Sir Gresham. Frank Whitson Fetter. "Some Neglected Aspects of Gresham's Law." *The Quarterly Journal of Economics* 46.3 (1932): 480–95. *JSTOR*. Web.

[41] John Kenneth Galbraith on Gresham's law. Galbraith.

bills of equal amount and one bill is wrinkled and the other is not, often people give out the wrinkled bill and keep the unwrinkled in their wallet: we *assign* a higher value to the latter even though both bills carry equal purchasing power.

1.7 What to Expect in Chapters to Come

To get a deeper understanding of what money is and what functions it performs, one has to define money is a more precise manner. Chapter 2 does this. It takes us to Modelville, a fictional town, and lets us observe the economic activities taking place in the microcosm of this fictional downtown on a Friday afternoon.

What forms have been used as money over the ages? How did we move from one form of money to the other? What led to the use of paper as money? When did paper currency become inconvertible into gold and silver? I go over the history of money in Chapter 3. Along the way, I keep money tied to the underlying economy. We revisit the Modelville and see how the economy of the whole town is functioning and what role money is playing.

The need for money arose because people wanted to exchange what they produced for what others had produced. Furthermore, for me to trade what I have produced for something that someone else has produced it must be the case that I have produced more than what I need. Think about it. When I only produce what I can consume then I have nothing left to trade. Same goes for others. When each produces only what each can consume, then there is nothing left to be exchanged.

But how is it that I am able to produce more than what I am able to consume? Well, simple: I specialize. Over time and with enough practice, I have learned ways that allow me to be more productive. Practice does have its payoffs.

Note that it is not enough that I specialize in the production of a particular product and produce more than what I can consume. There have to be others in the same situation for trade to take place. That is, others producing more than what they can consume and producing different products than what I am producing. If I can't find someone else whose products I want in exchange, the trade will not take place. Adam

Smith put it best over 250 years ago when he said that specialization was limited only by the extent of the market.[42] Smith wrote in 1776,

> When the market is very small, no person can have any encouragement to dedicate himself entirely to one employment, for want of the power to exchange all that surplus part of the produce of his own labour, which is over and above his own consumption, for such parts of the produce of other men's labour as he has occasion for. (Book I, Chapter III, p. 19)

Chapter 4 provides an explanation of how money has enabled us to accomplish division of labor and specialization, expand the extent of the market, and helped us realize gains from trade.

Of course, any talk of money, and paper currency, would be woefully incomplete without the discussion of the banking sector. Chapter 5 takes up this task. This chapter highlights the need for and importance of borrowing and lending and the roles of commercial banks and central banks in this arena. After presenting a brief history of commercial banking, I talk about the role that a bank plays in a modern economy. I talk about what interest really is and why has it been misrepresented as a social ill to be avoided at all costs? I discuss the differences between private borrowing and public borrowing, and the extent to which these differences can, or cannot be, exploited. Here, I introduce the reader to the Modern Monetary Theory, point out its roots in the mid-1940s economic literature,[43] and discuss its flaws.[44] I discuss in detail why lessons of a private borrower, say a household or a firm, may not be applicable to governments. I talk about why calls for a balanced federal budget are misguided.

One often hears about the dangers of the hegemony of a central bank when it comes to money. It is not uncommon to read in the press or watch it on TV someone implying that unelected central bankers are up

[42] The extent of the market. Adam Smith. *An Inquiry into the Nature and Causes of the Wealth of Nations*. Ed. Edwin Cannan. 1994th ed. New York: Random House, 1776. Print.

[43] Roots of Modern Money Theory. Abba P. Lerner. "Functional Finance and the Federal Debt." *Social Research* 10.1 (1943): 38–51. *JSTOR*. Web.

[44] Flaw in Modern Money Theory. John K. Galbraith. "Modern Monetary Realism." *Project Syndicate*, 2019, Sebastian Edwards. "Modern Monetary Disasters." *Project Syndicate*, 2019, Kenneth S. Rogoff. "Modern Monetary Nonsense." *Project Syndicate*, 2019.

to no good. That they have illicit motives. Chapter 6 expands on some of the topics discussed in Chapter 5. I go into more details about the functioning of central banks and the conduct of monetary policy. I talk about monetary policy and how it affects the economy. I use the Federal Reserve System (the Fed) as an example while discussing monetary policy. I talk about how the Fed conducts monetary policy and why it works at all. I talk about the importance of the independence of the Fed. I talk about what history teaches us about central banks that are influenced by national politics. I also talk about the limitations of monetary policy; what happens when the Fed cannot use its conventional tools. I discuss Zero-Lower-Bound, Quantitative Easing, the yield curve, and the debate about the interest rate target versus the inflation rate target.

While discussing inflation and deflation, I talk about why the former (in small doses) is necessary for an economy to function and the latter spells trouble. I highlight the perils in reinstituting gold standard as some have suggested over the decades. I show why the argument for backing currency by, say gold, will bring price stability, is not supported by empirical evidence. I provide examples from the nineteenth and the twentieth centuries when currency was backed by gold and silver and the lessons we have learned. For instance, one lesson that we have learned is that for prices to be stable the supply of money has to be elastic. The reason is that economic activity fluctuates over the course of a week, a month, a quarter, and a year. Backing currency by gold will lead to more price fluctuations, not fewer.

Humanity has experienced tremendous increase in living standards since the Industrial Revolution. Our lives are freer, more comfortable, safe, and enjoyable than anytime in recorded history.[45] What role did money play, if any, in this achievement? In Chapter 7, I offer evidence about the roles that money and related institutional arrangements have played.

One source of this achievement in standards of living is international trade—the ties between the domestic economy and the rest of the world. When one needs to exchange goods and service across borders, the need to evaluate the domestic currency in terms of other countries' currencies arises. How does this evaluation take place? Does having a strong domestic currency a "good" thing or a "bad" thing? Would it be better

[45] Economic growth and its fruits. Amartya Sen. *Development as Freedom*. Westminster, MD, USA: Alfred A. Knopf Incorporated, 1999. Print, Pinker, Pinker.

if we had a "world currency" so that we would not have to exchange one currency for another? After all, in the United States we have US dollar that is accepted in all fifty states. What does economic theory and practice tell us about such a "common currency area"? I go into these details in Chapter 8. I use the examples of the US dollar and the Euro. I discuss the history of the Euro and its possible future as predicted by the economic theory.

Back to the question of why people want to hold hard currency in times of crises.

One can understand preferring physical assets—gold, silver, piece of land, etc.—over pieces of paper, as the interaction between Dr. Paul and Dr. Bernanke highlights. Why faith in intrinsically worthless piece of paper with pictures of, most often, dead people? Galbraith's answer: Its scarcity due to convertibility into gold and silver. It was the convertibility of the paper money into gold and silver that put a limit on the money that could be printed. (I hasten to note here that the institution of central banks combined with our understanding of how the economy works has rendered the need to back paper by gold or silver obsolete.) "The worthlessness of the paper is a detail," he writes.[46] While true to some extent, it raises another question: In times of crises why do people want to hold an intrinsically worthless piece of paper today when it is not convertible into gold and silver? It is true that some policy makers as well as members of public want it to be convertible but they still hold the same intrinsically "worthless" paper. I will argue that the reason behind both phenomena is the desire and need for physical contact in times of crisis. I pick up this topic in Chapter 9, the final chapter of the book. Chapter 9 also makes some concluding remarks.

At the outset, I would like to impress upon you dear reader, that the key to understanding what money is, and to avoid confusions, is to always keep money tied to the underlying economy.

[46] Faith in a worthless piece of paper. Galbraith (p. 63).

Works Cited

Adams, John, and Lester J. Cappon. *The Adams-Jefferson Letters: The Complete Correspondence Between Thomas Jefferson and Abigail and John Adams*. Chapel Hill, NC: Published for the Omohundro Institute of Early American History and Culture, Williamsburg, VA, by the University of North Carolina Press, 1987. Web.

Ashraf, Mohammad. *Formal and Informal Social Safety Nets: Growth and Development in the Modern Economy*. New York, NY: Palgrave Macmillan, 2014. Print.

Bocquet-Appel, Jean. "When the World's Population Took Off: The Springboard of the Neolithic Demographic Transition." *Science* 333.6042 (2011): 560–61. *JSTOR*. Web.

Carneiro, Robert L. "The Evolution of Complexity in Human Societies and Its Mathematical Expression." *International Journal of Comparative Sociology (Brill Academic Publishers)* 28.3 (1987): 111–28. Web.

de Roover, Raymond. *Gresham on Foreign Exchange: An Essay on Early English Mercantilism with the Text of Sir Thomas Gresham's Memorandum for the Understanding of the Exchange*. Cambridge: Harvard University Press, 1949. Web.

Dunbar, Robin. "Neocortex Size as a Constraint on Group Size in Primates." *Journal of Human Evolution* 22.6 (1992). Print.

Edwards, Sebastian. "Modern Monetary Disasters." *Project Syndicate*, 2019. Print.

Fetter, Frank Whitson. "Some Neglected Aspects of Gresham's Law." *The Quarterly Journal of Economics* 46.3 (1932): 480–95. *JSTOR*. Web.

Galbraith, John K. "Modern Monetary Realism." *Project Syndicate*, 2019. Print.

———. *Money: Whence It Came, Where It Went*. Boston: Houghton Mifflin, 1975. Print.

Hammond, Bray. "Jackson, Biddle, and the Bank of the United States." *The Journal of Economic History* 7.1 (1947): 1–23. *JSTOR*. Web.

Kudo, H., and Robin Dunbar. "Neocortex Size and Social Network Size in Primates." *Animal Behaviour* 62.4 (2001): 711–22. Print.

Lehmann, J., A. H. Korstjens, and Robin Dunbar. "Groups Size, Grooming and Social Cohesion in Primates." *Animal Behaviour* 74.6 (2007): 1617–29. Print.

Lerner, Abba P. "Functional Finance and the Federal Debt." *Social Research* 10.1 (1943): 38–51. *JSTOR*. Web.

Pinker, Steven. *The Better Angels of Our Nature: Why Violence Has Declined*. New York: Penguin Books, 2011. Print.

———. *Enlightenment Now: The Case for Reason, Science, Humanism, and Progress*. New York: Penguin Books, 2018. Print.

Primm, James N. *A Foregone Conclusion: The Founding of the Federal Reserve Bank of St. Louis*. Federal Reserve Bank of St. Louis, 1989. Print.

Rogoff, Kenneth S. "Modern Monetary Nonsense." *Project Syndicate*, 2019. Print.

Sen, Amartya. *Development as Freedom*. Westminster, MD, USA: Alfred A. Knopf Incorporated, 1999. Print.

Smith, Adam. *An Inquiry into the Nature and Causes of the Wealth of Nations*. Ed. Edwin Cannan. 1994th ed. New York: Random House, 1776. Print.

Zhu, Zhaoyu, et al. "Hominin Occupation of the Chinese Loess Plateau Since About 2.1 Million Years Ago." *Nature* 559.7715 (2018): 608–12. Web.

CHAPTER 2

Imagine a World Without Money

This chapter starts with a scene from a fictional downtown where a festival is underway. The reader is then asked to imagine a scenario where money did not exist and barter was the only way to buy and sell goods and services. Then, I introduce the concept of money: What attributes something that can function as money needs to have. I introduce the reader to a fictional money called Pecuna. The purpose of creating a new name for currency is to start afresh and tie it to the economy from the very beginning. Existing forms of currency—dollar, pound, euro, Renminbi, etc.—have well-established characters, in and of themselves. This makes it more difficult to make the very important point that to properly understand money, it has to be tied to the underlying economy.

2.1 A Scene from Downtown Modelville

In this capital city, Modelville (established 1400), every first Friday of the month during summer the city corners off about three blocks in downtown. Vehicular traffic is blocked from 6:00 p.m. to 10:00 p.m.—only pedestrians are allowed. Bicyclists are also allowed, even if they are wearing skintight cycling gear. Small vendors of all sorts set up their tent-shops. Vendors selling t-shirts with funny-captioned messages are definitely there. Sometimes the jokes printed on t-shirts are really quite funny when you read them for the first time. But having these jokes printed on a t-shirt and reading them over and over again? That's a

M. Ashraf, *Money*,
https://doi.org/10.1007/978-3-030-50378-9_2

different matter. There is something about jokes; they have very short life span. They can stop being funny about the second or third time you encounter them. Jokes are not like music. Music, even disco music, has a lot longer life span. Maybe the gods of art put a curse on comedians. Perhaps the comedians made fun of gods. Or maybe other gods made fun of gods of art and they took it out on comedians. Who knows? Gods are touchy that way.

There are vendors selling jewelry, paintings and photographs, pieces of woodwork and metalwork, and blown glass, and other receptacles of dust. There are food trucks selling authentic street food. They are selling tacos, and pretzels, and shish kabobs, and gyros. And there are local craft beer stands.

No fortune-tellers though! It's not dark enough yet.

People are browsing and buying these pieces of jewelry and paintings and photographs and woodwork and metalwork and blown glass, but mostly browsing. Some are just people-watching and commenting on the attires of those who are buying this and that and those who are browsing. For some people-watchers, murder is perhaps forgivable, sartorial misdeeds are not. A hardcore buy-local crowd is here to support the local artisans and artists, walking around with a pint of local craft beer in one hand and a cell phone in the other. They are taking selfies and attaching pictures with texts and post them on *Facebook* and *Twitter* and *Snapchat* and chat with friends via *iChat* and *FaceTime*, storing these pictures in *iCloud* and *Google Drive*, and what have you. They want to be in the moment but perhaps not in the place. They enjoy the *now* and let others know that they are enjoying the *now*. *Facebook* and *Twitter* and *Snapchat* and *FaceTime* let them share their picture and comments for free. It is free, right? You do have to sign up, of course. But sign-up is free as well. So it is free then, right?

People browsing and buying this and that come from all walks of life. Some are local business owners, some work in firms that make some part of what makes *iCloud*, and *Google Drive*, and *iChat*, and *FaceTime*. Some own firms that make parts make *FaceTime* and *iCloud*. Some are attorneys who work in law firms that give advice to people on all matters of the law. Some are teachers who teach students how to learn. They frown upon students when they text and use *iChat* and *Facebook* and *FaceTime* in class using their cell phones. Some work in banks that take deposits and make loans to the brewers who make local craft beers, and t-shirts vendors who print funny jokes on t-shirts made in some foreign country, and jewelers who make jewelry using local stones, and food truck owners who make tacos and shish kabobs and pretzels and gyros. Some are retired. They saved parts of their incomes when they were working and deposited those savings in banks that made loans to vendors who brew beer in breweries that use hops grown in some state that has some capital and some downtown. They ferment hops in large steel fermentation systems made of stainless steel made in some other foreign country so that the hops and other ingredients turn into beer that they can sell on this first Friday.

Men in business suits, with necktie knots loosened. It is 6:00 p.m., after all. And women in business suits and heels. After all, this is how one gets together with colleagues to socialize at 6:00 p.m. right after work. And men in shorts and flip-flops, and women in shorts and flip-flops. And men in jeans and sneakers. And women in jeans and sneakers. This is the evening before the weekend after all. Men in jeans and starched shirts untucked, and women in summer dresses and heels. This is how one goes on a date after all. All are texting back and forth. Everyone is sending text messages with pictures attached to each other; men and women in their 50s and 60s and 70s too. Men and women in their 50s and 60s and 70s read their text messages using font size 20—an ocular equivalent of a toupee. No reading glasses for them. They are not *that* old, they tell themselves.

Oh the humanity!

Why on the first Friday of the month, you ask? Because most get paid on monthly basis and this is the first Friday after getting paid. The weekend starts tomorrow. They got paid for making parts that make *iCloud*, and *Google Drive*, and *Snapchat*, and *FaceTime*, and *Facebook*, and the handles that bar tenders pull to pour local craft beer, and bank employees for working in banks that accept deposits and make loans, and shoe store workers who sell shoes that were made in some foreign country, and employees who work in a clothes stores where they sell shorts and shirts and business suits and neckties. But why not on the first of the month? That would be nice except the first of the month may not fall on a weekend eve. Most people don't have to work over the weekend. They can relax and not worry about being hungover and not having had enough sleep when they go to work the next day. Of course, some people do work over the weekend but they are usually paid extra for working over the weekend. So they are compensated for working over the weekend, unless they work in service jobs. In service jobs, weekend work is common and expected.

People are buying local craft beers, and shish kabobs, and hotdogs, and tacos, and pieces of jewelry, and woodwork, and metalwork. They are paying with dollar bills, and credit cards, and debit cards, and checks, and *Apple Pay*, and *Google Pay*, and Bitcoins. In exchange for a piece of paper with certain writing on it, or a swipe of a piece of plastic with some writing on it, or just by bringing their cell phones closer to another gadget which makes a beeping sound the sellers hand over their local craft beers, and shish kabobs, and tacos, and jewelry made of precious metal, and studded with precious stones to the buyers.

Everyone is happy. The brewers will take these bills and swipes and beeps to the sellers of the hops and other ingredients and buy more hops and other ingredients. The sellers of the hops and other ingredients will accept these bills and swipes and beeps, and hand over the hops and other ingredients to the brewers. The brewers will brew more beer for the next first Friday. The artists—the painters and the woodworkers and the metal-workers—will exchange these dollar bills and swipes and beeps for more art supplies and make more art for the first Friday of the next month. The buyers are buying and the sellers are selling. The sellers are accepting these dollar bills, and credit card and debit card swipes, and beeps of *Apple Pay* and *Google Pay* and Bitcoins in exchange for whatever they are selling.

Freeze!

2.2 Barter, Again

Imagine that you are able to make everyone freeze in action and remove their methods of payment—the dollar bills and the credit cards and the debit cards and *Apple Pay* and *Google Pay* and Bitcoins. As if you were able to airbrush these, not only from the picture but also from the memories of the buyers and sellers. The buyers don't know what a dollar bill is, or what a credit card is, or a debit card is, or what an *Apple Pay* is, or what a *Google Pay* is, or what a Bitcoin is, and neither do the sellers.

Local craft beer brewers want to sell beer and the hardcore buy-local crowd wants to buy local craft beer. But the exchange does not take place. Local craft beer brewers want to be paid so that they can buy hops from the hops growers to brew beer for the first Friday of the next month. Some in the hardcore buy-local crowd make parts that make *iCloud* and *FaceTime* and *Snapchat* and *Google Drive* and *iChat* and *Facebook*. They can exchange these parts for pints of beer but local craft beer brewers do not need the parts that make *iCloud* and *FaceTime* and *iChat* and *Google Drive*.

Attorneys are some of the men in business suits with neckties loosened and women in business suits. They want to exchange legal advice for pints of beer but the brewers of craft beer do not need their advice, at least not right now. Schoolteachers are some of the men in jeans and sneakers and women in jeans and sneakers and dresses and flip-flops. They want to exchange lessons that teach students how to learn but local craft beer brewers don't want to exchange beer pints for lessons on how to teach students how to learn.

Why do local craft beer brewers not want to exchange pints of beer for parts that make *iCloud* and *iChat* and *Google Drive* and *Snapchat*? The local craft beer brewers need something that they can exchange for hops to brew beer for the first Friday of the next month. The farmers who grow the hops do not want to exchange hops for parts that make *iChat* and *Google Drive* and *FaceTime* and *iCloud* because they want something that they can exchange for seeds and fertilizers and fuel for their tractors and harvesters.

Why do local craft beer brewers not want to exchange pints of beer for legal advice and lessons on how to teach students how to learn? Local craft beer brewers don't want exchange pints of beer for legal advice and lessons on how to teach children how to learn for the same reason that they don't want to exchange pints of beer for parts that make *iCloud* and *iChat* and *Google Drive* and *Snapchat*. The local craft beer brewers need something that they can exchange for the hops that they need to brew beer for the first Friday of the next month. The farmers do not want legal advice and lessons on how to teach students how to learn. They want something that they can exchange for the seeds and the fertilizers and fuel for their tractors and harvesters. There is a term for this. It is called "double-coincidence of wants." For an exchange to take place between two individuals, the first individual has to offer what the second individual wants and the second individual has to offer what the first individual wants.

And even if the local craft beer brewers were willing to exchange pints of beer for parts that make *iCloud* and *iChat* and *FaceTime* and *Google Drive* and *Facebook* because the farmers who grow the hops are willing to exchange hops for parts that make *iCloud* and *FaceTime* and *Google Drive* and *Facebook* because the farmers, in turn, can exchange parts that make *iCloud* and *FaceTime* and *Facebook* and *Google Drive* for fertilizers and fuel for their tractors and harvesters, deciding how many pints of beer are worth how many parts that make *iCloud* and *iChat* and *FaceTime* and *Google Drive* and *Facebook* is hard. Men in suits with loosened ties and women in suits and heels, and men in jeans and sneakers and women in jeans and sneakers, will have to know the quality of beer brewed by local craft beers brewers and the local craft beer brewers will have to know the value of each part that makes *iCloud* and *iChat* and *Snapchat* and *Facebook* and how each part fits into what makes *iCloud* and *Snapchat* and *Facebook* and *iChat*. The local craft beer brewers are experts in brewing beer; they are not in the parts that make *iCloud* and *iChat* and *Snapchat* and *Facebook*.

Of course, the brewers of local craft beer can hire experts who can evaluate the parts that make *iCloud* and *iChat* and *Snapchat* and *Facebook*. The brewers of local craft beer, however, will have to find experts on evaluating the parts that make *iCloud* and *iChat* and *Google Drive* and *Facebook* who are willing to exchange their expert opinion for pints of beer. This may not be an easy task. And even if the local craft beer brewers are able to find such experts who satisfy their libation needs with locally brewed craft beer, it will just increase the cost of transaction because they will have to pay part of the beer brewed to the experts.

And the painters and photographers and woodwork artists and metalwork artists and blown glass artists and jewelers who use precious metal and stones to make stone-studded jewelry, they want to sell their art, and men in business suits and loosened neckties and women in business suits and heels and men in jeans and flip-flops and women in jeans and flip-flops wearing novelty t-shirts want to buy the art. But the exchange does not take place. The sellers do not have any need for what the buyers have to offer in exchange for the art.

There may be a jeweler selling her stone-studded jewelry in this capital city on this first Friday on this cornered off three blocks of downtown where no vehicular traffic is allowed except, of course bicyclists wearing skintight bicycling gear, who needs to teach her child to how learn. But how much is a piece of stone-studded jewelry worth in terms of lessons that teach students how to learn? And there may be a metalwork artists who is selling her metal artwork who needs legal advice from men wearing business suits and loosened neckties and women wearing business suits and heels but how much is a piece of metalwork worth in terms of legal advice?

And what if the jeweler who makes jewelry with precious metals and stones does not need the lesson plans on how to teach her child how to learn right now? She needs that advice two years from now or ten years from now. Her child is too young or has not even been born. She wants to be prepared and ready when she needs these lesson plans. Can she store these lessen plans for the next two years or ten years? Can the metalwork and woodwork artists store the legal advice to use when and if they need it?

We have not talked about the hardcore buy-local crowd taking selfies and posting pictures on *Facebook* and *Snapchat* using *iPhones* and *Android* devices with services provided by Verizon and AT&T and Sprint. How will they pay their monthly phone bills? We have not talked about the t-shirt vendor who buys t-shirts made in some foreign country by workers with multisyllabic names with numerous letters stuck in the spelling, which are supposed to be silent, just to trick the non-native speakers either. How will he pay the t-shirt makers in that foreign country who buy fabric which is used to sew the t-shirts from another foreign country, who buy cotton to make that fabric from yet another foreign country? It is already becoming unbearably complicated in this small corner of a downtown of a capital city with only a handful of vendors selling a handful of stuff.

In the United States in 2017, there were over 1000 types of different non-farm occupations that employed around 147,000,000 workers.[1] Remember we talked about the North American Product Classification System (NAPCS) in Chapter 1?[2] It is the product classification system that the United States Census Bureau, in partnership with its Canadian and Mexican counterparts, uses to classify various products produced in the three-country region. In case you are wondering, locally brewed craft beer falls under the main product category of "Food, beverage, and tobacco products, except raw farm products," and the "Beer, ale, and malt beverages" sub-category. This sub-category's NAPCS code is 11101260106.

It should not come as a surprise that there are numerous brewers who brew "Beer, ale, and malt beverages" in the Unites States, far too many

[1] Employment Statistics. https://data.bls.gov/cgi-bin/dsrv (Accessed: May 19, 2018).

[2] North American Product Classification System. https://www.census.gov/eos/www/napcs/index.html (Accessed: May 21, 2018).

to list here. Let us focus on one particular form of libation: craft beer. In 2017, there were 6266 craft breweries in the United States. They brewed 24,868,276 barrels of craft beer of over 150 distinct styles.[3] They differed by taste, color, clarity, aroma, alcohol content, and by origin.

As we saw in Chapter 1, the system in which people exchange stuff for other stuff is called a barter system. I bring up barter here again to emphasize the need for a numeraire in a complex modern economy. Barter is easy when you just have a handful of products. It becomes very complicated very quickly—evaluating products in term of other products. Take a very simple situation: Suppose you have three products, say, coffee, chairs, and wine. Assuming that there is only one kind of coffee and only one kind of chairs and only one kind of wine, an admittedly strong assumption because coffee differs by region, by roast, and so on. So do chairs and wine. In this very simple situation for exchange to take place, you will need to evaluate coffee in terms of chairs, coffee in terms of wine, and chairs in terms of wine. Three evaluations and you are done. When you have 10 products, you will need to perform 45 evaluations. When the number of products increases to, say, 100, you need to perform 4950 such evaluation. For 1000 products, you will need 499,500 such evaluations. Recall the formula I presented in Chapter 1—$\left[\frac{n\times(n-1)}{2}\right]$, where n is the number of products. Just plug in numbers and see how quickly the complication increases.

It seems almost not worth for the local craft beer brewer to brew beer, and the t-shirt vendor to print funny phrases on t-shirts, and the jeweler to make stone-studded jewelry, and the metalwork and woodwork artists and painters and photographers to create art, and try to sell them in exchange for parts that make *iCloud* and *iPad* and *iChat* and *Google Drive* and *Facebook*. Who wants all the headaches of evaluating products in terms of other products? But what a waste of talent would that be if the brewer stopped brewing beer and the jeweler stopped making jewelry and the painters stopped painting. Not only that, life would certainly be less enjoyable without art and wine and beer.

Unless they can come up with some common tool that allows them to exchange what they have to offer with what they want to buy—a common medium of exchange, if you will; some yardstick that allows

[3] Craft brewery data. Brewers Association. https://www.brewersassociation.org/statistics/national-beer-sales-production-data/ (Accessed: May 19, 2018).

them to evaluate what each has to offer in terms of what each wants to buy—a common unit of account, if you will; and some way to transfer the purchasing power of what they have to offer from now to the future without losing most, if any, of its value—a store of value, if you will.

2.3 Enter Money!

As we saw in Chapter 1, anything can be used as money as long as it has these three characteristics. First, it can serve as a medium of exchange—people are willing to exchange their artworks and their lesson plans and their pints of beer for this thing. Second, it can serve as a unit of account, or a yardstick—artworks and lesson plans and pints of beer can be evaluated in terms of this thing. This allows the local craft beer brewers and the people who make parts that make *Snapchat* and *iChat* and *Facebook* evaluate the relative values of what the sellers and buyers have to offer each other.

Note that these two characteristics—a medium of exchange and a unit of account—are related. For the exchange to take place, the buyer and the seller have to be able to evaluate the stuff in relative terms.

The third characteristic of something that can serve as money is a store of value. That is, people can store the purchasing power of what they have to offer from now to a future date. The jeweler who makes stone-studded jewelry may not need tips for how to teach her child how to learn right away. She needs them in a few years, as we saw earlier. How can she preserve the value of her precious stone-studded jewelry for the next few years when her child becomes of age? The teacher who is willing to exchange her lessons for stone-studded jewelry will have to stay close by so that when the jeweler's child comes of age she can offer her services. However, if the teacher can exchange the jewelry for something that can be used later by the jeweler to exchange for lessons the problem will be solved. The teacher will get the jewelry right away, and the jeweler will be able to buy lessons when her child needs them.

I used the phrases "a medium of exchange," "a unit of account," and "a store of value" for a reason. I did not coin these phrases; students in first-year macroeconomics course are familiar with these phrases, or at least they should be. Memorize these phrases and what they represent. These phrases will be very helpful throughout the rest of the book. Memorization is a crucial tool for learning no matter how poorly some new fad speaks of memorization. We memorize our names and the names of our parents and our children's names. We memorize where we live. We memorize proper etiquettes. And when we can't remember these pieces of information, we are called senile. We need treatment, we are told. Strange. Isn't it?

I also mentioned that anything that has these three characteristics can serve as money. As long as the thing being used as money is limited in quantity and it cannot be easily replicated, it can serve as money. As we will see in Chapter 3 in more detail, over the centuries, numerous things have been used as money. From seashells to stones to food grain to cigarettes to cans of tuna to clay tablets with special marks on them to pieces of paper to verbal promises of returning the favor. You name it and it has, somewhere in some shape or form, probably been used as money. In the coming chapters (specifically Chapters 3–5), I will go over the various forms of money that have been used and how they served the purpose.

Let me expand on the "limitedness" of something that can serve as money and why it is important that its replicability may not be that easy. Let us walk back to the first Friday gathering. I bet by now you are tired of this first Friday. I am tired of it too, but we must continue. I promise I will be brief. I will not bring up the bicyclists in their skintight attire unless it is absolutely necessary.

Remember the first characteristic of something that can be used as money, i.e. a medium of exchange? That is, something that people are willing to accept in exchange for their stuff—a pint of local craft beer, a stone-studded piece of jewelry, and so on. Suppose that I offer the brewer a certain thing in exchange for a pint of beer. By way of giving that thing a name, let us call it "Pecuna." And while we are at it, let us represent it by $\mathbb{P}$ when needed. Suppose also that the brewer can also create a Pecuna effortlessly if she wanted. I just thought of Pecuna and it was in my hand, as if by magic. The same way the brewer just thinks of Pecuna and it is there. It is in her hands. She is not imagining it. It really is in her hands. And just like me, or the brewer, everyone else can do the same; just think of Pecuna and it is there. And the number of Pecunae does not matter either; however, many Pecunae you want they are there. Pecunae are in unlimited supply. In this case, the brewer will have no incentive to exchange a pint of beer for a Pecuna.

Not only that, in such a situation a Pecuna stops being a yardstick to evaluate pints of beer in terms of, say a lesson to teach a child how to learn: It stops being a unit of account. Why? This is because if I can just think of Pecunae and they are there, in unlimited quantity, why not offer ten Pecunae for a pint of beer? Why not 20 million Pecunae? Or a billion Pecunae? Just pick a number. In fact, the brewer does not need to exchange a pint of beer for any number of Pecunae. As we saw, she can just think of Pecunae and they are there in the palm of her hand. So the limitedness of Pecunae is a must.

What about the ease of replicability? The thought experiment that we conducted earlier where all you needed to get any number of Pecunae was to just to think about Pecunae and they were there in the palm of your hand. Pecuna had instant replicability with zero cost of replication. Note that the zero cost of replication, the ease of replication, and limitedness, while related in the present situation, are not identical. An example may help. Think of copying a piece of writing, say an electronic version of this book. Assume that you came across an electronic copy of this book on the Internet. You could download it on your computer an unlimited number of times with practically zero (or very close to zero) cost. All you needed was an Internet-connected computer. Each copy will be identical. This, however, may be protected by copyright laws making it illegal to download unless you have paid for it, thus making it limited.

There is another related quality that needs mentioning here. That is of having a way to make sure that people do not "double-spend." By double-spend, we mean that one cannot use the same, say, dollar bill or Pecuna to buy a pint of locally brewed beer as well as a stone-studded piece of jewelry. Why is the ability to stop double-spending important? Suppose that the price of a pint of beer is five dollar and the price of a piece of jewelry is five dollars. You buy a pint of beer in exchange for a five-dollar bill. The brewer hands you the pint of beer and you hand her the five-dollar bill. Suppose now that you could buy a pint of beer *and* a piece of metal artwork with the *same* five-dollar bill. This is not because the price of a pint of beer or the price of the metal artwork has decreased, but because the exchange of the five-dollar bill and a pint of beer or a piece of jewelry did not take place. As another thought experiment, imagine that you showed a five-dollar bill to the brewer and she handed you a pint of beer, and you showed the *same* five-dollar bill to the jeweler handed you the piece of jewelry. The vendors are being ripped off. As we shall see in Chapter 3, to make sure that double-spending does not take place, blockchain technology, the software underlying cryptocurrencies, has a verification system in place. This verification system, however, significantly slows the speed with which transactions can take place.

I mentioned evaluating pints of beer in terms of a lesson to teach a child how to learn. This is just another way to establishing the price of a pint of beer in terms of lessons. In a barter system, as we saw above, we are establishing the price of one product in terms of the other product. However, it turned out to be quite a task: The more we thought about it, the harder it became. How many lessons for how many pints of beer? How many parts that make *iCloud* and *iChat* and *Facebook* for how many stone-studded pieces of jewelry? So much so that vendors even considered just giving it up and not vend at all.

Now, however, that we have Pecunae at our disposal we can determine the price of a pint of beer or a piece of stone-studded jewelry or an artwork and so on, in terms of Pecunae. We can even divide each Pecuna into however small a piece we want. We can establish a system which makes it absolutely clear the price of stuff that a vendor is selling. Remember we represented Pecuna by ℙ? So when we want to write the price of, say a pint of beer, to be 5 Pecunae, we can write it as 5ℙ. And when we want to write a given fraction of a Pecuna, say one-fifth of a Pecuna, we can write it as ℙ5. In this system, when ℙ is preceded by a number then that means that each Pecuna is being multiplied by that number, and when ℙ is followed by a number then that means that each Pecuna is being divided by that number; 20,000ℙ will mean 20,000 Pecunae, and ℙ20 will mean one-twentieth of a Pecuna.

Suppose that the brewer is willing to sell you a pint of local craft beer for five Pecunae, or 5ℙ. And the attorney charges 200 Pecunae, or 200ℙ, for each hour of legal advice. As we saw earlier, for the brewer to sell a pint of beer to the attorney she had to have a need for legal advice. That is, there has to be a double-coincidence of wants. Now this need not be the case. The attorney gave legal advice for, say two hours, and had 400 Pecunae, or 400ℙ, in his pocket. He can give 5ℙ to the brewer and get a pint of beer. In a similar fashion, the teacher gets paid, say 50 Penciae for ten lessons, or 50ℙ, and the jeweler sells each piece of jewelry for 4 Pecunae, or 4ℙ. The teacher may buy a piece of stone-studded jewelry from the jeweler for 4ℙ without the jeweler having to buy a lesson for one and one-quarter pieces of jeweler, or 1.25ℙ. Dividing a piece of jewelry into a quarter will quite likely decrease the value of jewelry significantly. As a result, it may keep the exchange from taking place; the teacher may only want just one piece of jewelry as opposed to one and one-quarter pieces—the equivalent of the value of one lesson.

What if the jeweler does not want any lessons right now but in a few years? The jeweler can hold on to the Pecunae that she earned on the first Friday and buy the lessons when she needs them. This way the teacher can buy and enjoy wearing the stone-studded jewelry now and the jeweler can buy the lessons later when her children become of age.

Things are in order again. Men in business suits with loosened neckties and women in business suits and heels are browsing and buying artwork while holding a pint of beer in one hand and cell phone in the other. They were paid Pecunae for giving legal advice and they are using these Pecunae to buy local craft beer and photographs of sunsets and trees and lakes and art pieces made of metal and wood. Retired men in jeans and sneakers and retired women in jeans and sneakers earned Pecunae when they were working. They saved part of their incomes in Pecunae. Now they are browsing and buying artwork while holding a pint of beer. They are paying the local craft beer brewer with Pecunae that they had saved. And men who make parts that make *iCloud* and *iChat* and *Facebook* and *Google Drive* and *FaceTime*, and women who make parts that make *iCloud* and *iChat* and *Facebook* and *Google Drive* and *FaceTime* are browsing and buying artwork while holding a pint of beer in one hand and a cell phone in the other. They are taking selfies that they post on *Snapchat* and *Facebook*, and the like. They are paying for the artwork and the locally brewed craft beer and their phone bills with Pecunae that they earn making parts that make *iCloud* and *iChat* and *Facebook* and *Snapchat* and *Google Drive*.

But wait a minute, you say. All you have done is introduced money into the picture and called it Pecuna as opposed to calling it dollar or pound or euro or Renminbi. Yes, I have. But in the process I made you think what money basically is, and what purpose it serves. Did I not? And coming up with the name "Pecuna" and writing about it was fun for me as well. As promised, I did not mention one particular group of people who use a particular mode of transportation wearing a particular attire.

Now that we have a basic understanding of what money is and what it does, in the coming chapters of this book I will go over a brief history of money and we will look at the numerous forms of money used in the history of humankind. We will see what role commercial banks and people play. We will explore who decides how much of money should be in an economy and why. We will see why a central bank is needed. Along the way, I will try to clarify various misconceptions that have become the go-to tools in the toolkits of conspiracy theorists, pulpit hucksters, and grifters of all stripes.

While we head out to dig deeper into the realm of all things money, it is important to keep in mind that the main purpose of money is to exchange goods and services. It is worth reminding ourselves that anything that serves as money has three main characteristics—a medium of exchange, a unit of account, and a store of value. The root cause of confusion is the untethering of money from goods and services.

By the way, in case you haven't figured it out, *iCloud* and *iChat* and *Facebook* and *Snapchat* and *Google Drive* and many other similar products that claim to be free are not free at all. The companies that produce these products are some of the most profitable companies on the planet. If they were giving their products for free, they wouldn't be earning any revenue, let alone a profit. In fact, these companies would not even exist. One way these companies earn revenue is to sell your information to other companies that want to advertise their products. Those advertisers then send their advertisements to only a select group of customers whom they consider likely purchasers of their goods and services. Why advertise horse feed to a city dweller and a street bike to a farmer. Firms pay for this information because it makes advertising more efficient. And you as the target of these advertisements are probably also better off as well. As a city dweller you do not want to hear about a special on horse feed. Your inbox is flooded with unsolicited advertisements as it is. Same goes for the farmer. She does not want to hear about a sale on street bikes.

CHAPTER 3

A Brief History of Money

This chapter presents a brief history of the various forms of money that humans have used over thousands of years. These range from precious metals and stones, to stone disks, to clay tablets, to food grain, to animal skins, to paper, and to the latest and newest, i.e., cryptocurrency, and everything in between. I go over the role that banks play in creating money, and why it is important. This chapter also presents a brief history of the use of paper currency in the United States. While reading this chapter, keep reminding yourself that the moment we divorce money from the underlying economy, confusions arise and even simple concepts can become overwhelming.

3.1 Categories of Money

I use the adjective "brief" in the title of this chapter advisedly. A complete history would take many volumes, and people have other things on their to-do-lists. Brief, however, need not be dumbed down.

As we learned in previous chapters, the need for money arose out of the desire to trade. People produced more than what they could consume and wanted to exchange what they produced for what others had produced. And as the number of goods and services increased, exchanging stuff for other stuff become way too complicated. They needed a numeraire. Something that could serve as a yardstick and if need be, the purchasing

M. Ashraf, *Money*,
https://doi.org/10.1007/978-3-030-50378-9_3

power of today's production could be transferred to the future without losing much, if any, of its value.

Over thousands of year of recorded human history, numerous objects have been created and used to serve as money. Perhaps "numerous" does not convey the scale. Some examples as comparison may help.

According to the American Kennel Club, there are over 200 breeds of dogs. All descending from wolf, by the way. No jackals, coyotes, or foxes involved.[1] While humans over the recorded history have worshiped tens of thousands of gods,[2] they do not stand a chance in front of the various forms of money. There are more than 10,000 saints in the Catholic Church,[3] with the capability to perform pretty much any kind of miracle that you can think of. St. Brigid of Kildare could turn water into beer. Apparently, she could also perform abortions, without any pain.[4] At the time of this writing, Bitcoin is one of over 2200 cryptocurrencies. Total market value of cryptocurrencies, as of June 20, 2019, was $293,534,971,125, according to CoinMarketCap.[5] It is a safe bet, though, that the types of money that have existed throughout human history will handily beat this number. Over time as economies changed and our understanding of how the economy works grew, so did the things that could be used as money. Primarily, however, money may be divided into two main categories—commodity money and non-commodity money.

Commodity money is probably the oldest form of money. It has some intrinsic value: It can be used for something other than just money. Take the example of, say, food grain. Obviously, food grain can be used to sustain life. One may, however, also use it to evaluate other goods and services. Suppose that in some part of the world people are using cups of

[1] Number of dog breeds. Richard Dawkins. *The Greatest Show on Earth: The Evidence for Evolution*. New York, NY: Free Press, 2009. Print.

[2] Number of gods. Robert Wright. *The Evolution of God*. New York, NY: Little, Brown, 2009. Print.

[3] Number of saints in the Catholic Church. http://www.uscatholic.org/articles/201310/how-many-saints-are-there-28027 (Accessed: May 23, 2018).

[4] St. Brigid of Kildare. https://www.nytimes.com/2018/05/19/opinion/sunday/ireland-abortion-referendum.html?rref=collection%2Fsectioncollection%2Fopinion&action=click&contentCollection=opinion&region=rank&module=package&version=highlights&contentPlacement=4&pgtype=sectionfront (Accessed: May 23, 2018).

[5] Number of cryptocurrencies. https://coinmarketcap.com/ (Accessed: June 20, 2019).

wheat to evaluate other goods and services. Of course they would have to agree upon the size of a cup and a standard would have to be developed. Once, however, they have an agreed upon size of a cup, food grain can be used as money.

Non-commodity money, on the other hand, does not have any intrinsic value. Its sole purpose is to serve as a medium of exchange, a unit of account, and a store of value. Fiat money is among these forms of money. I will expand on the concept of fiat money in the coming pages. For now, fiat money is a form of money that has been made money by fiat—by the authority, in almost all cases, of the government. The term "legal tender" is used for the form of money that has been recognized by the legal system, usually a government. Legal tender means that this method of payment has been accepted by the legal authority of the land and government dues paid in this form will be accepted. Furthermore, private parties legally cannot refuse to accept this in exchange for goods and service. Take a look at any denomination US dollar bill. Depending upon the vintage of the bill, usually in one corner of the bill it reads "THIS NOTE IS LEGAL TENDER FOR ALL DEBT, PUBLIC AND PRIVATE." Take another look at the dollar bills of various denominations in your wallet. Now think about what you don't see with a naked eye. Studies show that numerous forms of bacteria are found on these bills, from those found in human mouths to those causing acne. Over 80 percent have traces of cocaine and other illicit drugs.[6]

Let me now dig a bit deeper and go briefly over the history of money. I will start with commodity money.

3.2 About 11,000 Years Ago

Remember why we need money? We need money to exchange goods and services when we have produced more than what we can consume (or less of the goods and services than we want); we want to be able to measure the value of what we are exchanging; and we want to transfer the value of what we have to a future date. Think of human ancestors when they became sedentary, established villages, and were able to grow more grain than they could consume.

[6] Drugs on currency. http://journals.plos.org/plosone/article?id=10.1371/journal.pone.0175527 (Accessed: May 28, 2018).

Studies show that our human ancestors spread out of Africa around 70,000 years ago. It took another 60,000 or so years for humans to domesticate plants. The earliest signs of crop cultivation are found in the Near East around 9000 BCE. These dates have been established through carbon dating of the remains found in archeological excavations.[7] As we learned in Chapter 1, studies trace the emergence of farming "in seven or eight regions across the world, almost simultaneously at the beginning of the Holocene: in the Levant, in North and South China, in New Guinea and Ethiopia, and in eastern North America, Mesoamerica, and South America, all during the chronological window from 11,500 to 3500 years ago."[8] Studies also show that the earliest domesticated crops include emmer wheat, einkorn wheat, and barley. Eventually, with trial and error and selective breeding, they were able to grow more than they could consume. Gradually, other crops were domesticated and traded. Trade took place not only within a given community but with the neighboring communities as well.

It is quite likely that our human ancestors began domesticating even earlier and that the traces are lost in time. After all, as is usually the case, as our scientific understanding increases and we develop better techniques of discovery, our knowledge about historical events increases as well. Discoveries of fossilized human remains in archeological studies have shown it repeatedly. Here are just two such examples. In 1974, scientists discovered the skeletal remains of a member of the *Australopithecus afarensis* species. They nicknamed these skeletal remains "Lucy." Lucy was estimated to have lived about 3.2 million years ago.[9] At the time, Lucy was the oldest known ancestor. Later in 1994, scientists discovered the *Ardipithecus ramidus* remains. They nicknamed it "Ardi," and estimated that

[7] Earliest domesticated crops. Daniel Zohary and Maria Hopf. *Domestication of Plants in the Old World: The Origin and Spread of Cultivated Plants in West Asia, Europe and the Nile Valley*. 3rd ed. Oxford: Oxford University Press, 2000. Print.

[8] Emergence of farming. Jean Bocquet-Appel. "When the World's Population Took Off: The Springboard of the Neolithic Demographic Transition." *Science* 333.6042 (2011): 560–61. *JSTOR*. Web.

[9] Discovery of Lucy. http://humanorigins.si.edu/evidence/human-fossils/fossils/al-288-1 (Accessed: April 8, 2020).

the specie lived about 4.4 million years ago.[10] So I would not be surprised if we find evidence of even earlier domestication of crops down the road.

Back to money. One of the earliest forms of commodity money was metal. Gold, copper, and silver were the most desired metals to be used as money. It is well known that kings of Lydia around the latter part of eighth century BCE used metal coins. These included gold, silver, and copper coins. John Galbraith, citing Alexander Del Mar's *History of Monetary Systems*, writes that it is possible that India had used coins a lot earlier, perhaps hundreds of years earlier. He bases his contention on references found in Hindu epics.[11]

Another commodity that has served as money is tobacco. While tobacco leaves could be used for smoking, they were also used as money. Even if you were not a smoker you would accept tobacco in exchange for what you produced because others were willing to accept tobacco in exchange for what others were producing and wanted to sell. In this part of the world, pretty much from the very beginning of the first permanent English settlement in 1607, Jamestown, all the way to the last decade of the twentieth century, tobacco has served as money in one form or another. In fact, tobacco was declared legal tender by the General Assembly of the colony in 1642.[12]

R. A. Radford was a prisoner of war during World War II. He presents a fascinating account of how prisoners traded goods that were provided to them by their captors and the Red Cross in Prisoner of War camps. Cigarettes became the currency of choice. Prices were quoted in terms of cigarettes and exchanges took place. Both buyers and sellers used cigarettes in exchange, even those who did not smoke.

In the US prisons, cigarettes were being used as money until the Department of Justice, Bureau of Prisons banned smoking in prisons.[13] Perhaps not surprisingly smoking was not banned for those inmates who could claim a religious exemption. Be it the payment of tax or school

[10] Discovery of Ardi. http://humanorigins.si.edu/evidence/human-fossils/species/ardipithecus-ramidus (Accessed: April 8, 2020).

[11] Use of coins in India. John K. Galbraith. *Money: Whence It Came, Where It Went*. Boston: Houghton Mifflin, 1975. Print.

[12] Tobacco as money in Virginia. John K. Galbraith. *Money: Whence It Came, Where It Went*. Boston: Houghton Mifflin, 1975. Print.

[13] Cigarette ban in prisons. https://www.federalregister.gov/documents/2014/12/08/2014-28620/smokingno-smoking-areas (Accessed: May 29, 2018).

curriculum, religion often gets a special treatment. Soon after the rule went into effect on January 7, 2015, Ramen noodles replaced cigarettes and became the choice to serve as money.[14]

Cowries and other seashells were not only used as ornaments they were also a much used form of money. Marion Johnson[15] notes that cowries were in use in some parts of West Africa at least up until the late 1960 and early 1970s. The word "cowrie" or "cowry" has Indian roots. Spelled phonetically it would sound like "***kowdi***" in Punjabi, the language spoken in the Punjab province of the Indian subcontinent which is now divided between India and Pakistan. In Hindi and Urdu, if one were to spell it phonetically one would spell it as "cowrie" except that "r" is pronounced almost as "rt" but not quite. That particular sound, to my knowledge, is not represented by any English alphabet. Merriam-Webster writes that the word cowrie is pronounced as ***kauṛī*** in Hindi and Urdu.[16] Pronunciations often have this hurdle to cross and written language often fails us. Thankfully the pronunciation is not that crucial in this case. While not in use as currency by the end of the twentieth century, the words ***kauṛī and kowdi*** are still used to refer to something of little or no value.

Countries that used cowries had somewhat strange convention when it came to counting cowries. Johnson (1970) writes,

> Cowries in the north were generally counted in groups of five, which could be withdrawn from a heap by the fingers of one hand. These groups were then put together in piles of 60, 80 or 100, according to local convention; to make matters more confusing, the pile was generally known by the word for hundred. In Bambara, the 'hundred' was 80, at least when cowries were being counted. There is no record of how old this system of counting may be; it was certainly in existence at the end of the eighteenth century—[Mungo] Park noted that in Bambara 'it is curious that in counting the cowries, they call 80 a hundred; whilst in all other things they calculate by the common hundred'. (p. 38)

Johnson (1970) continues,

[14] Ramen noodles as money. Michael Gibson-Light. *Must Work for Food: The Politics of Nutrition and Informal Economy in an American Prison*, 2016. Print.

[15] Use of cowries as currency. Marion Johnson. "The Cowrie Currencies of West Africa: Part 1." *The Journal of African Studies* 11.1 (1970): 17–49. Print.

[16] Merriam-Webster pronunciation of cowrie. https://www.merriam-webster.com/dictionary/cowrie (Accessed: May 31, 2018).

> The fullest account of the Bambara counting system is given by the French officer Mage, who travelled nearly to Segu in 1866. Cowries, he writes, have a special system of numeration: 'They are counted by 10s and at first sight it seems that the system of numeration is decimal.' But they were counted according to the following table:
>
> 8 × 10 = 100
> 10 × 100 = 1,000
> 10 × 1,000 = 10,000
> 8 × 10,000 = 100,000
> which meant that 100,000 was in reality only 64,000, that 10,000 was only 8,000, that 1,000 was only 800, and 100 only 80. (p. 38)

Cowries also played an important role in West African slave trade. Jan Hogendorn and Marion Johnson in their book *The Shell Money of the Slave Trade* provide a fascinating look at how cowries were used across the world.[17] In the Introduction of their book, Hogendorn and Johnson write:

> The shell money of the slave trade consisted of the thousands of little cowrie shells, most of them fished in the lagoons of the far-off Maldive [*sic*] Islands of the Indian Ocean. They came to West Africa in a journey lasting a year or more, shipped initially by Arab merchants who took them to North Africa for export across the Sahara, and later by the European trading companies who carried them to Lisbon, Amsterdam, or London as ballast. Thence they were shipped by the barrel-load to West African coast, where they were an indispensable currency before, during, and after the slave trade, in purely quantitative terms overshadowing all others...For a very long period of time, the shells were actually better suited to transactions of extremely low value than were metallic coins, because it was all but impossible to mint a coin with worth as low as an individual cowrie. (The smallest British coin just before the colonial period was the farthing, equal to one quarter of a penny. It was about the same value as 25 to 32 cowries in southern Nigeria.)

The quality of cowries to be used in very small-value transactions was highly useful and desirable. Indeed, the ability of a form of money that can

[17] Cowries and other shell monies. Jan Hogendorn and Marion Johnson. *The Shell Money of the Slave Trade*. Cambridge: Cambridge University Press, 1986. Print.

be divided into smaller fractions without each fraction losing its proportional value remains a highly desirable quality even in today's modern monies.

One of the reasons behind the creation of the euro was to be able to make transactions across borders of the euro area without having to go through the hassle of converting one currency into another and bearing the exchange-rate risk. I will have more to say about the exchange-rate risk in Chapter 8. For now suffice it to say that the price of each country's currency in terms of another country's currency is subject to risk; prices of currencies in other currencies vary quite a bit.

To cite a specific example, the price of the US dollar in terms of the European euro from March 1, 2017 to March 1, 2018 oscillated between 1.0691 euros per US dollar and 1.234 euros per US dollar, with an average of 1.1627 euros per US dollar. It may not seem large enough of a swing to register for an average individual. However, when hundreds of billions of dollars are at stake this can make an executive of a company involved in international trade sweat bullets. So much so that she/he may decide to hold off on writing contracts with a European company. Just as an example, during the same time period the US exports to Germany, which uses euro, were over \$60,119.885 million with an average monthly exports of \$4624.607 million.[18] And this is just the volume of exports to just one country in the European Union. Instability in exchange rate can be extremely detrimental to international trade. We will see more details about exchange rates in Chapter 8. Cowries had a built-in quality. A cowrie is a cowrie whether it is West Africa or India or Europe.

And of course gold and silver have had a long history of being used as money. The first known coins are traced to Ephesus, a Greek city located in Asia Minor, around seventh century BCE. They were made of electrum. Electrum is a naturally occurring alloy of gold and silver. Electrum coins were also used in Lydia around the same time period. While these coins tended to be of irregular sizes and shapes, they "...were minted according to a strict weight-standard. The denominations ranged from one stater (weighing about 14.1 grams) down through half-staters, thirds, sixths, twelfths, 1/24ths and 1/48ths to 1/96th stater (about

[18] Exchange rate and export data. www.stlouisfed.org (Accessed: June 3, 2018).

0.15gm)."[19] "Stater," by the way, was the name of these coins, just as we call a unit of currency "dollar" in the United States or "pound" in the United Kingdom or "rupee" in India, and so on.

Coins made of gold, silver, and other precious metals contained the amount of metal according to the market value of the metal. For instance, the amount of gold contained in a gold coin was stamped on the coin. Any deviations would not, and did not, work. It made perfect sense to melt the coin if the stamped value of a gold coin were to be lower than the amount of gold it contained and sell the gold. This would have led to a shortage of coins. On the other hand, if the gold contained in a coin were to be lower than the stamped value then no one would accept it in exchange. With the advances in metallurgical technology, likenesses of humans and animals could be stamped on coins. That, of course, meant that kings wanted their faces stamped on coins. To this day monarchs (and monarch wannabees) have their pictures on their country's currencies and wherever else they can leave their marks. The British currency has the picture of Queen Elizabeth; Jordanian dinars have Jordanian kings imprinted; so did the Saudi kings; and of course the North Korean currency has the face of its supreme leader; and so on. Who knows what insecurities they hide!

In the United States, we do not have picture of living persons on currency. In 1866, the US Congress passed a law prohibiting the printing the portrait of a living person on the US currency, bonds, or securities.[20] The reason the Congress had to take action was due to what appeared on a five-cent note.

Spencer M. Clark was the Chief Clerk in the United State Treasury Department's National Currency Bureau (now known as Bureau of Printing and Engraving) from 1862 to 1868. His responsibilities included, of course, printing the US currency. In 1864, the US Treasury printed five-cent notes. His portrait ended up on those notes. Public did not take it kindly.

But it does not mean that the powerful haven't tried to put their likeness wherever they can.

[19] Electrum coins in Lydia. http://britishmuseum.org/explore/themes/money/the_origins_of_coinage.aspx (Accessed: June 3, 2018).

[20] Portraits on currency. https://www.treasury.gov/resource-center/faqs/Currency/Pages/edu_faq_currency_portraits.aspx (Accessed: June 22, 2018).

In anticipation of the summit scheduled for June 12, 2018 between the US President Donald Trump and the North Korean leader, Supreme Leader Kim Jong Un, the White House released a commemorative coin in May 2018. The coin depicted the two men facing each other.

Printing the pictures of a country's founders on its currency is one thing, a king or queen putting his or her own picture on the country's currency is quite another.

Back to the precious metals being used as money.

Gold has had an especially hallowed position in the United States from the very beginning of the nation's history. For some gold's hallowed status is metaphorical, for other it is literally so. It is an act of God. James Ledbetter in his 2017 book, *One Nation Under Gold: How One Precious Metal Has Dominated the American Imagination for Four Centuries*, tells the story of American infatuation with gold in detail. Talking about the gold rush of the mid-nineteenth century, he writes:

> The embrace of material wealth acquired with minimum suffering appears at odds with Christian teaching, and there were some who believed that the temptations of western metals led America down the wrong path. Certainly for nineteenth century Christians who believed that gambling, alcohol, and prostitution were grave offenses to God, the early gold settlements of the West readily looked like the epicenters of sin. Yet for most Americans, the material wealth associated with gold rush was not any cause to abandon any sense of being God's chosen nation. On the contrary, it implied that gold and silver were a national birthright, at once proof that America is a divinely promised land—and the very means to realize the promise. It may sound strange to a modern secular ear but Americans in the Third Great Awakening believed that gold and silver were deliberately placed beneath the Earth's surface by a benevolent God. Many believed that the fact that precious mineral resources are located in some places—say, the Rocky Mountains—and not others was a form of divine choosing; it of course followed from that premise that mining and using those riches to create American wealth was part of His plan that Americans had an obligation to fulfill. (p. 23)

No discussion of money will be complete without mentioning the example of money used on the Island of Yap. Economics professors love to give this example when they introduce the concept of money in introductory economics classes. There is a reason for the infatuation of the professoriate. The money used by the Islanders and their customs have all the features upon which professors want to stress. These stone discs have another immediate advantage: Showing pictures of these huge stone discs to students tends to get the attention even those students who can barely keep their eyes open in economics classes.

Yap, an island in the Pacific Ocean, uses large stone discs as money.[21] Locals call these discs *fei*. These stone discs are made of limestone found in another island about 400 miles away and chiseled into discs with hole in the middle so that a wooden pole may be inserted to carry the discs. The diameters of these stone wheels range from one foot to twelve feet. Yes, they are that large. It is certainly worth doing a Google search and looking at the pictures of *fei*.

As can be imagined, these large stone discs are rather hard to move from one place to another. Indeed, the islanders rarely, if ever, move these discs. Once the buyer and seller settle on the price of the good or service exchanged, the buyer transfers the ownership of the *fei* to the seller by making it public. They don't even make any mark on these discs. It just becomes public knowledge that this stone disc now belongs to the seller of a given good or service.

In fact, the discs do not even have to be on the island. According to the oral history, over a 100 years ago a large stone disc was being transported to Yap from a neighboring island where it was chiseled into shape. Due to a violent storm that arose the raft on which the disc was being brought to Yap sank along with the disc. The men transporting the disc survived and attested to the value of the disc. The islanders acknowledged the ownership of the disc even though it never touched the ground.

Another very interesting event took place when the German government purchased the island from Spain in 1898. The island had marked paths good enough for walking barefoot but not up to the German standard. The German government officials asked the local chiefs to repair these paths. The local chiefs, however, did not pay much attention to those orders. Milton Friedman (1991) quotes from *The Island of Stone Money*, written in 1910 by an American anthropologist, William Henry Furness:

> At last it was decided to impose a fine for disobedience on the chiefs of the districts. In what shape was the fine to be levied? … At last, by a happy

[21] Island of Yap. Milton Friedman. *The Island of Stone Money*. E-91-3 ed. Stanford University: The Hoover Institution, 1991. Print.

> thought, the fine was exacted by sending a man to every failu and pabai throughout the disobedient districts, where he simply marked a certain number of the most valuable fei with a cross in black paint to show that the stones were claimed by the government. This instantly worked like a charm; the people, thus dolefully impoverished, turned to and repaired the highways to such good effect from one end of the island to the other, that they are now like park drives. Then the government dispatched its agents and erased the crosses. Presto! the fine was paid, the happy failus resumed possession of their capital stock, and rolled in wealth.

So how did we get from the form of money that had some intrinsic value—commodity money—to the form of money that did not have any intrinsic value—non-commodity money? The *fei* after all did not have any intrinsic value in the sense gold, silver, copper, or other precision stones had. One can use, say, gold and silver to make jewelry or cap a decaying tooth. But a large stone disk?

Here it helps to remind ourselves that one of the characteristics of something that can serve as money is a medium of exchange. As long as people are willing to exchange their products and services for this thing, whatever it happens to be, it can function as money. And *fei* is no different. People were willing to accept *fei* in exchange for their product just as they were willing to accept tobacco or gold or silver or squirrel pelts or cakes of salt or the baked-clay tokens over 9500 years ago in the "Mesopotamian region of Sumer" where "ancient accountants kept track of farmers' crops and livestock by stacking small pieces of baked clay,… One piece might signify a bushel of grain, while another with a different shape might represent a farm animal or a jar of olive oil."[22]

We will return to this "accounting view of money" in coming chapters. This view will help us better understand, at least partially, some of the modern forms of money. For now, some more historical perspective.

A very short review of the history of banking is helpful to understand this transition from commodity money to non-commodity money. I will focus this primer on Western Europe, especially Italy, France, and Spain, since this is the part of the world where banking started and flourished.

All the way up until the fifteenth and sixteenth centuries, gold was one of the preferred forms of money. There was a problem with this

[22] Backed-clay tokens. https://news.nationalgeographic.com/2017/03/money-human-origins-journey-humankind/ (Accessed: June 10, 2018).

metallic form of money; its susceptibility to theft. Not everyone had a safe at home in which to put it. However goldsmith, given the nature of their profession, had a solution. One could deposit gold with goldsmiths for safekeeping. Of course the depositor had to pay a fee but it was still better than having one's gold stolen. The goldsmith would write a receipt indicating that such and such depositor had deposited this much gold with such and such goldsmith.

3.3 Modelville in the 1500s

Let me tell a tale. Tales make concepts palatable and lessons memorable.

We are in the early 1500s in a village, called Modelville, where residents used gold as money. Yes, it is the same Modelville we spent an evening in its downtown in Chapter 2. In this chapter, as opposed to exploring the microcosm of a three-block area of the downtown, we will take a bird's eye view of the whole town.

Let's give the residents of Modelville names and descriptors. Names alone, like acronyms, are convenient tools, but without descriptors they rarely, if ever, provide any useful information.

Ismael the ironsmith set up an iron smithing shop in Modelville. He made wrought iron fences. His customers paid Ismael the ironsmith with gold, the form of money used in Modelville. Ismael the ironsmith earned five ounces of gold during January 1500 by making wrought iron fences for his customers. Since he did not want to keep the gold in his house or in his shop, he deposited the five ounces of gold with Gloria the goldsmith. Gloria the goldsmith wrote a receipt to acknowledge the deposit. Everyone in Modelville called each receipt a Pecuna. For recordkeeping purposes, the residents used the symbol ℙ as a shorthand. Let's also make each Pecuna equal to one ounce of gold. That is, 1ℙ is equal to 1 ounce of gold, 2ℙ is equal to 2 ounces of golds, and so on. So Gloria the goldsmith wrote five receipts, one receipt per ounce of gold. That is, 5ℙ.

Yes, it is the same name that we gave to the "thing" that was used to exchange goods and services, to evaluate goods and services, and to transfer purchasing power from now to a later date in Chapter 2. And this is why we called the numeraire Pecuna and used ℙ to represent Pecuna.

Back to Ismael the ironsmith. Ismael the ironsmith often needed new iron smithing tools. Whenever Ismael the ironsmith needed to buy iron smithing tools from Terri the toolmaker, he would go to Gloria the goldsmith, submit the receipts issued by her (i.e., Pecunae) and withdraw his gold. Ismael the ironsmith would take the gold to Terri the toolmaker and exchange gold for tools. Since Terri the toolmaker did not have a safe in her home either, she would take gold to Gloria the goldsmith for safekeeping and get a receipt for each ounce of gold deposited as a proof of deposit (i.e., Pecunae). And so the life continued in Modelville. Everyone used gold to make transactions and everyone had the same issues with gold; it was susceptible to theft. So everyone used the safekeeping services provided by Gloria the goldsmith, or some other goldsmith, to keep their gold safe. It is worth pointing out that the number of goldsmiths does not matter. The model works the same whether there is one goldsmith or 1000 goldsmiths. Here, for the ease of exposition, I will use Gloria the goldsmith as a representative of all goldsmiths.

Suppose that at the beginning of our story, say January 1500, there were 100 ounces of gold and that these 100 ounces were deposited with Gloria the goldsmith who had issued 100 receipts, one receipt for each ounce of gold deposited. That is, there were 100 Pecunae in Modelville. We can say that the quantity of money in January 1500 was 100. We can count in terms of ounces of gold or in terms of the number of receipts (i.e., Pecunae) that have been issued by Gloria the goldsmith. Either way, the quantity of money is 100.

Life continued in this way for some time. When one resident of Modelville wanted to buy something from another resident they would take the deposit receipts that were issued by Gloria the goldsmith to her, get their gold, exchange it for the product. The seller would, again, deposit the gold with Gloria the goldsmith and get deposit receipts (i.e., Pecunae). This practice was a bit cumbersome though. For a transaction to take place there were these two extra steps of converting deposit receipts into gold and then converting gold into deposit receipts. People realized that as long as they could get their gold deposited with Gloria the goldsmith whenever they needed, they could just exchange goods and services using the deposit receipts. This certainly simplified the commercial life in Modelville. It was simpler for buyers as well as sellers to exchange goods and services for deposit receipts; no going back and forth to withdraw and redeposit gold. And it was simpler for Gloria the goldsmith as well. She did not have to exert time and effort to convert deposit receipts into gold when a depositor wanted her gold back or when someone wanted to deposit his gold for safekeeping. The gold stayed in Gloria the goldsmith's safes. Now of course the new bearer of the deposit receipt had to pay the safekeeping fee since he was the one who was the rightful owner of gold kept in Gloria the goldsmith's safes. All in all, it was much simpler than withdrawing the gold deposits, making the exchange, and redepositing the gold.

As of now the quantity of money in our model village, Modelville, is still 100. It's just that deposit receipts (i.e., Pecunae) are functioning as money. People could borrow and lend just like before, it's just that now all they needed were Pecunae as opposed to physical gold. Anyone who had the Pecunae could convert them into gold whenever they wanted. Not much had changed. Life continued.

Let's move about six months closer to the present—from January 1500 to June 1500.

Ever since Steward the student was a child he was fascinated by the wrought iron fence outside his school. Steward the student graduated from school in June 1500. In school, Steward the student learned how to read and write and how to do arithmetic. Now he wanted to become an ironsmith and learn how to make wrought iron fences. Steward the student asked Ismael the ironsmith if he would take Steward the student as his apprentice. Ismael the ironsmith agreed. Steward the student needed tools to start his apprenticeship. He needed a couple of hammers and tongs. But he did not have any money to buy the required tools. Steward the student did not need to buy his own anvil. Ismael the ironsmith had a spare one that Steward the student could use. Steward the student went to Gloria the goldsmith and asked for a loan of five ounces of gold so that he could buy iron smithing tools from Terri the toolmaker. Gloria the goldsmith and Steward the student agreed on the terms of the loan, the interest rate and the length of loan, etc. Steward the student got the loan to buy iron smithing tools from Terri the toolmaker. Steward the student could have gotten five ounces of gold from Gloria the goldsmith. Terri the toolmaker, however, was willing to accept deposit receipts issued by Gloria the goldsmith (i.e., Pecunae). Terri the toolmaker was certain that she could get the gold whenever she needed by presenting the receipts to Gloria the goldsmith. For Terri the toolmaker, those receipts were as good as gold. So Steward the student got deposit receipts worth five ounces of gold. That is, Steward borrowed 5ℙ from Gloria the goldsmith.

Yes, "as good as gold." Language has a way of preserving cultural and historical fingerprints. A US dollar is called a "buck" because pieces of buckskins and hides were used as money during the colonial times.

Something happened here. In January 1500, the quantity of money was 100 in Modelville. There were as many ounces of gold as there were the deposit receipts. In June 1500, the quantity to money increased to 105. Why? Because the ounces of gold were still 100 but there were 105 receipts. And because everyone is using receipts as money in Modelville, what matters is the number of receipts (i.e., Pecunae). Gloria the goldsmith had created money by issuing more receipts than there were deposits of gold. In fact, this is how commercial banks create money even today. Commercial banks create money by issuing more loans than they have deposits.

It sounds fishy. Doesn't it? Except that it's not. Here is why:

Issuing more loans than Gloria the goldsmith has deposits is obviously beneficial for her. She earns interest on the loans that she has extended. It is beneficial for the depositors as well. With these loans being made the depositors have to pay lower safekeeping fees. Indeed, depending upon the loans and the length of time for which loans are extended, they may even get a share of the interest that Gloria the goldsmith is earning. As long as Gloria the goldsmith is upfront and transparent about the loans she is extending, both Gloria the goldsmith and the depositors are better off. Transparency is the key in this situation. We will learn more about this in coming chapters.

It is better for Steward the student as well. Without this loan he could not have purchased iron smithing tools from Terri the toolmaker. And without Steward the student buying tools he would not have been able to learn how to make wrought iron fences. True, Steward the student might have found some other job but his talent would have been wasted.

In fact, there is more to it. Steward's ability to get a loan has two types of consequences—right now and further down the road. Right now, with increased demand of iron smithing tools, Terri the toolmaker may end up hiring more workers or ask existing workers to work more hours, or a combination of the two. Either way, the demand for Teri the toolmaker's tools, and by extension, the demand for workers who make iron smithing tools has increased. As a result, the incomes of both Teri the toolmaker and the toolmaking workers have increased. Put another way, the overall income level in the Modelville economy has increased. It started with Modelvillites depositing their gold with Gloria the goldsmith and, in turn, Gloria the goldsmith issuing more loans than she had deposits. So on and so forth.

The consequences down the road are perhaps even more important for everyone in Modelville. With Steward the student being able to apprentice with Ismael the ironsmith, Steward learned how to make wrought iron fences. Along the way Steward the student developed better techniques. And when someone in the generation after wanted to learn how to make wrought iron fences Steward the student taught that student. So on and so forth. That knowledge had the chance to extend to the next generation, and generations after that. Indeed, this is how knowledge—the main ingredient of growth and development—accumulates and spreads. The residents of Modelville had a lot larger pool of knowledge and a lot higher income levels in the Modelville economy for generations to come. And of course, a lot of beautiful wrought iron fences. So it is better for the society as a whole as well.

Suppose now that Steward the student is not able to get a loan from anyone to buy iron smithing tools from Terri the toolmaker. Gloria the goldsmith does not issue Steward the student receipts worth five ounces of gold either; she has only 100 ounces of gold in her safe and she does not want to issue more receipts (i.e., Pecunae) than there is gold. This is even though Gloria the goldsmith can verify whether or not Steward the student will return the loan along with the interest with a great degree of certainty. According to her information, the demand for wrought iron fences is growing, and based on the reputation of Steward the student, Steward is a smart and hardworking young man. He is expected to do well once he learns how to make wrought iron fences. Given these factors Steward will be able to return the loan along with the interest payment. Not only that, her experience based on her meticulous records of deposits and withdrawals tells her that not many people come to withdraw their gold deposits. Even then Gloria the goldsmith does not issue receipts worth five ounces of gold because she does not want to issue more receipts (i.e., Pecunae) than there is gold sitting in her safes.

In this scenario, everyone loses. Gloria the goldsmith loses because she cannot earn the interest. Savers lose because they have to pay higher safekeeping fees. Steward the student loses because he cannot learn how to make wrought iron fences and expand his skillset that could lead to higher income. The toolmakers lose because there are fewer toolmaking jobs. And society as a whole loses because the pool of knowledge is smaller than it would have been. And of course there aren't many beautiful wrought iron fences. Everyone loses.

I know I am repeating "*i.e.* Pecunae" in parentheses way too many times. I want the reader not to forget that we are calling those deposit receipts Pecunae, that each Pecuna is equal to one ounce of gold, and that Pecunae are being used as money—to exchanged goods and services, to evaluate goods and services, and to transfer purchasing power from today to tomorrow.

But what if everyone who had a Pecuna went to withdraw their gold from Gloria the goldsmith? Will she have enough gold? Obviously not. There were only 100 ounces of gold and there were 105 Pecunae outstanding. That is, there were 105 deposit receipts in Modelville. Gloria the goldsmith would have a problem only when everyone went to get their gold at the same time. But why would everyone go to get their gold at the same time? Residents of Modelville will only want their gold if they had any doubt about the convertibility of their receipts. Otherwise why would they want to hold gold in their houses where it is susceptible to theft? A mechanism has to be developed such that Modelville's residents' gold is safe, and that they know that their gold is safe.

Enter central banks.

One of the main roles that a central bank in an economy plays is that it makes sure that commercial banks are playing by the rules, and that people know that commercial banks are playing by the rules. Everything is transparent. This generates a degree of confidence in the economy. I will come back to commercial banks and the roles that central banks play in the coming chapters. For now, let's move closer still to the present and talk about the paper currency used in the United States.

3.4 Paper Currency in the United States

The Bureau of Engraving and Printing is the source of designing and printing paper currency. The bureau is also responsible for printing invitations to attend inauguration events, award certificates, forms, various identification cards, and security documents of the various branches of the US government.[23] The Bureau also maintains a detailed record of currency issued in the United States. The Bureau does not, however, produce coins. All coins are produced by the US Mint.

[23] The Bureau of Engraving and Printing. https://www.moneyfactory.gov/uscurrency/history.html (Accessed: June 26, 2018).

History tells us that military expeditions have always been expensive endeavors. While these ventures may be necessary at times, not many are willing to pay for such enterprises. One way out of this dilemma is to issue promissory notes: IOUs that promise to repay the bearer later on. Massachusetts Bay was the first of the thirteen original colonies to issue paper currency in 1690. Other colonies soon followed.

Of course the counterfeiters were not far behind either. It is much cheaper and easier to counterfeit a buck than to earn one, otherwise why would someone counterfeit? One way to deter counterfeiting is to make it harder to make the exact replica. Benjamin Franklin found a deterrent in the design and the printing techniques. In 1739, Franklin printed Colonial notes with hard to counterfeit features. Governments that were unable to adopt techniques that would make counterfeiting hard faced the inevitable. And they still do.

The Continental Congress issued paper currency to fund the Revolutionary War. The currency was denominated in Spanish milled dollars. The currency of the Continental Congress became known as the "Continental." While the Spanish dollars, made of one ounce silver, had milled edges and other markings making them harder to counterfeit, the paper currency issued by the Continental Congress denominated in these dollars did not have any such safeguards. Counterfeiters counterfeited and the Continental currency lost all its value. As I mentioned above, language has a way to preserving history. Anything that was worthless was said to be not worth a Continental. The protection of the public trust in a country's currency is paramount. The US Secret Service was originally established in 1865 as part of the US Treasury to ensure that counterfeiting did not take place and the public had trust in the country's currency.

In 1792, the Coinage Act was passed. Along with establishing a monetary system at the federal level, the Act set the value of the US dollar in gold (24.75 grains of gold) and silver (371.24 grains of silver).[24] Silver was overvalued. Gold left the country. Gresham's Law was in action.

On July 17 and August 5, 1861, the Congress passed certain Acts that asked the US Treasury to issue the "Demand Notes." They were called Demand Notes because the bearer was promised to be paid in gold coins on demand. The reason for issuing Demand Notes was to finance the

[24] Coinage Act of 1792. (2015). In J. S. Olson and A. O. Mendoza. *American Economic History: A Dictionary and Chronology*. Westport, CT: Greenwood (Accessed: June 26, 2018).

Civil War. They remained in circulation for only a year or so, from the summer of 1861 to the spring of 1862, and disappeared from circulation soon after the end of the Civil War.

In 1862, the Treasury issued the US Notes. These notes were not redeemable in gold or silver. The National Bank Act of February 25, 1863 created the Comptroller of the Currency and National Currency Bureau. The Act authorized the Comptroller of the Currency to charter National Banks and issue National Bank Notes.

Data show that when storms, hurricanes, and other natural and human-made disasters hit a region people withdraw money from banks; they want to hold on to physical bills. It could be that people think that storms may knock out power lines making credit card machines and ATMs useless. It could also be that people just want to hold on to physical objects that they consider valuable in times of uncertainty. During the Civil War people held on to coins, which usually were of smaller denomination, because of the precious metal they contained. The result was a shortage of coins in circulation. To remedy this situation, the Congress authorized public to pay US government debts using postage stamps. This created a shortage of postage stamps. To deal with this situation, the Congress issued notes in denomination of 3, 5, 10, 15, 25, and 50 cents. These were called "Fractional Notes." These notes were issued by the newly formed Bureau of Engraving and Printing. Earlier on these Fractional Notes looked very similar to postage stamps. In fact they were referred to as "postage notes." Later on they were designed to look like currency and the pictures of the founding fathers along with other luminaries appeared on these notes. This is when Spencer M. Clark's picture, the Chief Clerk in the US Treasury whom we met earlier, ended up on a five-cent note.

An act of the US Congress on March 3, 1863 authorized the Treasury to issue Gold Certificates. They were deposit certificates. Just like the practices of the goldsmiths of the fifteenth and sixteenth centuries (remember Gloria the goldsmith from a few pages back?), people could deposit gold at the Treasury and get a receipt certifying that this much gold was deposited. The original purpose of issuing Gold Certificates according to the Bureau of Engraving and Printing Website was[25]

[25] Gold Certificates. https://www.moneyfactory.gov/images/FactSheet_GoldCertificate_20130502.pdf (Accessed: June 27, 2018).

> to accumulate gold coin in the Treasury during the Civil War when gold was scarce. However, Treasury receipts from customs duties, which were always paid in gold, were enough to meet the needs of the Government. As a result, the first Gold Certificates were not issued until after the Civil War in November 1865. The notes became popular with merchants and banks that had to move large sums of gold; paper notes were easier and cheaper to transport.

Just as it is with gold, carrying silver is also cumbersome. In 1873, an act of the US Congress left out silver dollars from the list of legal tender. It was termed as "Crime of '73." An uproar, now known as the Free Silver Movement, followed. The proponents were the silver miners and the mid-western farmers. On February 28, 1878, the Bland-Allison Act was passed.[26] The Act authorized the issuance of Sliver Certificates. The first series of the Silver Certificates was issued in 1878. These were issued in $10, $20, $50, $100, $500, and $1000 denominations. In 1886, the second series Silver Certificates was issued. The denominations were $1, $2, and $5. In 1896, the last of the $20, $50, $100, $500, and $1000 denominations of Silver Certificates were issued. Some argue that the Free Silver Movement was also the motivation behind *The Wonderful Wizard of Oz*, the 1900 children's book written by L. Frank Baum. The author never confirmed or denied the reports. The inscription "IN GOD WE TRUST" first appeared on Silver Certificates printed in July 1957. June 4, 1963 (77 Stat. 54) was the end of Silver Certificates. The Act repealed all previous Acts pertaining to the purchase of silver coins and bullion. Silver Certificates were replaced with Federal Reserve Notes to which I turn next.

3.5 The Creation of the Federal Reserve System

The Federal Reserve Act of December 23, 1913 established the central bank of the United States, the Federal Reserve System, or the Fed, for short.[27] The Act has 31 sections with numerous subsections. While not exactly a beach read, it is certainly worth a read if one wants to get a

[26] Silver Certificates. https://www.moneyfactory.gov/images/FactSheet_SilverCertificate_20130425.pdf (Accessed: June 29, 2018).

[27] The Federal Reserve Act. https://www.federalreserve.gov/aboutthefed/officialtitle-preamble.htm (Accessed: June 29, 2018).

better understanding of the concept of money. Or one may watch videos if one is so inclined.[28]

The Fed has a unique structure. It is a public and private partnership. The Fed has, what is called, a dual mandate. It is responsible for a stable price level and high employment. Under its mandate to maintain a stable price level, the Fed manages the quantity of money (money supply) in the United States. The act of changing the quantity of money in the United States is called monetary policy. So the Fed is the official body that conducts monetary policy.

The above brief description of the establishment of the Federal Reserve System may give the impression that it was a smooth sailing. Quite the contrary. Establishing a national bank was quite an ordeal. The country went through a few iterations before it settled on the Fed. First it was the First Bank of the United States. It was established in 1790 after the ratification of the Constitution in 1788. It operated till 1811. The First Bank of the United States was authorized to issue paper currency. Before the establishment of the First Bank of the United States, there were a number of entities issuing their currency; even drugstores got into the action. It allowed customers to buy merchandize from the drugstore. Understandably it created a lot of confusion. The First Bank of the United States was a private bank. This created controversy. Once its charter ran out in 1811 it was not renewed. Then there was the Second Bank of the United States. It was chartered in 1816 to operate for 20 years. Andrew Jackson was the president of the United States by the time its charter ran out. President Jackson did not renew the charter.

The US currency has gone through many changes over the years. These changes include new designs and security features to make it harder for the counterfeiters to counterfeit. Today each denomination bill bears the signatures of the US Secretary of Treasury and the US Treasurer. It may be a matter of pride but sometimes it has a social cost. On November 15, 2017, Steve Mnuchin and his wife, Louise Linton, went to the Bureau of Engraving and Printing to see the first one-dollar bill bearing his signature. His wife tweeted pictures of the couple holding an uncut sheet of one-dollar bills. Linton was wearing expensive designer clothes. The pictures had some unwanted results when Ms. Linton shared the picture on her social media platform. As opposed to "likes," she received

[28] The Fed. https://www.federalreserve.gov/aboutthefed.htm (Accessed: June 29, 2018).

contempt for, in some individuals' views, at the unearned stature of the couple.[29]

Let me now turn to cryptocurrencies. As mentioned before, at the time of this writing, there are over 2200 types of cryptocurrencies. Bitcoin and Ethereum are probably the most popular cryptocurrencies. Remember money issued by drugstores? Well, a digital counterpart of that is Dentacoin, a cryptocurrency to be used at dentists. It claims to revolutionize dentistry. According to the Denatcoin Website, "Dentacoin aims at improving dental care worldwide and making it affordable through crowd power."[30] On January 8, 2018, its market cap (i.e., the total value of Dentacoins measured in US dollars) was $1,910,300,000, according to the data provided by the Website, CoinMarketCap.[31] The market cap ranged between $4,964,020 on August 11, 2017 and $121,431,000 on July 2, 2018, according to CoinMarketCap.[32]

The technology behind these cryptocurrencies is called blockchain. To explain what blockchain technology is let me take you back to the first Friday of the month in that capital city, Modelville. Remember the thought experiment with barter—a system of buying goods and services with other goods and services? It became pretty complicated pretty quickly. To make transactions, we decided to use Pecunae instead. We also had to make sure that people could not "double-spend" the Pecunae they had. That is, one could not buy a pint of locally-brewed beer and a stone-studded piece of jewelry with the *same* Pecunae. The Pecunae, or the US dollar, or the British pound, or the European euro, prevent this from happening by exchanging these currencies, either in paper form or in electronic form, for goods and services.

Now imagine a large record book that keeps track of all the transactions made with a given Pecuna. People cannot spend the same Pecuna more than once. When someone purchases something from someone else, Pecunae change hands; Pecunae go one way and the product goes the other way. Blockchain technology allows us to keep track of who bought

[29] Steve Mnuchin and his wife holding uncut dollar bills. https://abcnews.go.com/Politics/treasury-secretary-steve-mnuchin-wife-internet-sensation-posing/story?id=51189079 (Accessed: June 26, 2018).

[30] Dentacoin. http://www.dentacoin.com/ (Accessed: July 3, 2018).

[31] Dentacoin market cap. https://coinmarketcap.com/ (Accessed: July 3, 2018).

[32] Number of cryptocurrencies. https://coinmarketcap.com/ (Accessed: June 20, 2019).

what from whom and for how much in electronic form. Furthermore, blockchain allows the buyers and sellers to remain anonymous; it uses cryptographic pseudonyms. This last quality has made cryptocurrencies the darlings of a segment of the society that distrusts the government and the banking sector, not to mention those who want to trade in contraband—illicit drugs, arms, and so on. The Russians used Bitcoin to pay for servers, domain name, etc., when they hacked into the Democratic National Committee servers and Hillary Clinton's 2016 presidential campaign.[33]

There are a few problems with cryptocurrencies that make them unlikely to take the place of your everyday money. Remember the three characteristics that something that serves as money has to have—a medium of exchange, a unit of account, and a store of value?

As a medium of exchange, while cryptocurrencies, especially Bitcoin, are gaining popularity, they are far from being accepted by general public. There are reasons behind this. One is that it takes a lot longer for a transaction to take place. This is due to the verification system inherent in blockchain technology. For instance, at the time of this writing, Bitcoin could handle only a few transactions per second. Compare this to tens of thousands of credit card transactions per second and tens of thousands of cash transactions per second. The problem was at display at the North American Bitcoin conference held in January 2018 in Miami. The organizers of the conference stopped taking Bitcoins for tickets to attend the conference because it was taking too long to process each transaction.[34]

Oh the irony. Bitcoins not being accepted at a Bitcoin conference!

Another related problem that has arisen with an increased use of Bitcoin is the processing fee. Bitcoin transactions used to be free. According to Joseph Bonneau, an assistant professor of Computer Science at the New York University, and his co-authors, by the end of 2017 it

[33] Russians used Bitcoin to hack into the DNC servers. https://www.nytimes.com/2018/07/13/technology/bitcoin-russian-hacking.html?login=email&auth=login-email (Accessed: July 23, 2018).

[34] Bitcoin conference stops accepting cryptocurrencies. https://www.cnbc.com/2018/01/10/bitcoin-conference-stops-accepting-cryptocurrency-payments.html; https://slate.com/technology/2018/01/the-most-important-blockchain-conference-of-the-year-wont-take-bitcoin-for-last-minute-sales.html (Accessed: July 9, 2018).

was averaging around $20 and went as high at $400 per transaction.[35] Now, transaction fees are not uncommon. Each time you use a credit card (Visa, Master Card, American Express, etc.) the vendor is charged a transaction fee by the credit card company. Sometimes the vendor passes all or part of the fee to the consumers. But those charges are miniscule compared with $20 per transaction, on average, charged by Bitcoin and its cousins. Not only that, the fees charged by credit card companies are far more predictable and set in advance. By law credit card companies are required to let the merchants know how much they are being charged for each transaction. Similarly, merchants are required by law to make their customers aware of the transaction fee that the customers have to pay to use a credit card.[36]

How about using cryptocurrencies serving as a unit of account? That is, evaluating goods and services in terms of cryptocurrencies. Bitcoin and other cryptocurrencies are failing on this front as well. Here is why? Imagine using a yardstick (or a meter rod) to measure the distance between two fixed points. One would expect that whenever one measures the distance, the measurement is the same, say, five yards and three inches. Remember that the points are fixed. What if the length of the yardstick were to change pretty much randomly? Every time you measure the distance it is different, except by chance. Sometime it is longer and sometime it is shorter. Sometime the measured distance is five yards and ten inches, sometimes the measured distance is twenty yards and seven inches, and everything in between and beyond. You will never be confident of the measured distance between two fixed points. Because the length of the yardstick itself is changing, sometimes the change is mere inches and at other times the change is in thousands of yards. The yardstick is pretty worthless in this scenario. The same is true of evaluating goods and services in terms of Bitcoins and other cryptocurrencies. As we saw earlier, the market cap of Dentacoin ranged between $4,964,020 on August 11, 2017 and $121,431,000 on July 2, 2018. The price of

[35] Bitcoin transaction fees "Five Myths about Bitcoin." http://www.chicagotribune.com/business/columnists/ct-biz-bitcoin-myths-20171215-story.html; https://www.washingtonpost.com/outlook/five-myths/five-myths-about-bitcoin/2017/12/15/7a506742-e044-11e7-8679-a9728984779c_story.html?noredirect=on&utm_term=.e2b5a663e6fb (Accessed: July 9, 2018).

[36] Credit card transaction fee. https://usa.visa.com/support/consumer/visa-rules.html (Accessed: July 9, 2018).

each Dentacoin ranged between $0.000317 on August 11, 2017 and $0.000391 on July 2, 2018. It peaked on January 8, 2018 at $0.005874 per Dentacoin. In case you are wondering during the same period the price of each Bitcoin ranged between $2727.13 on August 11, 2017, with a market cap of $44,950,800,000, and $6380.38 on July 2, 2018, with a market cap of $109,273,000,000. Bitcoin peaked at $19,475.80 per Bitcoin on December 17, 2017, with a market cap of $326,141,000,000 (so far).[37] By way of comparison, the price of each UK pound on August 11, 2017 was $1.2988, and on July 2, 2018 it was $1.3133.

Why so many gyrations in the prices of cryptocurrencies? The reason lies in the third characteristic of something that can be used as money: a store of value. As I mentioned earlier, not many people are using cryptocurrencies as a medium of exchange or as a unit of account. Most people who own cryptocurrencies are hoping that when the use of cryptocurrency, especially the particular cryptocurrency that they are holding, i.e., Bitcoin, Ethereum, etc., becomes common, the demand for their particular cryptocurrency will increase. Given that there is a set maximum quantity of each cryptocurrency to be issued, each unit of that cryptocurrency will become more valuable.

Caution is in order, however. The issuers of Bitcoin have announced that the maximum number of Bitcoins issued will not exceed 21,000,000. At the time of this writing, there were 17,143,787 Bitcoins in circulation according to the Website www.coinmarketcap.com.[38] Issuers of other cryptocurrencies also have a preset maximum quantity. This is a myth, argue Joseph Bonneau and his co-authors. They write:

> The currency's original design calls for the 21 million units to be slowly created over the next 100 years or so. But the protocol can be amended by community consensus—a majority of participants in the bitcoin network—as has already occurred several times, such as an update that helped users specify payment conditions. So far, the bitcoin community has fiercely

[37] Prices of Bitcoin and Dentacoin. https://coinmarketcap.com/ (Accessed: July 9, 2018).

[38] Quantity of Bicoin. https://coinmarketcap.com/ (Accessed: July 11, 2018).

> defended the planned finite supply and is notoriously change-averse. But politics among users, not math, keeps things that way for now.[39]

So people are holding these currencies as assets. Now, as the expectations of people who hold a cryptocurrency, say Bitcoin, change, so does its value in terms of US dollars (and other currencies). Expectations, not grounded in reality, can be fickle. Furthermore, as we will see in the coming chapters, fixed quantity of a form of money is not a feature. It is a bug. As our understanding of how the economy works, and how the financial sector and the goods and services sector interact has improved, flexibility in the quantity of money has proven to be a much desired feature.

Some readers may be wondering why did I pick August 11, 2017 and July 2, 2018 as the start and end dates, respectively. The reason is simple: I started talking about Dentacoin above as an example of various cryptocurrencies, and I continued the example. The earliest price data for Dentacoin are available starting August 11, 2017, and at the time of writing this part of the book, July 2, 2018 was the latest date for which data were available.

"But wait" an attentive reader may be wondering. "You mentioned that banks create money by issuing more loans than they have deposits and that the central bank changes money supply without mentioning the 'how' and 'why,' and just moved on. You also mentioned that everyone in Modelville would have been worse off had Gloria the goldsmith not issued loan (i.e., created money) to Steward the student without going into much detail. Could you expand on that? What is the mechanism? More importantly, where is the evidence that the economy suffers when banks do not issue loans?" Relax, you, the attentive reader. I will go over the details in the coming chapters. Be patient.

[39] Maximum Quantity of Bitcoin "Five Myths about Bitcoin." http://www.chicagotribune.com/business/columnists/ct-biz-bitcoin-myths-20171215-story.html; https://www.washingtonpost.com/outlook/five-myths/five-myths-about-bitcoin/2017/12/15/7a506742-e044-11e7-8679-a9728984779c_story.html?noredirect=on&utm_term=.e2b5a663e6fb (Accessed: July 9, 2018).

Works Cited

Bocquet-Appel, Jean. "When the World's Population Took Off: The Springboard of the Neolithic Demographic Transition." *Science* 333.6042 (2011): 560–61. *JSTOR*. Web.

Dawkins, Richard. *The Greatest Show on Earth: The Evidence for Evolution*. New York, NY: Free Press, 2009. Print.

Friedman, Milton. *The Island of Stone Money*. E-91-3 ed. Stanford University: The Hoover Institution, 1991. Print.

Galbraith, John K. *Money: Whence It Came, Where It Went*. Boston: Houghton Mifflin, 1975. Print.

Gibson-Light, Michael. *Must Work for Food: The Politics of Nutrition and Informal Economy in an American Prison*, 2016. Print.

Hogendorn, Jan, and Marion Johnson. *The Shell Money of the Slave Trade*. Cambridge: Cambridge University Press, 1986. Print.

Johnson, Marion. "The Cowrie Currencies of West Africa: Part 1." *The Journal of African Studies* 11.1 (1970): 17–49. Print.

Wright, Robert. *The Evolution of God*. New York, NY: Little, Brown, 2009. Print.

Zohary, Daniel, and Maria Hopf. *Domestication of Plants in the Old World: The Origin and Spread of Cultivated Plants in West Asia, Europe and the Nile Valley*. 3rd ed. Oxford: Oxford University Press, 2000. Print.

CHAPTER 4

Saving, Lending, Borrowing, and the Banking Sector

This chapter goes through the details of money creation. After showing the benefits of saving, borrowing, and lending, I talk about fractional-reserve banking. I introduce the reader to the basic mechanics of money creation. I go over the concepts of price level, inflation, deflation, and disinflation. The reader learns that while decreasing prices may *sound* like a good thing, a decreasing price level holds the seeds of economic stagnation.

4.1 Saving, Borrowing, and Lending

Recall again why we need money in an economy. We need money to exchange goods and services. We need money to evaluate goods and services. And we need money so that we can transfer purchasing power from today to the future. In other words, for something to function as money it has to have three characteristics. It can function used as a medium of exchange. It can serve as a unit of account. And it can be used as a store of value. In Chapter 2, we saw that without money, which we named Pecuna, venders (the brewers of craft beer, the t-shirt sellers, the stone-studded jewelry sellers, the painters, the metalworkers, the woodworkers) had trouble selling their wares.

Let's go back to Modelville and see how Gloria the goldsmith is doing. Yes, she makes jewelry from gold, but she also makes loans to those who want to borrow. And Stewards, the students of the Modelville, borrow so

M. Ashraf, *Money*,
https://doi.org/10.1007/978-3-030-50378-9_4

that they can purchase tools from Terries, the toolmakers. So on and so forth. Gloria the goldsmith creates money by issuing more receipts (i.e., Pecunae) than she has deposits of gold. I also mentioned that modern-day commercial banks created money the same way: Commercial banks create money by issuing more loans than they have deposits. Let me go into more detail about saving, borrowing, and lending. Here, an example may clarify point further. If you have had an introductory course in macroeconomics, you were quite likely given a similar example. A refresher, however, would be helpful.

Let's bring our sixteenth-century Modelville to the present. It is a thriving town. Pecuna is the currency of the day. When Modelvillites have more income than they consume, they save the rest. They use banks to make deposits. They use banks to borrow when they need more than what they have. When they deposit their saving in a bank, the bank pays them interest. And when they need to borrow, the bank charges the borrowers interest. All borrowing and lending is conducted using Pecunae, the currency of the day.

Modelville has residents of all ages, from newborn babies to the retired, and everyone in between. Those who are just entering college and those who have just graduated. Those who have been earning a living for two decades or more and those who are just entering the labor market. Modern-day Ismael the ironsmith has been working for over two decades. Over time while his needs have grown, his income has also grown. Usually what happens is that over the course of our lives, we have a disparity between our income and our consumption. When we are starting out in the labor market, our income tends to be lower than our consumption. We make up the difference by borrowing. Our consumption, though, tends to be relatively smooth as compared with our income. A stylized picture of income and consumption may look something like presented in Fig. 4.1.

Here is a stylized depiction of the lifecycle of our representative Modelvillite. Let's call her Molly. She graduates from college at age 21. For the sake of simplicity, suppose that Molly did not borrow any money, i.e., Pecunae, to go to college and she is graduating without any debt. Molly finds gainful employment. In this diagram, for visual ease, I am representing her income by a solid line and her consumption by a dotted line.

Molly needs a reliable car to commute to work, she needs professional looking clothes, and she needs a place to stay. Since she is starting out,

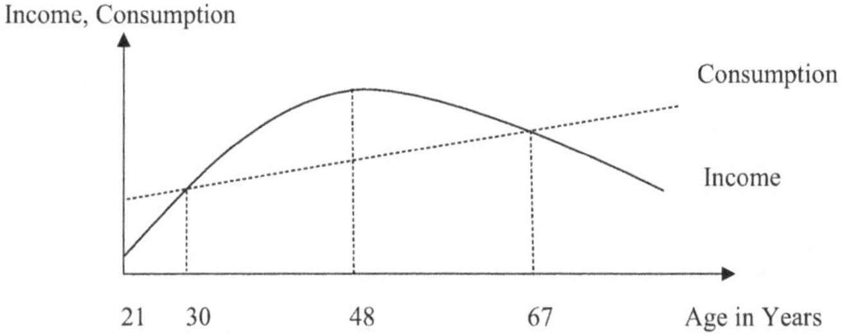

Fig. 4.1 Income and consumption (Figure prepared by the author)

she does not have any savings of her own. Her consumption is higher than her income. This is represented by the vertical distance between the dotted line and the solid one. As Molly gains experience her level of skills increases and with that her income increases as well. By age 30, her income and her consumption are the same—the vertical distance between the dotted line and the solid line has disappeared. As she gains experience and develops new skills, her income keeps on increasing. This is a combination of effort and skills. Her income peaks at 48. After that her income starts to decline. This could be due to fewer hours worked or a depreciation in skills or a combination these (and other) factors. She retires at age 67. After that her income falls below her consumption and she starts withdrawing her savings to fill the gap between her income and consumption. In fact, after her retirement Molly does not have any labor income. Any income Molly has it is from the interest that she is earning from her savings.

The point to be made here is that our income and consumption are asynchronous. When our income is lower than our consumption, we can support our consumption by borrowing. In return, we pay interest to those who lend us. And when our income is higher than our consumption, we can lend the saving to those who want to borrow and, in return, they pay us interest. It helps both borrowers and lenders. Of course, here we are abstracting from a number of complications. But then again, this is just to get us started. I will add complications in due time and the picture will become more realistic.

4.2 The Creation of Money

Back to Modelville. Let's pick a date just to anchor our discussion, say, January 1, 2018. And just as the residents of Modelville in the 1500s deposited gold with Gloria the goldsmith of the day, the residents of Modelville of the 2000s deposit Pecunae with the modern-day Gloria the goldsmith. Let's call him Bob the banker. And let's give Bob's bank a name. Let's call it Bob's Bank. (We, economists are very creative. There is no stopping when the creative juices are flowing. Move over Shakespeare!)

Modelvillites do this for safekeeping. In the Modelville of 1500s, the residents used gold as money. In the Modelville of today, the residents use Pecunae as money. An important point to keep in mind is that while the "thing" that is being used as money has changed, the purpose remains the same, that is, to exchange goods and service, to evaluate goods and services, and to transfer purchasing power from now to a future date.

On January 1, 2018, the residents of Modelville had deposited 100,000ℙ with Bob the banker for safekeeping and he had issued receipts to the depositors. Now that we are in the 2000s, let's call these receipts checks because this is what these receipts are. These days when we open an account in a bank and make a deposit, the bank issues a checkbook. Debit cards issued by a bank are just electronic versions of checkbooks. Whenever someone wants to buy something from someone else (a grocery store, a coffee shop, pay for dry cleaning, or what have you), they can swipe their debit card (or write a check if they want to annoy people behind them in line in a grocery store). Now, if someone does not trust the person who is writing the check, i.e., the buyer, they can ask for cash. In that case, the buyer can go to the bank, cash the check, and present cash to the seller. This, however, adds another step before the transaction can take place. It increases transaction costs. So as long as the seller trusts that the buyer has enough funds in the bank to cover the check and that the bank will be able to cash the check whenever the seller presents the check to the bank, the seller is willing to accept the check in exchange for the stuff she is selling. The same way whenever someone in Modelville wants to buy something from someone, they hand over a receipt (i.e., a check) of the required amount to the seller. The seller can take the check and hand over the stuff she is selling to the buyer. If not, the seller can ask for cash, i.e., Pecunae.

On January 1, 2018, then, the total amount of money in Modelville is 100,000ℙ. And just as Gloria the goldsmith had realized that not many depositors of gold withdrew gold to make transactions during the 1500s, Bob the banker of the 2000s has come to the same realization: Not many depositors withdraw Pecunae to make transactions. Most of the time most of the deposited Pecunae just sit in a vault in Bob's Bank. This means that when someone goes to Bob the banker of the 2000s to borrow money so that she could buy a car, or a house, or pay for school, all the borrower needs is a checkbook. And as long as the seller is confident that when and if she needs to withdraw Pecunae she can do so and the check will be honored by Bob the banker, she will be willing to part with her goods for a check.

When our representative resident of Modelville, Molly, started her new job and needed a reliable car to commute to work, she went to Bob the banker and borrowed 20,000ℙ on January 15, 2018. And since Bob the banker is a trustworthy banker, Molly was satisfied with having just a receipt book (i.e., a checkbook) which she could use to buy the car she wanted. And since the seller of the car had the same level of confidence in Bob the banker, he was willing to accept a receipt (i.e., a check) in exchange for his car. Just as Gloria the goldsmith of the 1500s had created money by issuing more loans that she had deposits, Bob the banker of the 2000s has created money equal to the amount of 20,000ℙ by issuing more loans than he has deposits. Total quantity of money in Modelville on January 15, 2018 is 120,000ℙ. It is the sum of 100,000ℙ original deposits against which receipts (i.e., checkbooks) were issued, and 20,000ℙ loan made to Molly from Modelville. This has happened because everyone in Modelville is using checks to buy goods and service, and the sellers of goods and services are willing to accept checks in exchange for their goods and services. The Modelvillites are not withdrawing and using Pecunae to make transactions. The checks are serving as money. And just as Bob the banker in our fictional town of Modelville has created money by issuing more receipts, in this case a loan to Molly, than he has deposits, actual modern-day banks everywhere create money by issuing more loans than they have deposits.

4.2.1 Fractional Banking and Money Creation

When Bob the banker kept part of the deposits and issued loans for the remainder, he engaged in what is called "fractional banking." The term comes from the fact that banks keep a fraction of the deposits and make loans of the rest. Let's try to understand this concept in more detail.

Suppose that Bob the banker keeps 20 percent of deposits to meet the demands of depositors who may stop by to withdraw Pecunae to make transactions (or those to whom his depositors have written checks to buy goods and services), and makes loans for the rest. Whatever Bob the banker kept to meet the withdrawal needs of his depositors are called "reserves," and the ratio that is kept as reserve—in this case, 20 percent—is called "reserve ratio." Had Bob the banker not made any loans, we would have 100,000ℙ as reserves. In this case, the reserve ratio would have been 100 percent. On the other extreme, had Bob the banker lent 100,000ℙ the reserves would have been zero and the reserve ratio would have been zero percent. How does Bob the banker decide what fraction of deposits to keep? We shall address this question in more detail later. For now, suffice it to say that just as Gloria the goldsmith in Modelville of the 1500s estimated the amount of gold to keep to meet the demands of depositors, Bob the banker of the 2000s (along with the central bank of an economy) performs similar estimation.

Suppose now that some other Modelvillite also needed a loan. They came to Bob the banker. After agreeing on the terms of the loan, Bob the banker made the loan. Keep in mind that everyone is using checks to make transactions so that checks are serving as money. No one is using cash. This means that whoever borrowed from Bob the banker needed just a checkbook and not cash. Just as Molly, in our earlier example, did not need Pecunae to purchase her car, others who have borrowed do not need Pecunae to make transactions. All they need is a checkbook (or checkbooks if they are more than one). So Bob the banker issued checkbooks allowing the borrowers to write checks worth 80,000ℙ. One can also think this way: The borrowers received Pecunae and deposited those back in Bob's Bank, and Bob the banker issued checkbooks.

Note also that it does not matter whether Bob the banker made several loans to many individuals that amounted to 80,000ℙ, or loaned the whole 80,000ℙ to one individual. Also, just as in the case of the goldsmith (Chapter 3), it does not matter whether there is one bank or a thousand banks. The results stay the same. To keep things simple, suppose that there is one person who got the loan of 80,000ℙ. Also suppose that every bank in Modelville keeps 20 percent of deposits as reserves.

Continuing our example, now suppose that someone who borrowed 80,000ℙ bought widgets worth 80,000ℙ and wrote checks for the same amount. The seller of those widgets deposited the checks in her account. Suppose that the seller of the widgets maintains an account at, say Caroline's Bank. She deposited the check worth 80,000℗ in her account. Caroline's Bank kept 20 percent in reserves and made loans of the remainder—Caroline's Bank kept 16,000℗ in reserves and lent out 64,000℗. Again, the borrower did not need Pecunae; all he needed was a checkbook. He bought goods worth 64,000℗ from someone and wrote a check for the amount drawn at Caroline's Bank. The seller of these goods had an account at Danielle's Bank. Danielle's Bank kept 20 percent as reserves and lent the remainder—Danielle's Bank kept 12,800℗ as reserves and lent 51,200℗. So on and so forth.

By way of summarizing, Table 4.1 presents these numbers.

Let's go over Table 4.1. Columns [1] through [5] list "Stage," "Name of Bank," "Deposit," "Reserve," and "Loan," respectively. At Stage 1, deposits, reserves, and loans are all zero at Bob's Bank. At Stage 2, someone deposits 100,000℗ at Bob's Bank. The amount of deposits increases to 100,000℗ (see Column [3]), and so does the amount of reserves (see Column [4]). At this point, since Bob the banker has not extended any loans, the amount of loans is zero (see Column [5]). At Stage 3, Bob the banker keeps 20 percent (i.e., 20,000℗) in reserves and issues loans worth 80,000℗. As we saw earlier, just as in the case of Gloria the goldsmith of the 1500s, as long as the borrower is reasonably certain that checks drawn at Bob's Bank will be accepted, all the borrower wants

Table 4.1 Money creation

[1] *Stage*	*[2]* *Name of Bank*	*[3]* *Deposit*	*[4]* *Reserve*	*[5]* *Loan*
1	Bob's Bank	0	0	0
2	Bob's Bank	100,000	100,000	0
3	Bob's Bank		20,000	80,000
4	Caroline's Bank	0	0	0
5	Caroline's Bank	80,000	80,000	0
6	Caroline's Bank		16,000	64,000
7	Danielle's Bank	0	0	0
8	Danielle's Bank	64,000	64,000	0
9	Danielle's Bank		12,800	51,200
...	...	...	...	...
...	...	...	...	...
	Total	500,000	100,000	400,000

Table prepared by the author. We are assuming that reserve ratio is 20 percent; goods and services are bought and sold using checks

is a checkbook, and not Pecunae. The borrower, now, buys some widgets from someone and writes a check in the amount of 80,000ℙ.

Move to Stage 4. Note that at this point Caroline's Bank has zero deposits, zero reserves, and zero loans. The seller of the widgets maintains an account at Caroline's Bank. She deposits the check at Caroline's Bank. When the seller of the widgets deposits the check worth 80,000ℙ (see Stage 5), deposits as well as reserves increase from zero to 80,000ℙ. The amount of reserves is 80,000ℙ because Caroline's Bank has not extended any loans yet—the amount of loans is zero (see Column [5] at Stage 5). At Stage 6, Caroline's Bank keeps 20 percent of 80,000ℙ (i.e., 16,000ℙ) and extends loans worth 64,000ℙ (see Stage 6, Column [5]). The individual who borrowed 64,000ℙ from Caroline's Bank buys some goods from someone and writes a check in the amount of 64,000ℙ.

Move to Stage 7. Note, again, that at this point, the amount of deposits, reserves, and loans at Danielle's Bank is zero. Move now to Stage 8. The seller of the goods maintains an account at Danielle's Bank. She deposits the check for 64,000ℙ in her account at Danielle's Bank. The amount of deposits increases accordingly to 64,000ℙ. Since Danielle's Bank has not extended any loans yet, the reserves also increase to 64,000ℙ. In Stage 9, Danielle's Bank keeps 20 percent of deposits as reserve, i.e., 12,800ℙ, and makes loans for the remaining 51,200ℙ. And so on.

At this point, it will be helpful to think of the total amount of deposits, reserves, and loans in all the banks. A few points to note about Table 4.1. One, at each stage the amount lent keeps on getting smaller. The reason is that at each stage a part of the deposit is kept as reserve. Recall that we are assuming that the reserve ratio is 20 percent. That is, each bank keeps 20 percent of the deposits as reserves, and extends loans for the remainder.

Two, the *total* amount of deposits keeps on increasing, even though the initial deposit was only 100,000ℙ. But this increase does not continue forever. The reason is that at each successive stage there are fewer and fewer Pecunae left to be loaned. When all is said and done, with an initial deposit of 100,000ℙ the banking system (i.e., all the banks combined) is able to issue loans worth 400,000ℙ, and the total amount of deposits now is 500,000ℙ. And since checks serve as money—a medium of exchange, a unit of account, and a store of value—the amount of money in the Modelville economy has increased from 100,000ℙ to 500,000ℙ.

Three, the process will stop when the total amount of reserves reaches 100,000ℙ, the amount of initial deposit. As always, we are holding everything else constant. That is, no changes in reserve ratio, no influx of new deposits, and no one withdraws Pecunae. Everyone is making transactions using checks. It is easy to see that the total amount of money in the economy will be affected when a borrower withdraws cash or a bank keeps more or less than 20 percent.

How did I come with this total number? While one could keep on calculating the amount of deposits and loans at each stage and add all the deposits and loans, there is a better way. Here is the formula that I used.

$$D = \left(\frac{1}{rr}\right) \times R \tag{4.1}$$

In "change-form," the equation may be written as

$$\Delta D = \left(\frac{1}{rr}\right) \times \Delta R \tag{4.1'}$$

In this equation, ΔD represents change in deposits, *rr* represents the reserve ratio, and ΔR represents the changes reserves. The quantity $(\frac{1}{rr})$ is called the money multiplier. It tells us that a given change in reserve, ΔR, will lead to a change in deposits, ΔD, by a multiple, $(\frac{1}{rr})$, of ΔR. Note that the way the equation is written it states that when changes in reserves, ΔR, is multiplied by the inverse of the reserve ratio, $(\frac{1}{rr})$, the money multiplier, it leads to a change in deposits, ΔD. That is, the change in deposits, ΔD, "depends" upon the change in reserves, ΔR, given the reserve ratio. There is a method to this madness. As we will see in the next chapter (Chapter 5), central banks, in order to change money supply, change the amount of reserve, which in turn leads to changes in the quantity of money in the economy.

It is instructive to remind ourselves that since everyone is using checks to buy and sell goods and service, to evaluate goods and services, and to transfer purchasing power from now to a future date, checks are serving as money. Furthermore, the amount of deposits at various banks in the economy is a measure of the total quantity of money in the economy.

4.2.2 *What Could Go Wrong?*

Well, one thing that could go wrong is that when depositors find out that Bob's Bank and other banks have issued more loans than there are Pecunae deposits, they could panic and may want to withdraw their Pecunae. Obviously not everyone will be able to get their Pecunae. There are only 100,000ℙ and there are 500,000ℙ worth of receipts (i.e., checks) in the economy. This is what economists call a "bank run."

Bank runs are self-fulfilling. Suppose that a Modelvillite fears for whatever reason—it could be an actual news about the financial health of Bob's Bank or it could just be a rumor—that his deposit at Bob's Bank is not safe. He goes to withdraw his Pecunae. Bob's Bank gives the depositor his Pecunae. His neighbor, who also happens to have an account at Bob's Bank, hears about his concerns. "It is better to be safe than sorry," she reasons. Yes, she will be losing the interest income that she is getting but it is better to lose the interest income than the whole deposit. She decides to withdraw Pecunae from her account. Suppose that Bob's Bank is able to return her deposits as well. The third neighbor, who also maintains an account at Bob's Bank, reasons the same way and decides to withdraw his Pecunae. Recall that Bob's Bank is keeping only 20 percent as reserves. Eventually Bob will run out of Pecunae. Not everyone will be able to get their deposits back.

A bank run may not stop with Bob's Bank. The news of people withdrawing their deposits spreads throughout Modelville. Everyone is trying to withdraw her/his deposits at the same time, regardless of where they keep their deposits. "If Bob's Bank is in trouble, Caroline's Bank may also be in trouble, and Danielle's Bank, and so on," they reason. Now we have a full-blown system-wide bank run. In the absence of more information about the financial health of a given bank, this is a perfectly valid way to think.

If everyone, however, were certain that they would be able to get their Pecunae back whenever they needed, no one would want to withdraw. Why? Remember the reason that Modelvillites deposited their Pecunae at Bob's Bank, and other banks, in the first place? They did not want to keep Pecunae in their houses and shops. So if there were some body—some agency, some guarantee, some law—that could assure the Modelvillites that their deposits would be safe and that they would be able to get them when they needed, they would not run to Bob the banker to get their deposits back.

This is where a central bank that is not influenced by changing political winds comes in. The independence of a central bank is extremely important for the health of any economy for several reasons.

A well-functioning central bank provides assurance to the residents of an economy that their savings at banks are safe. This assurance stops bank runs from taking place. Take the example of the central bank of the United States—the Federal Reserve System, or the Fed, for short. Before its establishment in 1913, bank runs were common occurrences. (I will go into more details about the establishment of the Fed in Chapter 5.) It is also important that depositors know that the actions of the central bank are not influenced by the politicians in power. Even a hint that the central bank's actions are to appease the powers to be may further worsen the situation.

One way to provide this assurance is to let people know that when a commercial bank falls on hard times and needs funds to support withdrawals, the central bank will be there to help the bank out. Just having such an assurance is often enough for people not to run to their banks and withdraw funds.

Another way that a central bank creates confidence in the commercial banking sector is by making sure that banks are following the rules. When they are lending funds to someone, they are making sure that the borrower has a reasonable chance of repaying the loan. In our example, the central bank makes sure that Bob the banker is not lending money (i.e., Pecuane) to a borrower who does not have a reasonable chance of repaying the loan along with the interest. That is, Bob the banker makes sure that Molly from Modelville has a job that pays enough to cover her interest and principal. The central bank will ask Bob the banker not only to appraise Molly's potential for repayment but also keep an eye on her after she has received the loan so that she is not slacking off.

Economists have specific terms for these two situations. (We have terms for everything, don't we?) Suppose that Bob the banker, even after due diligence, extended the loan to someone who could not reasonable repay the loan. In such a situation, we would say that Bob the banker has made an "adverse selection." That is, he ended up extending loan to someone he actually wanted to avoid.

Now suppose that Bob the banker made sure that Molly from Modelville was trustworthy, and that she had a job that paid enough not only to cover her living expenses but also the principal and the interest. However after Molly received the loan she started to slack off. She started to become tardy which increased the possibility of her losing her job. Or instead of making her monthly payments Molly started spending her salary on frivolous items. This situation is referred to as "moral hazard." It arises after the loan has been made.

A central bank performs numerous other economically important function as well. I will return to these in due time.

4.3 Borrowing Short and Lending Long

We learned that just as the Modelvillites of the 1500s did not want to keep gold in their shops and homes and deposited their gold with Gloria the goldsmith for safekeeping, the Modelvillites of the 2000s deposit Pecunae in a bank because they do not want to keep Pecunae in their shops, offices, and homes. There is one difference. The depositors of the 1500s paid safekeeping fees while the depositors of the 2000s earn interest—a negative safekeeping fee. The question arises: How is a bank able to pay interest on deposits? The answer: They engage in what is called, "borrowing short and lending long." Indeed, this is how a bank earns profit. Here is how this works.

At this point, it is informative to think of a Modelvillite depositor as a lender to the bank. And when there is a lender, there is also a borrower on the other side of the transaction. In this situation, the bank is the borrower. When Modelvillites deposit Pecunae in a bank, usually they are depositing for a short period of time—a month, a year, and so on. Another way of putting this is that the depositors have lent their Pecunae, and a bank has borrowed, for a short period of time. The bank has "borrowed short." As we also learned that usually a depositor does not withdraw all of her or his Pecunae at the same time. Not only that, not all the Modelvillites withdraw their Pecunae at the same time. This means that a bank has Pecunae sitting in the vault. Modelvillites who need to borrow to start a business or buy a house are borrowing, and the banks are lending, for a longer period of time. For instance, when one borrows to buy a house, usually the loan is made for 20 or 30 years. Car loans are usually for five years. That is, banks are "lending long."

4.3.1 Illiquidity Versus Insolvency

Let me mention two concepts at this point—illiquidity and insolvency. First, "liquidity" in the financial parlance refers to the ease of converting one asset into another. What is an asset, you may ask? Anything that is subject to ownership is an asset. A house is an asset, and so is cash. A house is less liquid than cash. Why? This is because it is relatively harder to convert a house into another asset. Suppose you want to buy a car, another asset. While one can sell a house and, depending upon the price of the car and the value of the house, convert house into a car, it may, however, take some time. (It is also possible that the car dealer is willing to exchange the car for the house, i.e., barter. See Chapter 2 for more detail.) On the other hand, if you had cash, the car dealer would be more than happy to sell you the car for cash—convert cash into a car.

Illiquidity, the opposite of liquidity, refers to the situation when a bank (or any other entity) while financially healthy is not able to meet its withdrawal needs. It cannot convert some, or all, of its assets into cash. Its borrowers have legitimate ventures. They have businesses that are profitable, or have well-paying jobs and can make the mortgage payments. They, however, cannot pay back the loans right away. Their assets are illiquid.

Insolvency, on the other hand, refers to the situation when the borrower does not have assets that can cover the loan. Illiquidity can lead to insolvency. Suppose someone has borrowed to buy a house. The terms of the loan indicated that the borrower would pay off the loan in 30 years. This type of loan is often called as a 30-year mortgage loan. She is making monthly payments on time and does not foresee any issues down the road. She has the assets to cover the loan amount—her house and other assets are worth at least the amount of loan. While the borrower may not be able to repay the loan right away, she is perfectly capable of paying off the loan in due time, i.e., 30 years. The borrower, in this situation, will be considered "illiquid."

Now suppose that the lender asks the borrower to pay back the loan right away. The borrower cannot sell the house right away to pay back the loan. Assuming that the borrower does not have any other way to meet the demands of the lender, and tries to sell the house right away, it is likely that the price of the house will be far below than what it is worth. In this case, the borrower will be considered "insolvent." Illiquidity has turned into insolvency.

4.4 Perils of 100 Percent Reserve Banking

What if the people of Modelville, in order to avoid all the hassle, passed a law that forbade Bob the banker from making loans more than he had deposits? That is, the law only allowed 100 percent reserve banking, and banned fractional-reserve banking. Furthermore, the law also mandated that Bob could only make loans from the deposits that belonged to him or from the deposits of people who had agreed to make such loans.

In this case, on the plus side there is not any risk of a bank run. The depositors are paying an agreed upon fee to Bob the banker for safekeeping. Bob the banker will return the funds to depositors when they want their Pecunae back. On the negative side, however, everyone in Modelville is worse off. Here is why?

Molly is worse off because she is not able to take advantage of the knowledge and skills that she learned in college. Her education is going to waste. The employer is worse off because she needs an employee with the skillset that Molly has. But she can't hire Molly because Molly cannot get to work. This means that the firm cannot produce the goods and services that it wants to produce, sell those goods and services to those who want to buy, and earn profit. The savers are worse off because their savings are just sitting there in a vault in Bob's Bank and not earning interest that those savings could earn. Not only that, the savers have to pay Bob the banker for safekeeping. Their savings are being eroded over time. The residents of Modelville are worse off because the goods and services that the firm could produce are not being produced. They cannot purchase the goods and services they want and enjoy.

But why can't Molly from Modelville borrow directly from the depositors who have deposited their savings in Bob's Bank? Good question.

There are numerous reasons why this does not happen in Modelville, or any modern-day town, and why banks act as intermediaries between savers and lenders.

To start with, it is quite likely that Molly does not know who has 20,000ℙ saved. It is equally likely that the saver does not know Molly or does not know Molly well enough to lend her 20,000ℙ.

Remember we talked about adverse selection and moral hazard above? These situations arise from what economists call asymmetric information. That is, two or more parties in a transaction not having access to the same information—there is an asymmetry of information. In our example, Molly from Modelville knows more about her skills and her work habits than savers in Modelville do. Savers may want to lend to Molly but because they do not have enough information about her, they avoid lending to Molly. From their perspective, it is better to pay Bob the banker safekeeping fee and have savings eroded a bit than lose all or most of what they have saved. As a result, lending does not take place and everyone loses. Everyone, even Bob the banker who is being paid for safekeeping is worse off. Bob the banker can increase his earnings if lending were to take place.

Commercial banks have developed expertise to ensure, to the extent possible, that the borrowers have credible sources of income. Not only that, since a borrower's financial history is also important—one's financial history provides signals about one's financial future—commercial banks have access to the borrower's financial history. Has the borrower ever been late on any payments? How many, if any, checks have the borrower written that did not clear? What other loans does the borrower have? How many credit cards does the borrower have? Is the borrower making payments on time? Is the borrower stretched too thin to stay afloat in case there is a crunch? It all shows up in the borrower's credit report. True, any saver who is thinking of lending to someone can, in principle, gather that information, gathering information, however, is costly. Not only does it take time and financial resources to gather all the information needed, it takes time and expertise to make sense of the information. If a saver cannot assess the riskiness of a loan, they are better off not making the loan at all. And this is what many in such a situation end up doing. Indeed, this is exactly what happened during the 2007–2009 financial crisis. Even commercial banks could not assess the riskiness of some loans. So they stopped lending. Credit markets froze.

The story, however, does not end here. Suppose that Molly could not get the loan of 20,000ℙ to buy the car. This means that the car dealer will not be able to sell the car to Molly. And since the car dealer cannot sell the car, the car dealer will stop buying more cars to sell. The car dealer may have to lay off some sales staff along with the accountant. Why would you want an accountant if you are not selling any cars? So on and so forth. The economy grinds to a halt. In terms of Fig. 4.1, our representative Modelvillite, Molly's income curve shifts down because she is not able to find well-paying job that matches her training and expertise. And as her income curve shifts down, so does her consumption curve. Consumption, however, may not decrease proportionately. After all, she has to spend on basic necessities. The result is that her savings are lower if she saves anything at all. She has a job but she is not building a career. She is not accumulation human capital that leads to an increase in her income. The "hump" in the income curve is not much of a hump. Modelvillites, as a whole, are worse off. Since there are lower savings in the aggregate, there is lower lending: Stewards the students of Modelville, cannot borrow to buy tools from Terries the tool makers. Terries of Modelville cannot sell their tools. They have to lay some workers off. Laid off workers reduce their consumption of goods and services that they purchase as their incomes decrease. So on and so forth.

A decrease in saving and lending has negative consequences in the long run as well. As we saw when Terri the toolmaker could not sell her tools, she had to fire some workers. As it happens, our skills tend to decay when we do not use them. So the longer the workers stay unemployed the more likely they will lose their skills. This means that Modelville will have fewer skilled toolmakers. And since Stewards the students cannot borrow to buy tools they cannot acquire ironsmithing skills. There are fewer knowledgeable ironsmiths in Modelville. As older ironsmiths retire and pass away, ironsmithing skills are not transferred to the next generation. The overall pool of knowledge decreases in Modelville, making Modelville poorer in the long run.

These are not just fanciful musings of an academic economist. Empirical evidence supports this contention. The richest and most dynamic economies in the world also have the healthiest financial sectors. There is a long history, over 5000 years long, of these types of financial arrangements where savers and borrowers engage in mutually beneficial contracts. A detailed account of how such arrangements have helped civilizations over the millennia is provided by William N. Goetzmann in his book *Money Changes Everything: How Finance Made Civilization Possible.*[1]

A word of caution, however, is in order. While economic studies show a positive correlation between a healthy financial system and a healthy economy, they do not, to the best of my knowledge, show a causal relationship.[2] Another word of caution. The lack of evidence of causation does not mean that finance does not help promote economic growth. All it says is that we do not have enough evidence and the tools needed to

[1] William N. Goetzmann. *Money Changes Everything: How Finance Made Civilization Possible*. Princeton, NJ: Princeton University Press, 2016. Print.

[2] Yongseok Shin. "Finance and Economic Development in the Very Long Run: A Review Essay†." 56.4 (2018): 1577–86. Web.

establish that evidence that finance is a causal factor in economic growth. Statistical analyses show that finance does explain the economic growth of societies but there could be other factors as well. Indeed, one major factor that comes up in studies over and over again is the depth and breadth of the pool of knowledge that a society has. This is commonly known as "technology."

I would like to make another point before we move on. Data show that as income grows, so does consumption. Take a look at Fig. 4.1 again. The consumption curve has a positive slope. This implies that consumption (and income) grows over time. There is no guarantee, however, that income and consumption will grow over time. Some countries, especially in Africa, have not been so lucky and their standards of living have declined over time. For instance, Fig. 4.2 shows Real Gross Domestic

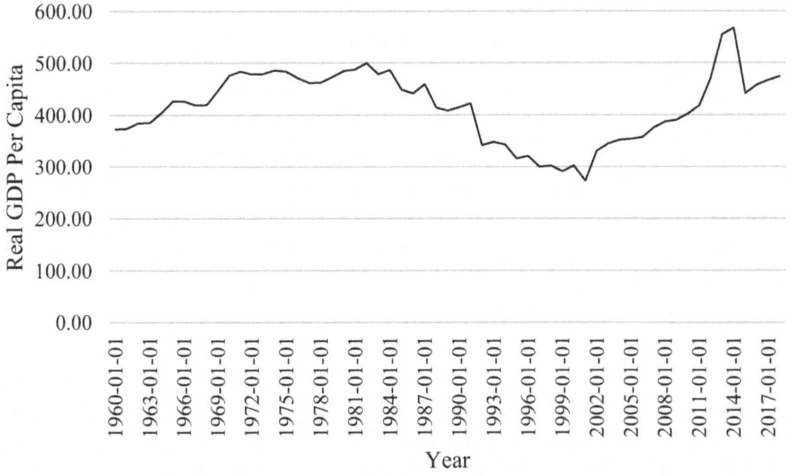

Fig. 4.2 Real GDP per capita of Sierra Leone (Figure prepared by the author. *Data Source* World Bank, Constant GDP per capita for Sierra Leone [NYGDPPCAPKDSLE], retrieved from FRED, Federal Reserve Bank of St. Louis. https://fred.stlouisfed.org/series/NYGDPPCAPKDSLE [Accessed: July 9, 2019])

Per Capita (a measure of per-person income, adjusted for inflation) in evaluated in 2010 US dollars, of Sierra Leone.[3]

Figure 4.2 makes a couple of points. First, there is no guarantee that income will keep on increasing over time. From 1960 to 1982, per capita income increased moderately and then it declined from 1982 to 2001. Income increased from 2001 to 2014, but then declined again. It seems to be recovering since the decline in 2014. Second, while income level bounces around a bit, the overall income level is flat. Note also that per capita income is very low. In Sierra Leone in 2014, inflation-adjusted per capita income was about 567 US dollars, the highest in the time period covered. By way of comparison, during the same year, inflation-adjusted per capita income in the United States was about 51,000 US dollars.[4] I will go into more details about Gross Domestic Product and related concepts in Chapter 7.

4.5 Optimal Quantity of Money

Now that we have at least a basic understanding of how economic activity and the quantity of money are related, and that having too little money in an economy will lead to an economic contraction, a question arises: How much money should be created? What if Bob the banker had loaned 30,000ℙ to Molly? How about 40,000ℙ? On the other hand, what if Bob the banker had lent only, say, 10,000ℙ to Molly? What is the optimal amount of money to be created? And relatedly: Who decides how much money should be created? We turn to these questions now.

Economists have pondered these questions quite a bit. First, let's say that there was only one car in Modelville that was for sale. And that 20,000ℙ was its "fair" price. (Why did I put the word *fair* in quotation marks? I will come back to this point.) In this case, Molly gets the loan of 20,000ℙ and buys the car. Suppose now that the seller of the car thinks that the value of the car is 30,000ℙ. And given our assumption that

[3] Sierra Leone real GDP per capita. World Bank, Constant GDP per capita for Sierra Leone [NYGDPPCAPKDSLE], retrieved from FRED, Federal Reserve Bank of St. Louis, https://fred.stlouisfed.org/series/NYGDPPCAPKDSLE, July 9, 2019.

[4] Real GDP per capita for the US in 2010 constant US dollars. World Bank, Constant GDP per capita for the United States [NYGDPPCAPKDUSA], retrieved from FRED, Federal Reserve Bank of St. Louis, https://fred.stlouisfed.org/series/NYGDPPCAPKDUSA, July 9, 2019.

there is only one car for sale in Modelville and that Molly needs the car to start her job, she will have to ask for a loan of 30,000ℙ from Bob the banker. Suppose that Bob the banker agrees to lend 30,000ℙ to Molly. Molly gets the loan and buys the car for 30,000ℙ. Is this a good thing? It depends.

What if Bob the banker were only willing to lend 10,000ℙ? Suppose now that there is only one buyer, Molly, and that the seller is in need of money. Under this situation, the seller of the car agrees to sell the car for 10,000ℙ. Is this a good thing? It depends.

Notice, first, what has happened in this example? The price of the car has changed to match the amount of the money that is created. It increased to 30,000ℙ in the first scenario and it decreased to 10,000ℙ in the second. Of course in a well-functioning economy there are millions and millions of goods and services being bought and sold every hour, perhaps every second, depending upon the size of the economy. So we are talking about the prices of millions and millions of goods and services.

If you look closely, even in this simple example there is more to the story. Molly is selling her labor to the firm that has hired her. Molly buys gas to run her car. She drives on the roads that have been paved by the town of Modelville. These roads have traffic lights and stop signs. These are managed by the town of Modelville. The town of Modelville had to pay to the construction company for the construction of roads and traffic lights and traffic signs. The construction company, in turn, paid to the workers that it hired. So on and so forth. And where does Modelville get the funds to pay for the roads, and traffic lights, and traffic signs? It charges taxes from the Modelvillites.

Now to the questions of whether the loan of 30,000ℙ is better or the loan of 10,000ℙ. One way to evaluate these alternatives is to see whether or not Molly's salary has changed accordingly. Take the example of an increase in the price of the car to 30,000ℙ. If Molly's salary increased proportionately to cover the monthly car payments, then Molly is neither better off nor worse off.

On the other hand, if Molly's salary did not adjust to account for the increase in the price of the car, then Molly is poorer than she would have been. Why? This is because now Molly, after making the monthly car payment, does not have as much left over as she would have had the price of the car not increased. When Molly accepted the job offer and signed on the dotted line, the offer was in terms of Pecunae, and not in terms of cars. The offer did not say that when/if the price of the car were to increase, the monthly salary would also increase proportionately.

What if the price of the car were to decrease to 10,000ℙ? In this case, Molly will be better off. Why? Molly's pay is still the same. She is still earning the same number of Pecunae per month. Now, however, after making the monthly car payments, Molly has more money left over to spend on other stuff.

This simple example may give the impression that a decrease in prices is good for everyone. After all people can purchase whatever they were purchasing before and still have money left over to buy other stuff. Upon reflection, however, one finds that things may not be this simple. To understand this relatively counterintuitive point, we need to take a step back. Before we do that, it is instructive to get an understanding of what prices of various goods and services really show.

4.5.1 Prices Serve as Signals

In a market economy, prices serve as signals. Prices tell buyers what to buy and tell producers what to produce. As buyers of goods and services, we compare prices of these goods and services and decide, given our ability and wiliness to purchase, what to purchase. As producers of various goods and services, given our ability and wiliness to produce, we decide what to produce. When Molly from Modelville, given her aptitude and resources, decided to go to college and major in a particular subject, her decision was based upon what her skills would be worth upon graduation. Of course, she did not know exactly how much she would earn but she had some idea based on the information she had at the time. When the firm that hired Molly from Modelville decided to produce what the firm was producing, its owners based their decision on the expected prices of the products that they would produce, given the expected prices of the inputs—prices of raw material, rent for the building, wages of labor, etc. Put simply, as producers and consumers we are looking at these signals and make our decisions to produce and consume.

Furthermore, we are (almost always) only looking at the products toward these signals are pointing. We are not aware of the sources of these signals. Sometimes, however, these signals are distorted. There could be a number of causes for these distortions. These distortions may include taxes, subsidies (i.e., negative taxes), tariffs (i.e., taxes on imported goods and services), monopoly power of firms, misinformation, externalities

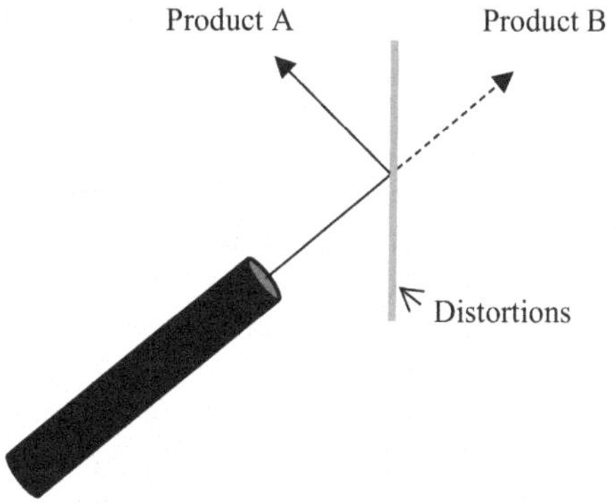

Fig. 4.3 Prices as signals (Figure prepared by the author)

(positive and negative), and so on. These distortions lead to misallocation of resources—they point toward the "wrong" product.

A way to understand this is to imagine that you are using a laser pointer to point toward an object. Suppose someone puts a mirror in between the laser pointer and the object which diverts the laser beam to a different object. Figure 4.3 makes this point graphically.

As depicted in Fig. 4.3, the laser beam is pointing toward Product B. However, due to distortions, depicted by a gray bar, the beam is diverted toward Product A. These distortions lead to misallocation of resources. In our example, these distortions could lead Molly from Modelville to major in a subject that, in reality, does not have good job prospects. These distortions could lead the producers of the firm that hired Molly to produce goods and services that, in reality, were not as profitable as the prices suggested when they made the decision.

4.5.2 *Overall Price Level, Inflation, Deflation, and Disinflation*

Before we move on, let me clarify what we mean by overall price level, inflation, deflation, and disinflation. It is important to note here that there is a difference between the price of a particular product and the overall price level. While the price of a particular product measures, as is obvious from the phrase, the price of that particular product, the *overall* price level provides a measure of the prices of all the goods and services in an economy. At the risk of brutal simplification, it is an "average" of all the prices that prevail in the economy, where average is calculated a certain way.

There are several measures of the overall price level. These include Gross Domestic Product Implicit Price Deflator (GDP deflator), Consumer Price Index (CPI), producer price indices (PPIs), among others. When we are creating an Index, we assign a given value, usually 100, to a variable. The purpose of creating an index is expositional ease.[5] The GDP deflator, for instance, is constructed by the Bureau of Economic Analysis. According to their definition, it "measures changes in the prices of goods and services produced in the United States, including those exported to other countries. Prices of imports are excluded."[6]

CPI is probably the most commonly reported measure of price level in the press. The Bureau of Labor Statistics constructs this measure, along with other price level measures. The Bureau defines CPI as "a measure of the average change over time in the prices paid by urban consumers for a market basket of consumer goods and services."[7] While these measures differ in details, they point in pretty much the same direction. In Fig. 4.4 (p. 91), I plot both data series, GDP deflator and Consumer Price Index. For both series, the index value has been set to equal 100 in 2012. I will cover these concepts in more details about these concepts in later chapters (Chapters 6 and 7).

Note that inflation is an increase in the overall price level, deflation is a decrease in the overall price level, and disinflation is a decrease in the rate of increase in overall price level.

Back to Modelville.

Let me go into a bit more detail about what may happen if the price level were to decrease.

Cary the car seller buys used cars, fixes them, and resells them. He is an upstanding citizen. He is honest and courteous, pays his bills on time, and he recycles.

Ever since Cary was a little boy, he liked cars. When he grew up and graduated from high school, he decided to follow up on his passion. He went to a trade school and learned everything there was to learn about cars. After he finished his training, he opened a car repair shop. Modelvillites are happy that there is a reliable and qualified car mechanic in town.

[5] Index value. https://www.bls.gov/cpi/technical-notes/home.htm (Accessed: July 11, 2019).

[6] GDP Deflator. https://www.bea.gov/data/prices-inflation/gdp-price-deflator (Accessed: July 9, 2019).

[7] Definition of CPI. https://www.bls.gov/cpi/ (Accessed: July 9, 2019).

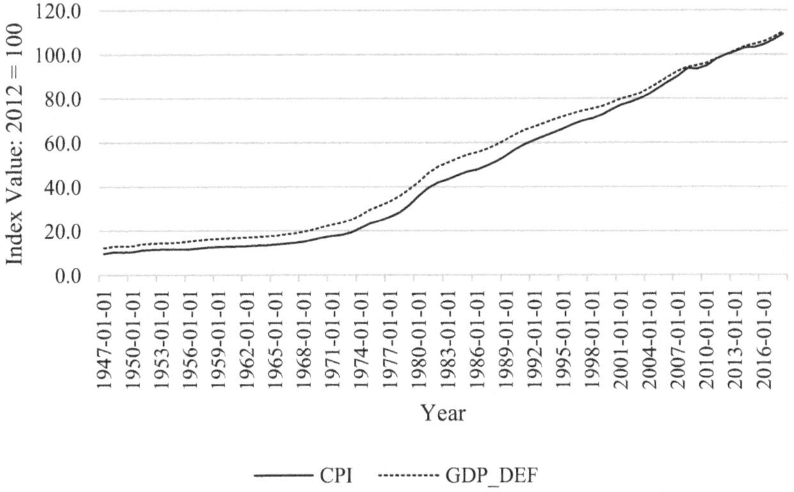

Fig. 4.4 GDP Deflator and Consumer Price Index (Figure prepared by the author. CPI is the Consumer Price Index. GDP_DEF is the GDP Implicit Price Deflator. *Data Source* GDP_DEF [US Bureau of Economic Analysis, Gross Domestic Product: Implicit Price Deflator (GDPDEF), retrieved from FRED, Federal Reserve Bank of St. Louis. https://fred.stlouisfed.org/series/GDPDEF]; CPI [US Bureau of Labor Statistics, Consumer Price Index for All Urban Consumers: All Items (CPIAUCSL), retrieved from FRED, Federal Reserve Bank of St. Louis. https://fred.stlouisfed.org/series/CPIAUCSL (Accessed: July 11, 2019)])

Before Cary the car seller opened his car repair shop Modelvillites had to take their cars to a car repair shop in a neighboring town. Now they can get their cars repaired locally. Whenever they need their cars repaired, they can drop off their cars at Cary's Car Repair Shop. He does an excellent job. So he gets a lot of repeat business.

Over the years, Cary the car seller has accumulated some savings. Sometimes when some Modelvillites want to buy new cars, they ask Cary if he would like to buy their old cars. Depending upon the car, Cary the car seller sometimes buys those cars. Some cars need some repairs. Cary the car seller repairs them and resells them. Usually Cary buys those cars with his Pecunae that he has saved. Sometimes, however, when the price of the car is more than what Cary the car seller has in savings and he deems the car worth it, he borrows the remainder from Bob the banker.

Bob the banker knows that the loans extended to Cary the car seller are safe. So Cary has no problem securing these loans.

Cary the car seller purchased a car for 15,000ℙ that needed repair worth 4000ℙ. This included parts as well as his labor. He had 10,000ℙ in savings and he borrowed the rest, 9000ℙ, from Bob the banker. He repaired the car. When Molly needed a reliable transportation, she stopped by Cary's Car Repair Shop. She knew that Cary the car seller would sell her a reliable car at a reasonable price. Molly from Modelville test drove the car and liked it. They agreed on a price of 20,000ℙ. Cary the car seller made 1000ℙ in this transaction. This is a payment for his savings and his skills.

Now imagine that Bob the banker only lent 10,000ℙ to Molly from Modelville, and that the price of the car declined to 10,000ℙ. It may seem like that the decline in the price of the car is a good thing. However, looked at the situation from the point of the overall economy this could be disastrous. Here is why?

First, Cary the car seller owes 9000ℙ in terms of Pecunae, not in terms of cars. When Cary borrowed from Bob the banker, the price of the car was 20,000ℙ. Translated in terms of cars, Cary borrowed 0.45 of a car. That is, 9000ℙ/20,000ℙ. Now that the price of the car has declined to 10,000ℙ, in terms of cars Cary the car seller borrowed 0.9 cars. That is, 9000ℙ/10,000ℙ. This is an increase of 100 percent. Cary the car seller's debt burden has increased by 100 percent. Cary the car seller is in financial trouble. His savings are wiped out. He has a few possible options. He could ask Bob the banker to accept only part of the original loan. After all, Bob the banker is a rich man. He is making money just by lending other people's money and charging interest. As bad a reputation as bankers have, and some deservedly so, bankers serve an important social and economic function. I will expand on this point below.

This option may spell doom for the economy. Remember that Bob the banker is functioning as an intermediary. Modelvillites who have savings deposit their savings with Bob the banker. These Pecunae are not his own Pecunae. And Bob the banker is lending only because the depositors have allowed Bob to lend. If Bob the banker takes back only part of the Pecunae, he is in effect taking only part of the Pecunae for the depositors. If this were to happen, in reality the depositors are the ones who are losing. True, Bob may also end up losing some of his money as well—he may not get payment for services rendered. Most of the losses, if not all, will be borne by the depositors. Depositors in the future may not deposit with Bob the banker. Or if they did they may say that they did not want their savings to be lent. They would rather pay a fee to Bob the banker for safekeeping than lose their savings.

If the savers were to take this route, Cary the car seller will not be able to get the loan and buy the car, fix it up and sell to Molly from Modelville. Molly would not be able to buy the car and commute to her job. As we saw earlier, Molly is worse off because she cannot take full advantage of her skills and training. The firm that wanted to hire Molly is worse off because it cannot produce goods and services it could have produced and earn profit. The Modelvillites are worse off because they cannot purchase the goods and services that the firm would have produced, and enjoy those goods and services. Cary the car seller is worse off because he cannot buy used cars, fix them, and sell them to those who could use a reliable transportation. Modelvillites who want to buy new cars and want to sell their old ones are also worse off. Now they do not want to buy a new car because they cannot sell their old ones. The new car dealers cannot sell their cars either. So on and so forth. Everyone in Modelville is worse off.

There is another problem with a decline in prices. Suppose that you are looking to buy a dining table. You have checked out a few tables online as well as in nearby furniture stores. It took you a few days but you found the one that you liked. While you were shopping around, you noticed that the price of the table had declined. When you first looked at it a few days ago, the price was 300ℙ. Now the price is 275ℙ. Unless you are in dire need for a dining table, chances are you would wait for a couple more days expecting that the price may drop even further. Just as you expected, a couple days later the price has, indeed, dropped. It dropped to 250ℙ. Now again, unless you are in dire need for a dining table, you would rather wait and see whether or not the price will drop even further. During this wait and see period, however, the furniture store is not able to sell the dining table. And since the furniture store is not selling dining tables, the proprietor is quite likely not to order any more dining tables. And since the dining table manufacturer is not able to sell dining tables to the furniture store, inventories at his shop start to pile up. He has to reduce the production of dining tables. In order to do that he asks the carpenters who work at his shop to reduce the hours. Depending upon how much inventories are piling up, he may even have to lay off a couple of carpenters. This reduces the incomes of the furniture store owner, the furniture manufacturer shop owner, and the carpenters. They are all worse off. Not only that, they buy fewer of goods and services that they purchase. So on and so forth. Everyone is worse off.

Is there any evidence that a decline in price level signals a possible disaster for the economy? Yes we do. We have empirical evidence of how a declining price level may lead to a decline in output going back to 1724 when the French government cut the price level by 45 percent. "The industrial sector experienced a contraction of 30 percent," writes Francois Velde.[8] "When the government changed course and increased the nominal money supply overnight by 20 percent ... and industry rebounded." Velde continues (p. 591).

Here, it bears repeating the difference between *level*, *change*, and the *rate of change*. Remember that the overall price level (e.g., GDP deflator, CPI, PPIs, etc.) represents the average level of prices prevailing in the economy. *Inflation* is an increase, *deflation* is a decrease in this level, and *disinflation* is a decrease in the rate of increase in price level.

So no, a decline in prices is not necessarily a good thing.

Are there any situations where a decline in prices may be beneficial for the economy? One must be careful in answering this question. First, as we saw there is a difference between the price of a particular product and the prices of many products—the *overall* price level. It is quite possible that the prices of certain goods and services are sending distorted signals—Cary the car dealer paid too much for the car; Molly from Modelville made a mistake in majoring in a particular subject area; the firm that hired Molly did not calculate costs of production and/or misread the market and the market price. In such situations, a correction of signals—decreases in these prices—is, indeed, desirable. Markets are great at information gathering. When, however, we are talking about the overall price level, things take an ugly turn when price level decreases. As we saw above, deflation can have serious consequences for the economy. When deflation takes hold, it becomes very hard to reverse that cycle. Experiences of Japan, the United States, and other countries show that.

Does this mean that inflation is desirable? The answer is a qualified yes. It depends upon the rate at which price level is increasing and how volatile these changes are. Most economists agree that *inflation rate*—percentage increase in price level—should be between 2 percent and 4

[8] Deflation in France in 1724. François R. Velde. "Chronicle of a Deflation Unforetold." *Journal of Political Economy* 117.4 (2009): 591–634. Web.

percent.[9] The Fed, for instance, tries to keep the inflation ration rate around 2 percent.[10] Uncertainty about inflation and/or inflation rates beyond 10 percent, however, are undesirable.

4.5.3 Who Decides and How

Now we turn to the question of who decides what is the optimal amount of money creation and at what rate it should be created? That is, who decides what is the optimal inflation rate? This is the job of the central bank of a country. We will pick up this topic in the next chapter in greater detail. We will use the Fed as an example and go through the tools that it uses to reach its objectives.

Now that we have developed an understanding of what money is, what role borrowing and lending play, and how commercial banks create money, going forward, we will look at the actual economies and their central banks, as opposed to the fictional economy of Modelville, and see how changes in money supply affect the economy.

Before we move on, it is worth repeating that money is not created for the sake of creating money. The purpose of money is to facilitate exchange of goods and service, to serve as a yardstick so that goods and services may be evaluated, and to be able to transfer purchasing power from now to a future date. While it is true that money may be held as an asset, its value depends upon the economy—the goods and services produced—it represents.

[9] Inflation rate target. Thomas M. Mertens and John C. Williams. "Monetary Policy Frameworks and the Effective Lower Bound on Interest Rates." *American Economic Review: Papers and Proceedings* 109.May (2019): 427–32. Print, Laurence H. Meyer. *A Term at the Fed: An Insider's View*. New York, NY: Collins, 2004. Print, Laurence H. Meyer. *Inflation Targets and Inflation Targeting*, 2001. Print.

[10] Fed's inflation rate target. "Monetary Policy: What Are Its Goals? How Does It Work?" https://www.federalreserve.gov/monetarypolicy/monetary-policy-what-are-its-goals-how-does-it-work.htm (Accessed: July 9, 2019).

Works Cited

Goetzmann, William N. *Money Changes Everything: How Finance Made Civilization Possible*. Princeton, NJ: Princeton University Press, 2016. Print.

Mertens, Thomas M., and John C. Williams. "Monetary Policy Frameworks and the Effective Lower Bound on Interest Rates." *American Economic Review: Papers and Proceedings* 109.May (2019): 427–32. Print.

Meyer, Laurence H. *Inflation Targets and Inflation Targeting*, 2001. Print.

———. *A Term at the Fed: An Insider's View*. New York, NY: Collins, 2004. Print.

Shin, Yongseok. "Finance and Economic Development in the Very Long Run: A Review Essay†." 56.4 (2018): 1577–86. Web.

Velde, François R. "Chronicle of a Deflation Unforetold." *Journal of Political Economy* 117.4 (2009): 591–634. Web.

CHAPTER 5

Central Banks, Monetary Policy, and the Economy

This chapter starts by providing a brief history of the Federal Reserve System (the Fed), the central bank of the United States. Then, I go over the tools that the Fed uses to conduct monetary policy. The chapter provides historical perspective of what we have learned over the years about the conduct of monetary policy and how it affects the economy.

5.1 A Brief History of the Federal Reserve System

History provides perspective, and details are important. A "Cliff Notes" version of history provides only an illusion of perspective. It removes the wrinkles and makes the reader think that the past was smooth. The Federal Reserve Act of 1913 established the Federal Reserve System, the central bank of the United States. Reading about the back and forth between the various interests when Federal Reserve Act of 1913 was in the making, one gets the impression that it was a wonder that the Act passed at all. It was, indeed, a feat.

The Federal Reserve Act of 1913 is officially entitled "An Act To provide for the establishment of Federal reserve banks, to furnish an elastic currency, to afford means of rediscounting commercial paper, to establish a more effective supervision of banking in the United States,

M. Ashraf, *Money*,
https://doi.org/10.1007/978-3-030-50378-9_5

and for other purposes."[1] The word "elastic" in the title of the Act is worth keeping in mind. As we will see in the coming pages, changing money supply as needed by the underlying changes in the economy is of great import for the stability and prosperity of the economy. Even though we have learned much about the havoc that a gold standard has unleashed over the years, its proponents somehow still believe in its virtues. We saw in Chapter 1 how Representative Ron Paul, Senator Ted Cruz, Congressman Alexander Mooney, among others, favored a gold standard. Fixed money supply under the guise of "sound money" has a long history with tortured explanations. Untying the US dollar from gold and silver has been considered immoral.[2] Beginning with the very founding of the nation Americans agreed that the country needed a stable currency and a strong financial system. What it meant to have a sound currency and a strong financial system, however, was not clear.

As we saw in Chapter 1, often "sound money" is mistakenly equated with having a fixed quantity of money. What our knowledge about the functioning of the economy, and the role money plays in the economy, has shown us that the type of money that meets the needs of a dynamic economy is sound money. This means that the quantity of money has to be flexible. As the needs of the economy change, so should the quantity of money.

The formation of the central bank had many roadblocks to overcome. There was the "First Bank of the United States," followed by the "Second Bank of the United States." Both were short-lived. Note also that the term "central bank" is a relatively modern term. It gained popularity around the 1940s. Barry Hammond notes that Alexander Hamilton, the main man behind the establishment of the Bank of United States, which later became known as the "First Bank of the United States" used the

[1] Official title of the Federal Reserve Act of 1913. https://www.federalreserve.gov/aboutthefed/officialtitle-preamble.htm (Accessed: July 11, 2019).

[2] Immorality of untying money from gold. James Ledbetter. *One Nation Under Gold: How One Precious Metal Has Dominated the American Imagination for Four Centuries*. London: W. W. Norton, 2017. Print, James N. Primm. *A Foregone Conclusion: The Founding of the Federal Reserve Bank of St. Louis*. Federal Reserve Bank of St. Louis, 1989. Print.

term "public bank." A commonly used term in the nineteenth century was "bank of issue."[3]

5.1.1 The First Bank of the United States

Alexander Hamilton, the Treasury Secretary, was of the view that for the young nation to survive, it was imperative that "foreign and domestic creditors" had confidence in the nation's fiscal affairs. In 1790, Hamilton presented the Congress "a plan to fund the national debt at par, assume the debts of the states and provide a national money supply through the agency of a national bank of issue modeled on the Bank of England."[4] Hamilton also saw similarities in the economic conditions of the United States at the time and those of England that prevailed during reign of King William, III. These included "weak state finances brought about by war and revolution; opposition from agrarian groups; the pressing need of the government for funds," writes H. W. Morgan.[5] The fact that the plan took the Bank of England as model was not an accident either. The founders of the new nation were of the English heritage and their knowledge of banking stemmed from the English banking system.[6]

The Bank of England, however, was not the only institution that Hamilton used as a model. The Bank of North America was another example. "The aid afforded to the United States by this institution during the remaining period of the war was of essential consequence; and its conduct towards them after the peace has not weakened its title to their

[3] Public Bank to Bank of Issue to Central Bank. Bray Hammond. "Jackson, Biddle, and the Bank of the United States." *The Journal of Economic History* 7.1 (1947): 1–23. *JSTOR*. Web (footnote 2).

[4] Hamilton's plan to establish a central bank. Primm. https://www.federalreservehistory.org/essays/first_bank_of_the_us (Accessed: July 15, 2019).

[5] Similarities between the United States and England. H. W. Morgan. "The Origins and Establishment of the First Bank of the United States." *The Business History Review* 30.4 (1956): 472–92. *JSTOR*. Web.

[6] Bank of England as model. H. W. Morgan. "The Origins and Establishment of the First Bank of the United States." *The Business History Review* 30.4 (1956): 472–92. *JSTOR*. Web.

patronage and favor," wrote Hamilton in support of his proposal.[7] The Bank of North America was established in Philadelphia in 1781. It had been issued charters by Pennsylvania, Delaware, Maine, New York, and the Continental Congress.

This was not Hamilton's first undertaking when it came to bank plans either. He had already written a similar plan for a state-chartered bank, the Bank of New York, in 1784. He would later serve on its Board of Directors. While Hamilton was not the only one proposing a central bank, he was certainly its strongest supporter.[8] According to the plan, the Bank would issue paper currency, provide banking services to public, collect tax revenues, and pay debts on the behalf of the government.

It must also be noted that Hamilton, by no means, was a starry-eyed supporter of a central bank. He had thought through the matter for quite some time, and he was well aware that such an institution was not a panacea. In a 1779 correspondence with Congressman John Sullivan from New Hampshire, Hamilton wrote[9]:

> I do not believe that the advantages will be so great in fact, as they seem to be in speculation. They will be limited by the means of commerce which the States produce; and these may not be so extensive in the beginning as the plan supposes. Besides this, the profits of the commerce will not be so large, in proportion, after the first or second year, as during those years; neither will it be possible to increase the paper credit in the same degree. But the Bank of England is a striking example, how far this may be carried, when supported by public authority and private influence.

The First Bank of the United States had a number of skeptics from the very beginning. "Banking and currency had been a central political issue since the first years of the Republic," writes James Primm.[10] The main difference lied in the vision for the country. Hamilton thought

[7] Hamilton citing Bank of North America as example. As quoted in H. W. Morgan. "The Origins and Establishment of the First Bank of the United States." *The Business History Review* 30.4 (1956): 472–92. *JSTOR*. Web.

[8] Hamilton's plan. H. W. Morgan. "The Origins and Establishment of the First Bank of the United States." *The Business History Review* 30.4 (1956): 472–92. *JSTOR*. Web.

[9] Hamilton's letter to John Sullivan. As quoted in H. W. Morgan. "The Origins and Establishment of the First Bank of the United States." *The Business History Review* 30.4 (1956): 472–92. *JSTOR*. Web.

[10] James Primm's book. Primm.

commerce and industry essential for the strength of a nation. In a letter to Robert Morris, Superintendent of Finance of the United States, Hamilton wrote[11]:

> Most commercial nations have found it necessary to institute banks; and they have proved to be the happiest engines that ever were invented for advancing trade. Venice, Genoa, Hamburg, Holland and England are examples of their utility. They owe their riches, commerce, and the figure they have made at different periods, in a great degree to this source. Great Britain is indebted for the immense efforts she has been able to make, in so many illustrious and successful wars, essentially to that vast fabric of credit raised on this foundation. 'Tis by this alone she now menaces our independence.

His opponents thought the very opposite. They thought that, "the very seeds of destruction were sown in commerce and industry."[12] Thomas Jefferson, for instance, envisioned the young nation to be an agrarian nation. The commercial nature of national bank did not sit well with his vision of the country. Another opponent, William McClay, a Congressman from Pennsylvania, called such an institution a "house of ill fame."[13]

The farmers in the South saw the plan to "fund the national debt at par, assume the debts of the states" as a transfer of wealth from the farmers in the South to the banking sector in the North since most of the wartime bonds were held by the latter.[14] James Madison, Secretary of State, Thomas Jefferson, and Attorney General, Edmund Randolph were of the view that the US Constitution did not allow the federal government

[11] Hamilton's letter to Robert Morris. As quoted in Morgan: 472–92.

[12] Commerce and industry as seeds of destruction. H. W. Morgan. "The Origins and Establishment of the First Bank of the United States." *The Business History Review* 30.4 (1956): 472–92. *JSTOR*. Web.

[13] "a house of ill fame." As cited in Primm.

[14] Skeptics of the plan to establish a central bank. https://www.federalreservehistory.org/essays/first_bank_of_the_us (Accessed: July 15, 2019).

to "charter corporations."[15] Hamilton, however, argued that the "Necessary and Proper" clause of the Constitution afforded such authority to the Congress. Section 8 of the US Constitution reads, in part[16]:

> The Congress shall have power to lay and collect taxes, duties, imposts and excises, to pay the debts and provide for the common defense and general welfare of the United States;
>
> ...
>
> To coin money, regulate the value thereof, and of foreign coin, and fix the standard of weights and measures;
>
> ...
>
> To make all laws which shall be necessary and proper for carrying into execution the foregoing powers, and all other powers vested by this Constitution in the government of the United States, or in any department or officer thereof.

President Washington was persuaded by Hamilton's arguments that the Constitution allowed such powers and that establishing a central bank was necessary.

The Bank of the United States (which later came to be known as the First Bank of the United States), was charted for 20 years by the Congress on February 25, 1791. Headquartered in Philadelphia, the Bank opened its doors on December 12, 1791. Branches in Baltimore, Boston, Charleston, and New York opened in 1792, Norfolk in 1800, Savannah in 1802, Washington, DC in 1802, and New Orleans in 1805.[17] At the time, most of government tax revenue came from customs duties. Indeed, that was the reason for establishing all branches, except Washington, DC, in port cities. These locations made it easier for the

[15] Constitution did not allow the federal government to charter corporations. James N. Primm. *A Foregone Conclusion: The Founding of the Federal Reserve Bank of St. Louis*. Federal Reserve Bank of St. Louis, 1989. Print.

[16] Necessary and Proper clause of the Constitution. https://www.archives.gov/founding-docs/constitution-transcript#toc-section-8 (Accessed July 14, 2019).

[17] Branches of the First Bank of the United Stated. https://www.federalreservehistory.org/essays/first_bank_of_the_us (Accessed: July 15, 2019).

government to collect taxes. Port-city locations also helped government to finance and promote international trade.

The First Bank of the United States had a capital of 10 million US dollars. This made it "not only the largest financial institution, but the largest corporation of any type."[18] The federal government provided two million and private interests would furnish the rest, "three-fourths of which they could pay for in government bonds."[19] Its Board of Directors had 25 members. Out of these, five members were appointed the government and 20 were chosen by the private investors who provided four-fifth of the capital.[20]

Over these years, there had been stability in the credit markets and the notes issued by the Bank were accepted throughout the country. In fact, notes issued by state banks were not accepted in the payment of taxes. The only notes acceptable were those issued by the First Bank of the United States. This, however, was not enough. Thomas Jefferson continued his opposition to the Bank on Constitutional grounds that issuing corporation charters was prohibited. The fact that most of the shares were held by foreign nationals did not help the matter either. Even though the foreign interests could not vote, to many it still seemed unpatriotic. Henry Clay, Speaker of the House, "struck an Anglophobic chord by pointing out that foreigners owned 70 percent of the Bank's stock," writes Primm.[21] In 1811 the re-charter bill failed by one vote.

It is noteworthy that initial public offering did not deliver the bank shares right away. It offered subscriptions, or "scrips" for short. These served as "a down payment on the purchase of bank stock…When the bank subscriptions went on sale in July 1791, they sold so quickly that

[18] The First Bank as the largest corporation in the country. https://www.federalreservehistory.org/essays/first_bank_of_the_us (Accessed: July 15, 2019).

[19] Capital of the First Bank of the United States. James N. Primm. *A Foregone Conclusion: The Founding of the Federal Reserve Bank of St. Louis*. Federal Reserve Bank of St. Louis, 1989. Print. https://www.newyorkfed.org/aboutthefed/history_article.html (Accessed: July 14, 2019).

[20] Composition of the Board of Directors of the First Bank of the United States. https://www.newyorkfed.org/aboutthefed/history_article.html (Accessed: July 14, 2019).

[21] Anglophobic chord. James N. Primm. *A Foregone Conclusion: The Founding of the Federal Reserve Bank of St. Louis*. Federal Reserve Bank of St. Louis, 1989. Print.

many would-be investors were left out, prompting fierce bidding in the secondary market for scrips."[22]

5.1.2 *The Second Bank of the United States*

Perhaps it is human nature that we often find order confining, and miss it only after we have lost it. Once the charter of the First Bank of the United States ran out, and the War of 1812 with Britain broke out, the chaotic days made all parties—ordinary citizens, state and national politicians, and business people alike, wish for the confining days of the First Bank of the United States. There wasn't any agency to regulate the banking industry anymore. As a result, credit issued by state-chartered banks expanded rapidly, and soon many of them would not redeem their notes. Former opponents of the Bank came around. Representative John C. Calhoun from South Carolina, who would later serve as the seventh Vice President of the United States from 1825 to 1832, and Henry Clay, Speaker of the House, along with "the financiers John Jacob Astor, David Parish, Stephen Girard, and Jacob Barker; Alexander Dallas, who would become secretary of the Treasury in 1814," led the charge.[23] Clay cited "force of circumstance and the lights of experience" the reason for his conversion.[24] The charter of the Second Bank of the United States passed both houses of Congress in 1816, albeit with a thin majority. James Madison was in the Congress when the First Bank of the United States was founded. He was a fierce opponent. Madison, now the President, signed the bill in April 1816.

For Madison, however, it was not a smooth road to conversion. He went back and forth. In the spring of 1814, Madison "reluctantly admitted to the need for another national bank" to finance the war.[25] He withdrew his support once peace talks were under way later that year, and so did the Congress. Again, once the economic health of the country

[22] Bidding war for scrips. https://www.federalreservehistory.org/essays/first_bank_of_the_us (Accessed: July 15, 2019).

[23] Supporters of the Second Bank of the United States. https://www.federalreservehistory.org/essays/second_bank_of_the_us (Accessed: July 15, 2019).

[24] Clay and "force of circumstances." https://www.newyorkfed.org/aboutthefed/history_article.html (Accessed: July 14, 2019).

[25] Madison supports the Second Bank of the United States. https://www.federalreservehistory.org/essays/second_bank_of_the_us (Accessed: July 15, 2019).

became a concern, the need to establish a central bank caught attention and, again, the proposal gained momentum.

The structure of the Second Bank of the United States was very similar to that of the First Bank of the United States. Just as the First Bank of the United States, the Second Bank of the United States was chartered for 20 years. The federal government provided one-fifth of the capital and four-fifth of the capital was provided by private investors, states, and businesses. One-fourth of the private capital was to be paid in gold or silver. As it was in the case of the First Bank, the make-up of the Board of Directors of the Second Bank was also proportional. The President appointed one-fifth of members and the Senate confirmed their appointment, and the rest, four-fifth, were chosen by the private investors. Just like its predecessor, the Second Bank of the United States served as a fiscal agent to the government—it collected taxes and paid its bills, and provided banking services to individuals and businesses. Furthermore, just as in the case of the First Bank of the United State, scrips—a "down payment" for the purchase of shares—were offered to investors.

There were some differences as well. One difference was that the Second Bank had a capital of 35 million dollars. The scrips went on sale in July of 1816 for a three-week period in twenty cities around the country. This time around though, scrips worth three million remained unsold after the sale period ended. This was perhaps due to the size of the capital—35 million versus 10 million. Stephen Girard, a Philadelphia banker ended up buying the leftover scrips.[26]

Another difference was the number of branches—twenty-five versus eight. This allowed the Bank to transfer funds and issue credit to a larger swath of the country. This, in turn, led to economic growth. In the end though, the fate of the Second Bank was the same as that of the First Bank. It closed its doors once the 20-year charter ran out.

Several reasons led to its demise.

> The private banks and their friends had helped to kill the first Bank of the United States twenty years before, but the strength they could muster against the second was much greater. Herein lies the principal difference between the situation of the old bank when Jefferson became president in 1801 and the situation of the second when Jackson became president in

[26] Scrips sale for the Second Bank of the United States. https://www.federalreservehistory.org/essays/second_bank_of_the_us (Accessed: July 15, 2019).

> 1829. Both men disapproved of the national bank and yet were inhibited by its being accepted in their own party and performing well its evidently important functions.

Writes Hammond.[27] While the commonly used term in the literature is "state banks," Hammond prefers using the term "private banks." In private banks, Hammond includes those banks that were owned by state governments (in whole or in part) and "units of the banking system." He reasons that, "functionally these 'state banks' ... differed little if any from the private banks."[28]

The first President of the Second Bank of the United States, William Jones, was one of the Bank's directors appointed by the President. (Nicholas Biddle, the Bank's third, and final President had also served as a government-appointed director.) Serving as a director, however, did not endow Jones with much knowledge about the functioning of a central bank. The Bank first lent too much credit, and then reversed its course in short order. This led to an economic turmoil. Jones resigned in 1819.

Langdon Cheves was the second President of the Bank. His tenure as a President was not much better either, at least not in the public opinion. By training Cheves was an attorney from South Carolina. He had served in the House from 1810 to 1815, and as speaker of the House from 1814 to 1815. When Cheves became the President, he:

> cut in half the number of second Bank banknotes in circulation, made fewer loans, foreclosed on mortgages, and exerted more control over the Bank's branches. He presented state banknotes for specie, a request that sent many state-chartered financial institutions into bankruptcy because they did not have enough gold and silver on hand to cover the redemptions. Another depression, characterized by deflation and high unemployment, ensued. Although the economic slump was part of a worldwide downturn, the Bank's policies magnified the contraction in the United

[27] Situational differences between the First Bank of the United States and the Second Bank of the United States. Hammond: 1–23.

[28] Private banks vs. state banks. Bray Hammond. "Jackson, Biddle, and the Bank of the United States." *The Journal of Economic History* 7.1 (1947): 1–23. *JSTOR*. Web (footnote 4, page 2).

States. Public opinion started turning against the Bank as many believed it contributed to the recession.[29]

Andrew Jackson was elected President of the United States in 1928. To say that he disliked banks and their functions would be an understatement. He believed that currency should only be gold or silver coins, and not banknote. His distrust had a personal reason. Two decades ago he sold some land in exchange for paper currency. The buyer went bankrupt and the notes became worthless. An important function of banks is issuing credit. Jackson, however, was also of the view that one should not buy anything on credit.

With regard to the Second Bank of the United States in particular, there were political reasons for Jackson's dislike. He thought that the Bank's power rivaled the government's power. Not only that, the directors of the Bank were not responsible to the voters.

When Jackson won the reelection in 1832, he made it clear that the Bank would not survive. Two actions by Jackson served as fatal blows. Four years prior to the expiration date of the charter of the Second Bank, the charter was sent to the Congress. While both houses of Congress approved the legislation, Jackson vetoed it. There were not enough votes to override the veto.

Second, soon after his reelection, Jackson ordered the withdrawal of the federal government funds from the Bank. He ordered that the funds be deposited in state banks. The law, however, did not allow Jackson remove deposits. Only Secretary of Treasury could take such an action. Jackson had to "get rid of two Treasury heads successively before he found a third who would execute his wishes."[30] This significantly limited the abilities of the Bank.

In April 1834, the bill to re-charter was defeated in the Congress. The Congress also voted to keep federal deposits in state banks. That was the end of the Second Bank of the United States.

[29] Langdon Cheves become president of the Second Bank of the United States. https://www.federalreservehistory.org/essays/second_bank_of_the_us (Accessed: July 16, 2019).

[30] Jackson removing deposits from the Second Bank. Bray Hammond. "Jackson, Biddle, and the Bank of the United States." *The Journal of Economic History* 7.1 (1947): 1–23. *JSTOR*. Web.

5.1.3 *The Independent Treasury Bill*

Andrew Jackson's successor and his Vice President, Martin Van Buren, was sworn into office on March 4, 1837. He was greeted by the Panic of 1837. Banks stopped converting paper currency into gold and silver. A depression followed. Van Buren's proposal was to free all federal government activity from the banking sector. He proposed creating branches of the United States Treasury—"sub-treasuries"—which would collect and disburse federal funds. An Act to provide for the collection, safekeeping, transfer, and disbursement of the public revenue, was passed by the 26th Congress of the United States in 1840. It authorized the creation of four offices of the "receivers-general of public money," and the officers to be appointed by President with the consent of the Senate. The Act required the creation of four sub-treasury locations—New York, NY; Boston, MA; Charleston, SC; and St. Louis, MO.[31] The Act would later become known as the "divorce bill."

"As it turned out, the divorce did not mean total separation," writes Primm.[32] The sub-treasuries often relied on the state banks to transfer funds. Salmon P. Chase was the Treasury Secretary during the Civil War. He relied on issuing paper money and borrowing to finance the War instead of raising taxes. This led to high inflation. A financial reform was called for again. And again, the creation of a central bank did not have public support. Chase proposed a network of "national banks." According to the plan, "five or more persons could obtain a federal bank charter by filing articles of association with the Comptroller of the Currency. Capital stock required, which had to be fully paid in before opening for business, ranged from $50,000 (later reduced to $25,000) for banks in towns of less than 6000 population to $200,000 for those in cities of 50,000 or more."[33] The 37th Congress passed the National Bank Act on February 25, 1863.[34] By 1913, when the Federal Reserve Act passed, there were about 7500 national banks. As large as the number

[31] The Independent Treasury Bill. http://legisworks.org/congress/26/session-1/chap-41.pdf (Accessed: July 21, 2019).

[32] The "divorce bill." Primm.

[33] A system of national banks. James N. Primm. *A Foregone Conclusion: The Founding of the Federal Reserve Bank of St. Louis*. Federal Reserve Bank of St. Louis, 1989. Print.

[34] The National Bank Act. https://fraser.stlouisfed.org/title/1111 (Accessed: July 21, 2019).

was, it paled in comparison with state banks, which reached about 17,000. The reasons for the expansion of state banks as compared with national banks were the relatively restrictive lending controls, rigorous capital, and reserve requirements. In spite of the controls (mostly on national banks), the banks extended credit extensively. The system proved inadequate for the prevention and spread of financial crises. The financial crises of 1873, 1893, and 1907 drove the point home.[35] The nation needed a central bank.

By then, there was widespread support for the establishment of a central bank. Primm reports that a poll conducted by Paul M. Warburg and published in the *Banking Law Journal* showed that "nearly 60 percent of the banker respondents favored a central bank."[36] As is usually the case, however, there were skeptics. O. M. W. Sprague wrote a long critique of the various proposals to establish a "European type" central bank. Concluding his discussion he wrote,[37]

> A central bank does not appear to either required [*sic*] or well suited to relieve our financial ills...The causes of the financial troubles in the United States are in large measure peculiar to this country. Certain general causes of financial disturbances, such as highly speculative character of many American economic activities, are beyond the control of the banks, however organized. (pp. 413–14)

5.1.4 National Monetary Commission and the National Reserve Association

On May 30, 1908, the 60th Congress of the United States passed the Aldrich-Vreeland Act. The bill was co-sponsored by Senator Nelson W. Aldrich from Rhode Island, and Representative Edward Vreeland from New York. Its purpose was to "amend national banking laws." There were objections to the bill. Robert Owen, US Senator from Oklahoma, and later Chair of the US Senate Committee on Banking and Currency, objected to the "various obstructions in the way of quick-circulating

[35] Inadequacy of the National Banking System. O. M. W. Sprague. *History of Crises Under the National Banking System*. Washington, DC: Government Printing Office, 1910. Print.

[36] Bankers' support for a central bank. Primm.

[37] Critique of central bank by Sprague. Sprague.

notes." He argued on the Senate floor that, "the method was unreasonable, cumbersome, and defeated the object of preventing panic, although useful in abating a panic after its occurrence" (p. 34).[38]

Section 17 of the bill established National Monetary Commission. It stated,[39]

> That a Commission is hereby created, to be called the "National Monetary Commission," to be composed of nine members of the Senate, to be appointed by the Presiding Officer thereof, and nine members of the House of Representatives, to be appointed by the Speaker thereof; and any vacancy on the Commission shall be filled in the same manner as the original appointment.

Aldrich served as the chair of the Commission. On October 14, 1911, Aldrich presented a revised plan to the Commission to establish the National Reserve Association. The original plan was presented on January 11, 1911. Primm (1989) argues that Frank A. Vanderlip of the National City Bank of New York was the actual author of the plan. "Senator Aldrich, choosing pride of authorship over good judgment, brought the proposal to the National Monetary Commission as his own," Primm writes.[40] According to the revised plan[41]:

> [T]he National Reserve Association of the United States...shall be the principal fiscal agent of the Government of the United States. The authorized capital of the National Reserve Association shall be 20 per cent of the capital of the banks eligible for membership (approximately 300 millions). The length of its charter shall be 50 years. The head office of the association shall be in Washington, D. C.

These were some of the steps that painstakingly led to the creation of the Federal Reserve System, the central bank of the United States. The National Reserve Association would serve as a template of the

[38] Objections of Owen. Robert L. Owen. *The Federal Reserve Act*. United State of America, 1919. Print.

[39] The creation of National Monetary Commission. [H.R. 21871]. http://legisworks.org/sal/35/stats/STATUTE-35-Pg546.pdf (Accessed: July 22, 2019).

[40] The actual author of the Aldrich plan. Primm.

[41] The National Reserve Association. https://fraser.stlouisfed.org/archival/1342/item/457504 (Accessed: July 22, 2019). See also Owen.

Federal Reserve System. It was a bi-partisan effort. Republican Senator Nelson Aldrich and Democrat Congressman Carter Glass would co-author "major versions of Federal Reserve legislation."[42]

5.2 The Federal Reserve System

Woodrow Wilson won the presidential election in 1912. Wilson was not clear about his views on the establishment of central bank. "He had stuck to generalities during the campaign," writes Primm. He went "no further than supporting the Democratic platform, which rejected the Aldrich plan and central banking while endorsing reform in principle."[43] Robert Owen (1919), chair of the Senate Committee on Banking and Currency, notes that Wilson ran on anti-central bank platform. Wilson declared that[44]:

> Banks exist for the accommodation of the public and not for the control of business. All legislation on the subject of banking and currency should have for its purpose the securing of these accommodations on terms of absolute security to the public and have complete protection from the misuse of the power that wealth gives to those who possess it. (pp. 69–70)

After his election, however, Wilson warmed up to the idea of establishing a central bank. Many discussions followed in the House and the Senate Committees on Banking and Currency. Owen (1919) further notes that, "the hearings on this bill before the Senate Committee filled three large volumes of 3,259 pages, and were not concluded until October 27, 1913" (p. 80).

After much back and forth between the House and the Senate, the bill finally passed both houses of Congress—the House on December 22, 1939, and the Senate December 23, 1913. A few hours later on December 23, 1913, President Woodrow Wilson signed the bill as well.

As the financial and economic needs have changed, and our understanding of the economy has improved since the passing of the 1913

[42] Co-authors of the Federal Reserve legislation. Primm.

[43] View of Woodrow Wilson on central bank during the campaign. James N. Primm. *A Foregone Conclusion: The Founding of the Federal Reserve Bank of St. Louis*. Federal Reserve Bank of St. Louis, 1989. Print.

[44] Wilson's anti-bank platform declaration. Owen.

Act, numerous amendments have been made to Act. Below I provide an outline of the structure, as it exists now, and highlight its main features.

5.2.1 Structure of the Federal Reserve System

The Federal Reserve System (the Fed) has a unique public and private partnership. Commercial banks that want to be members of the Federal Reserve System hold shares of stock in the Fed. When an entity buys a share of stock in a private company, it is buying a part of the said company. Broadly speaking, that entity in return gets part of the profit when the company earns profit and shares loss when the company suffers loss. One main difference in the case of the Fed is that this public and private partnership, however, is not formulated to earn profit. Rather it is formulated to serve the public interest. The Fed is not owned by the member banks. As we will see below, shareholding banks get voting privileges when it comes to picking members of boards of directors of the Federal Reserve Banks.

The Fed does not receive any appropriations from the Congress. The main sources of revenue of the Fed include interest on government bonds that it holds and service fees—check cashing and funds transfer services for depository institutions, etc. After meeting its expenses and keeping a surplus (a maximum of $10 billion), it transfers the earnings to the US Treasury. For instance, during 2015 the Fed transferred about $97.8 billion to the US Treasury.[45]

The Fed has three main entities—Board of Governors, Federal Reserve Banks, and the Federal Open Market Committee. The United States Congress oversees the Fed.

5.2.1.1 The Board of Governors[46]

There are seven members of the Board of Governors. (It was known as Federal Reserve Board up until the passage of the Banking Act of 1935.) The President of the United States nominates a member and the US Senate confirms the appointment. The length of the appointment

[45] Transfer from the Fed to the US Treasury. https://www.federalreserve.gov/abouttthefed/structure-federal-reserve-banks.htm (Accessed: July 26, 2019).

[46] Board of Governors of the Federal Reserve System. https://www.federalreserve.gov/aboutthefed/section10.htm (Accessed: July 24, 2019).

is 14 years. A term beings every two years on February 1st of even-numbered years. Terms of members overlap to ensure that institutional memory is preserved and passed on. Unless a member was appointed to finish an unexpired term of another member, no member who has served a full term is reappointed. In order to avoid conflict of interest, the Board members are prohibited from holding "any office, position, or employment in any member bank, except that this restriction shall not apply to a member who has served the full term for which he was appointed."[47]

The Chair and Vice Chair of the Board of Governors are picked from the members of the Board. They are appointed by the President and confirmed by the Senate. Each serves for four years and may be reappointed by the President and confirmed by the Senate. To date, William McChesney Martin remains the longest-serving Chair of the Board of Governors. He served as Chair from April 2, 1951, to January 31, 1970, under five different presidents. The second longest-serving Chair of Board of Governors is Alan Greenspan. He was the Chair from August 11, 1987, to January 31, 2006. Greenspan served as Chair under four different Presidents.[48]

5.2.1.2 Federal Reserve Banks

The Fed is divided into twelve geographic areas called Federal Reserve Districts. These divisions do not co-inside with state geographic boundaries. At the time of the founding, the geographic divisions were based on the economic activities in the area. Section 2 of the Federal Reserve Act dictated that, "'[t]he Reserve Bank Organization Committee,' shall designate not less than eight nor more than twelve cities to be known as Federal reserve cities, and shall divide the continental United States … into districts, each district to contain only one of such Federal reserve cities."[49] Each district has a Federal Reserve Bank, which is named after the city in which its headquarter is located. Table 5.1 provides the district number, names of the Federal Reserve Banks, and the geographic areas served by each Bank.

[47] Restrictions on Board members. https://www.federalreserve.gov/aboutthefed/section10.htm (Accessed: July 24, 2019).

[48] Tenures of William McChesney Martin and Alan Greenspan as Chairs of the Board of Governors. https://www.federalreservehistory.org/people (Accessed: July 24, 2019).

[49] Geographic organization of the Fed. https://www.federalreserve.gov/aboutthefed/section2.htm (Accessed: July 24, 2019).

Table 5.1 Federal Reserve Districts and Federal Reserve Banks

[1] *District*	*[2]* *Federal Reserve Bank*	*[3]* *Areas served*
1	Federal Reserve Bank Boston	Connecticut (excluding Fairfield County), Massachusetts, Maine, New Hampshire, Rhode Island, and Vermont
2	Federal Reserve Bank of New York	New York state, the 12 northern counties of New Jersey, Fairfield County in Connecticut, Puerto Rico, and the US Virgin Islands
3	Federal Reserve Bank of Philadelphia	[E]astern Pennsylvania, southern New Jersey, and Delaware
4	Federal Reserve Bank of Cleveland	Ohio, western Pennsylvania, the northern panhandle of West Virginia, and eastern Kentucky
5	Federal Reserve Bank of Richmond	Virginia, Maryland, the Carolinas, the District of Columbia, and most of West Virginia
6	Federal Reserve Bank of Atlanta	Alabama, Florida, Georgia, and portions of Louisiana, Mississippi, and Tennessee
7	Federal Reserve Bank of Chicago	Iowa, and most of Illinois, Indiana, Michigan and Wisconsin
8	Federal Reserve Bank of St. Louis	Arkansas and portions of six other states: Missouri, Mississippi, Tennessee, Kentucky, Indiana, and Illinois. The St. Louis Federal Reserve Bank serves most of eastern Missouri and southern Illinois
9	Federal Reserve Bank of Minneapolis	Minnesota, Montana, North and South Dakota, 26 counties in northwestern Wisconsin and the Upper Peninsula of Michigan
10	Federal Reserve Bank of Kansas City	Colorado, Kansas, Nebraska, Oklahoma, Wyoming, northern New Mexico, and Western Missouri
11	Federal Reserve Bank of Dallas	Texas, northern Louisiana and southern New Mexico
12	Federal Reserve Bank of San Francisco	Alaska, Arizona, California, Hawaii, Idaho, Nevada, Oregon, Utah, Washington, Guam, American Samoa, and the Northern Mariana Islands

Table prepared by the author. *Data Source* https://www.federalreserveeducation.org/about-the-fed/structure-and-functions/districts (Accessed: July 24, 2019)

Each Federal Reserve Bank is separately incorporated. As we saw earlier, the Fed is a public and private partnership. Commercial banks hold shares of stock in the Federal Reserve Bank that serves their district. According to Section 5 of the Federal Reserve Act, the "capital stock of each Federal reserve bank shall be divided into shares of $100 each." As the number of banks changes or the size of each bank changes, the number of shares of stock in a given Federal Reserve Bank also changes accordingly. The Act dictates that, "[w]hen a class member bank increases its capital stock or surplus, it shall thereupon subscribe for an additional amount of capital stock of the Federal reserve bank of its district equal to 6 per centum of the said increase." To ensure that no one bank has undue control over the decision making of a Federal Reserve Bank, the Act dictates that "[a]ny member bank which holds capital stock of a Federal Reserve bank in excess of the amount required on the basis of 6 per centum of its paid-up capital stock and surplus shall surrender such excess stock."[50]

Each Federal Reserve Bank is governed by a board of directors, which consists of nine members. There are three classes of the members of a board of director—Class A, Class B, and Class C. There are three members in each class of directors. Class A directors "shall be chosen by and be representative of the stockholding banks."[51] Class B directors "shall represent the public and shall be elected ...with due but not exclusive consideration to the interests of agriculture, commerce, industry, services, labor, and consumers."[52] Class C directors are appointed by the Board of Governors of the Federal Reserve System. They are elected to "represent the public ...with due but not exclusive consideration to the interests of agriculture, commerce, industry, services, labor and consumers."[53]

Depending upon the size of the district, some Federal Reserve Banks have several branches. For instance, the Federal Reserve Bank of Atlanta

[50] Amount and value of shares of stock in the Federal Reserve Banks. https://www.federalreserve.gov/aboutthefed/section5.htm (Accessed: July 26, 2019).

[51] Class A directors. https://www.federalreserve.gov/aboutthefed/section4.htm (Accessed: July 26, 2019).

[52] Class B directors. https://www.federalreserve.gov/aboutthefed/section4.htm (Accessed: July 26, 2019).

[53] Class C directors. https://www.federalreserve.gov/aboutthefed/section4.htm (Accessed: July 26, 2019).

is headquartered in Atlanta, with branches in Birmingham, Jacksonville, Miami, Nashville, and New Orleans.[54] The branches of the Federal Reserve Banks are overseen by their own boards of directors. The number of directors is "not more than seven nor less than three…of whom a majority of one shall be appointed by the Federal reserve bank of the district, and the remaining directors by the Board of Governors of the Federal Reserve System."[55] The Board of Governors of the Federal Reserve System may require a Federal Reserve Bank to close a given branch. In such a situation, the parent Reserve Bank will assume the business of the branch. It is worth noting that as individuals we cannot open an account in either the Federal Reserve Banks or any of its branches.

Why have so many directors? Decentralized nature of the Federal Reserve System and diversity of opinion; that is why. But why do we need a decentralized body? It is quite likely that economic conditions will not be the same in each district. What may ail one region, and the actions that remedy its ailment, may be different from that of another region. Indeed, it is a safe bet that economic conditions in different regions will be different. Yes, there are some national trends, but differences remain. The farmers of Midwest and industrial cities in the Northeast often do not face the same economic circumstances. Each needs representation in decision making. Since each Federal Reserve Bank and its branches serve their district, the directors are more intimately familiar with the economic conditions that may prevail at any point in time in their respective district.

5.2.1.3 The Federal Open Market Committee

The Federal Reserve Open Market Committee (FOMC) is the entity that conducts monetary policy. Here, let me remind you what monetary policy is. Recall from Chapter 3 that monetary policy refers to changes in the quantity of money in the economy. Recall also what we mean by "money." For anything to function as money, it has to have three characteristics—a medium of exchange, a unit of account, and a store of value. We spent some time in the preceding chapters (Chapters 2, 3, and 4)

[54] Branches of the Federal Reserve Bank of Atlanta. https://www.frbatlanta.org/about/atlantafed/branches.aspx (Accessed: July 24, 2019).

[55] Branches of the Federal Reserve Banks. https://www.federalreserve.gov/abouttheFed/section3.htm (Accessed: July 25, 2019).

exploring why money is needed in a modern economy. Because an understanding of these concepts is of great import, it would not be a bad idea to review these concepts before moving on.

How does the FOMC conduct monetary policy? We will spend much of the remainder of this chapter to answer this question. First, let me go over the basic structure of FOMC.

The FOMC typically holds eight meetings during the year in Washington, DC. If needed, additional meetings may be called by the President of the Fed. It has 12 voting members. All seven members of the Board of Governors and the President of the Federal Reserve Bank of New York are permanent members of the FOMC. The remaining four seats are filled by the 11 presidents of the Federal Reserve Banks. They serve a term of one year each on a rotating basis. Furthermore, all non-voting members attend the FOMC meetings and participate in discussions. "By law, the FOMC determines its own internal organization and, by tradition, the FOMC elects the Chair of the Board of Governors as its chair and the President of the Federal Reserve Bank of New York as its vice chair."[56]

In case you are wondering about the origin of the name of the Federal Open Market Committee, it comes from the fact that FOMC is responsible for conducting Open Market Operations. And what are Open Market Operations, you may ask? The Fed buys and sells existing government bonds in the open market—hence the term "open market"—to increase and decrease money in the economy, respectively. It is the main tool of the Fed to conduct monetary policy. We will go into a lot more detail about this and other tools the Fed has at its disposal to conduct monetary policy, and in turn, affect the economy. Let's dive right into it.

5.3 Monetary Policy

Recall that monetary policy is related to changing the quantity of money (often called money supply) in the economy. When the quantity of money changes in the economy, the forces of supply and demand interact and the cost of borrowing changes. That is, the interest rate changes. Note that interest rate is nothing more than the rental rate of purchasing power. When one saves, one is deferring purchasing goods and services. What one has saved has purchasing power. Instead of just letting the purchasing

[56] The structure of FOMC. https://www.federalreserve.gov/aboutthefed/structure-federal-open-market-committee.htm (Accessed: July 27, 2019).

power sit there, one might as well rent it to someone who wants to use it, all else constant. This, in turn, affects how much is borrowed to build factories, buildings, houses, machines, buy cars, appliances, and so on. If the cost of borrowing—the amount of interest one pays—is lower, it is more attractive to borrow. So people borrow more. The reverse happens when the cost of borrowing increases.

Let me give an example. Suppose that there are three projects—Project A, Project B, and Project C. If one were to undertake these projects, produce goods and services, and sell them, one may earn profit. Profit is the positive difference between the total cost of producing goods and services and the total revenue from the sale of those goods and services. Note that total cost is the cost per unit times the number of units produced. Analogously, total revenue is the price per unit times the number of units sold. Suppose a firm produces 100 units of a product and the cost of producing each unit is \$10, then total cost will be \$1000, which is \$10 times 100. Now suppose that the firm sells these 100 units for \$12 per unit, the total revenue will \$1200, which is \$12 time 100. The firm is earning a profit of \$200. The profit *rate* is just the difference between the total revenue and total cost divided by total cost. In this example to calculate profit rate, we divide the profit \$200, which, as we saw, is the difference between total revenue and total cost, by total cost, which is \$1000, that is, $\left(\frac{1200-1000}{1000}\right) = 0.2$. So the profit rate is 0.2. When we multiply 0.2 by 100, it gives profit rate per one hundred dollars, that is, 20 percent. This is how rate is reported, be it profit or interest. Often we also attach a time period. Usually, it is per year. Another term used in the literature for what we just calculated is the "rate of return." We will use the term rate of return in this example.

Another point worth mentioning here is that interest rate is what comes out by solving the expression that compares the difference between amount borrowed and the amount paid back, with the amount borrowed. Take this example. Suppose you borrowed \$950 with a promise to pay back \$1000 in a year. The difference of \$50 here is the cost of borrowing, or the interest paid on \$950. Put another way, it is the rent for using the purchasing power in those \$950. The interest rate in this example will be (approximately) 5.26 percent. How did I come up with this figure? I took the difference between the amount borrowed and the amount promised to pay back, and divided it by the amount borrowed, that is, $\left(\frac{1000-950}{950}\right) \approx 0.0526$. When you multiply this by 100, you will get 5.26

percent. As I mentioned earlier, interest rates and rates of return often have time periods attached to them—usually a year. In this example if the borrower borrowed this amount for a year, then the interest rate will be 5.26 percent per year. Note also the similarity between how we calculated the rate of return and how we calculated the interest rate. In fact, the formula is the same.

Back to our example. Suppose that each of our projects requires $1 million. Each project has a certain expected rate of return. Project A's expected rate of return is 10 percent; Project B's expected rate of return is 8 percent; and Project C's expected rate of return is 6 percent. I am using the adjective "expected" to highlight the fact that any project's rate of return beforehand is always expected. It is only after the fact that we find out about the actual rate of return. Holding all else constant, a higher profit results in a higher rate of return. On the other hand, a lower profit leads to a lower rate of return. Rate of return will be negative when there is a loss—total revenue is less than total cost. For the ease of exposition, let me put these figures in a table, Table 5.2.

Columns [1] through [4] in Table 5.2 list the project names, expected rate of return, the amount borrowed per project, and total borrowing, respectively. Just to clarify, Column [4] lists the total borrowing in the economy. This is the total sum borrowed for all projects.

At an interest rate of, say, 10.5 percent, none of the projects is profitable. As a result, the total amount borrowed is zero. Suppose now that the interest rate decreases to 9.5 percent. Since Project A's rate of return is higher than the borrowing cost, Project A is worth it. The total amount borrowed is $1 million. When interest rate decreases to, say, 7.5 percent, both Project A and Project B are worth starting. The total amount borrowed now is $2 million—$1 million for Project A and $1 million for Project B. Suppose now that the interest rate decreases

Table 5.2 Expected rates of return and amount borrowed

[1] Project name	*[2] Expected rate of return*	*[3] Amount borrowed*	*[4] Total borrowing*
Project A	10 percent	$1 million	$1 million
Project B	8 percent	$1 million	$2 million
Project C	6 percent	$1 million	$3 million

Table prepared by the author

further to, say, 5.5 percent. Now all three projects are worth starting. The total amount borrowed now is $3 million—$1 million for Project A, $1 million for Project B, and $1 million for Project C. As the interest rate decreases, holding all else constant, the total amount borrowed increase, and vice versa.

At this point, perhaps another concept should be clarified. That is the concept of "investment." In everyday life when people say that they have made an investment, it is quite likely that they are talking about buying shares of stock or buying a bond. (Below I will provide more details about what a bond is.) For economists, investment means an act of adding to the existing stock of capital plus changes in inventory, whereas "capital" includes roads, bridges, machinery, equipment, houses, apartment building, software, and so on.[57] These are the things that are produced to produce other goods and services. Inventory is the difference between output and sale. The reason firms hold inventories is to meet the unforeseen changes in demand. Capital represents the productive capacity of the economy. When we, as households, buy bonds and stocks, we are saving. The only "investment" that we as households make is buying a new house or a condominium, and so on. In our example of borrowing for the various projects, one can think of firms borrowing to add to the number of factories, machines, software, and so on. That is, they are investing. If a firm, however, borrows to acquire another firm, it will not be considered investment. Why? One way to think about it is to think in terms of the overall economy. When a firm acquires another firm, it is not adding to the existing stock of capital—machines, buildings, software, etc. The only thing that is happening is that the ownership is changing. From the point of view of the overall economy, the acquisition of one firm by another firm has not resulted investment.

We can say, then, that when the interest rate increase, the total quantity of investment decreases, and when the interest rate decreases, the total quantity of investment increases. Why is that? The reason is that, holding everything else constant, as interest rate decreases, the cost of borrowing decreases, and more and more projects become profitable. The reverse happens when interest rate increases.

[57] NIPA Handbook: Concepts and Methods of the US National Income and Product Accounts. https://www.bea.gov/resources/methodologies/nipa-handbook (Accessed: July 29, 2019).

5.3.1 *Tools of Monetary Policy*

The methods that the Fed uses to change the quantity of money in the economy are referred to as "tools of monetary policy." The Fed uses four main tools—Changes in Required Reserve Ratio; Changes in Discount Rate; Open Market Operation; and Interest on Required and Excess Reserve Balances. The first three are "old" tools in the sense that the Fed has been using these tools for quite some time. The fourth tool—Interest on Required and Excess Reserves held at the Federal Reserve Banks—was introduced in 2006. Then there are unconventional tools that the Fed used in the aftermath of the financial crisis and the Great Recession of 2007–2009. Let me go into more detail on these four monetary policy tools.

5.3.1.1 Changes in Required Reserve Ratio

Required Reserve Ratio is the percentage of deposits that depository institutions—"commercial banks, savings banks, savings and loan associations, credit unions, US branches and agencies of foreign banks, Edge corporations, and agreement corporations"[58]—are required to hold either as cash in their vaults, called "vault cash," or as deposits at the Federal Reserve Banks. The purpose of holding these reserves is to meet the withdrawal demands of depositors.

There is another important purpose that these reserves serve. Changes in the amount held as reserves lead to change in the amount of loans that a commercial bank can make.[59] We saw in Chapter 4 that when the percentage of deposits held as reserves increases, the bank is able to extend fewer loans. On the other hand, as the percentage of deposits held as reserves decreases the bank is able to extend more loans. We called it "reserve ratio" and represented it by rr. The inverse of reserve ratio, $(\frac{1}{rr})$, we called money multiplier. The Board of Governors has the sole authority to change the ratio of deposits that depository institutions must hold as reserves. Over the decades, as we have learned more about how monetary policy affects the economy, this requirement has changed. It depends upon the size the depository institution (amount of deposits),

[58] Depository institutions. https://www.federalreserve.gov/monetarypolicy/reservereq.htm (Accessed: July 27, 2019).

[59] Purposes of holding reserves. Joshua N. Feinman. "Reserve Requirements: History, Current Practice, and Potential Reform." *Federal Reserve Bulletin*. June (1993). Print.

Table 5.3 Reserve requirements by depository institutions

[1] *Liability type*	*[2]* *Requirement*	*[3]*
	% of liabilities	*Effective date*
Net transaction accounts		
$0 to $16.3 million	0	01-17-2019
More than $16.3 million to $124.2 million	3	01-17-2019
More than $124.2 million	10	01-17-2019
Non-personal Time Deposits	0	12-27-1990
Eurocurrency Liabilities	0	12-27-1990

Table prepared by the author. *Data Source* https://www.federalreserve.gov/monetarypolicy/reservereq.htm (Accessed: July 27, 2019)

its financial health, and location. Table 5.3 presents reserve requirements at present.[60]

Notice that the percentage of deposits that must be kept as reserves increases with the amount of deposits. Smaller banks with deposits below $16.3 million are not required to hold any reserves. Holding everything else constant, when the Fed increases the required reserve ratio, *rr*, the value of the money multiplier, $\left(\frac{1}{rr}\right)$, decreases, and the quantity of money supply decreases. The reverse happens when the Fed lowers the required reserve ratio, *rr*. It is worth mentioning here that the percentage also depends upon the type of deposit. I will refer the curious reader to the Federal Reserve's Website for details about the differences between these account types. Just as a clarificatory note about terminology, "Liability Type." As we saw earlier, when you deposit funds in a bank, you are in effect lending to the bank and the bank is the borrower. So the deposited amount is your asset and it is the liability of the bank.

At this point, a diagram will be helpful in visualizing the change in money supply. Figure 5.1 shows this change in money supply.

In terms of Fig. 5.1, when the Fed lowers the required reserve ratio, *rr*, and as a result the money multiplier, $\left(\frac{1}{rr}\right)$, increases. Holding all else constant, commercial banks are able to lend more. In terms of Fig. 5.1,

[60] Reserve requirements by depository institutions. https://www.federalreserve.gov/monetarypolicy/reservereq.htm (Accessed: July 30, 2019).

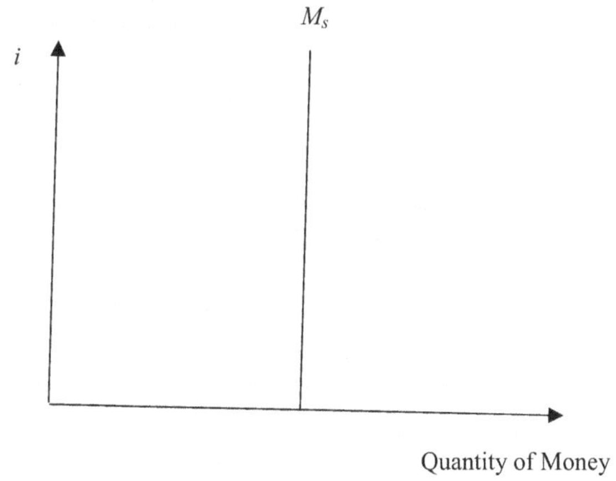

Fig. 5.1 Changes in money supply (Figure prepared by the author)

the money supply curve, M_s, shifts to the right. The reverse happens when the Fed wants to decrease the quantity of money supply.

Notice that in Fig. 5.1, I have Quantity of Money on the horizontal axis and the interest rate, i, on the vertical axis. The money supply curve, M_s, is drawn as a vertical line. This indicates that the Fed's decision to change money supply is not affected by the interest rate. Rather, the Fed affects the interest rate. As we saw earlier, changes in interest rates affect the economy by affecting the cost of borrowing, and in turn, the profitability of various projects. When interest rates increase, the cost of borrowing increases. As a result, fewer and fewer projects remain profitable, and the quantity of investment declines, holding all else constant. The reverse happens when the interest rate decreases.

5.3.1.2 Changes in Discount Rate

The Fed also serves as a "bankers' bank." What this means is that when a commercial bank needs to borrow, and for whatever reason it cannot borrow from other banks, it may borrow from the Fed. The interest rate that the Fed charges the commercial banks is called "discount rate." When the Fed wants to increase the supply of money in the economy, it lowers the discount rate. This makes it cheaper for banks to borrow and extend loans, all else constant. In terms of Fig. 5.1, the M_s curve shifts to the right. The reverse happens when the Fed wants to decrease money supply—the Fed raises the discount rate, leading to a leftward shift of the M_s curve.

5.3.1.3 Open Market Operations

While the two tools mentioned above can be used to affect money supply, the main tool that the Fed uses is Open Market Operations. This involves buying and selling of government securities in the open market, hence the term "Open Market Operations." A "security," by the way, is a financial asset—a bond or a share of stock—that can be bought and sold. It is instructive to remind ourselves that when we buy a bond we are lending funds, and when we sell or issue a bond we are borrowing funds. Furthermore, the price of a bond is the amount lent. Also recall that a bond is a promissory note: The borrower promises to pay back the loan and the interest at a given date. Here is how this tool works.

When we—individuals, firms, foreigners, foreign governments—lend to the US Treasury, we charge interest to the Treasury. The interest rates that we charge the Treasury depend upon the length of time for which the loans are made. The US Treasury borrows for short-term needs as well as for long-term needs. In Table 5.4, I have provided interest rates that prevailed on January 2, 2014 for various borrowing periods.

The top row of Table 5.4 lists "Maturity" and "% Yield." Maturity refers to the time period for which the loan is made. For instance, we can lend to the US Treasury for one month, or two months, all the way to 30 years. % Yield stands for yield to maturity. It is the interest rate that we charge the US Treasury for loans made for a specific time period. (Note that during 2014 the US Treasury did not issue Treasury bills for the two-month period. This is why it states "N/A" across from "2 M" in the % Yield column.) Why not just call it interest rate? The reason is that in calculating yield to maturity we use a particular way of calculating interest rate which is the most accurate. I will not go into this formula here. Curious reader is referred to the US Treasury's Website for details.[61]

By way of distinguishing between the various maturity dates and other features, promissory notes that mature up to 52 weeks (i.e., one year) are referred to as Treasury bills. Treasury bills are sold at a discount. What this means is that, when the Treasury bill matures, the lender gets the face value. This is the amount that the borrower promises to pay back. Face

[61] Yield to maturity calculations. https://www.treasury.gov/resource-center/data-chart-center/interest-rates/Pages/yieldmethod.aspx (Accessed: August 3, 2019).

Table 5.4 US Treasury interest rates (January 2, 2014)

[1] *Time to maturity*	*[2]* *%* *Yield*
1 M	0.01
2 M	N/A
3 M	0.07
6 M	0.09
1 Y	0.13
2 Y	0.39
3 Y	0.76
5 Y	1.72
7 Y	2.41
10 Y	3.0
20 Y	3.68
30 Y	3.92

Table prepared by the author. *Data Source* https://www.treasury.gov/resource-center/data-chart-center/interest-rates/Pages/TextView.aspx?data=yield (Accessed: August 3, 2019). Note that during 2014 the US Treasury did not issue Treasury Bills for the two-month period. This is why it states "N/A" across from "2 M" in the % Yield column

value is higher than what they have lent. An example may help. Suppose that the face value of Treasury bill is \$100.00, and amount lent is \$95.00. This means that the Treasury bill has been sold at a discount. We can write the formula as follows.

Interest Rate $= \left(\frac{F-P}{P}\right) = \left(\frac{100-95}{95}\right) \approx 0.0526$

In this formula, F represents the face value—the amount that the borrower promises to pay back at the maturity date, and P represents the price—the amount lent by the lender. When we multiply the result by 100, we get 5.26 percent. This is exactly the way we calculated interest rate above. Again, a reminder that while we talk about interest rate when discussing loans, interest rate is what pops out of solving this equation. This takes the difference of the promised amount, the face value, and the price of the bond, the amount lent, and compares it with the price of the bond.

Promissory notes whose maturity date is greater than a year and up to ten years are called Treasury notes. Treasury notes pay interest every six months. Finally, promissory notes whose maturity date is greater than ten years are called Treasury bonds. Similar to Treasury notes, Treasury bonds

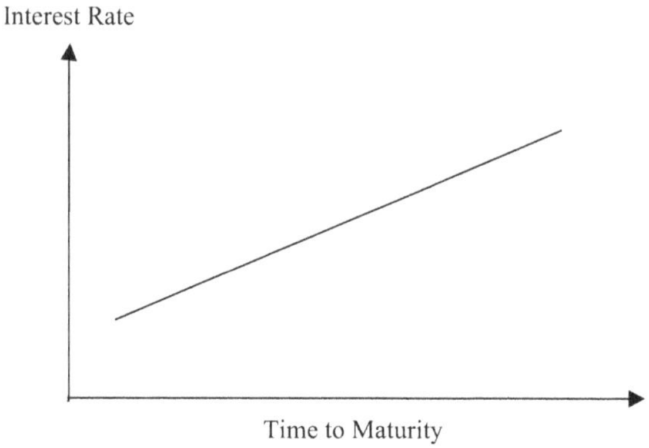

Fig. 5.2 A stylized yield curve (Figure prepared by the author)

also pay interest every six months.[62] Treasury notes and bond are also known as "coupon bonds." The term comes from the fact that the holder of these promissory notes would tear out a coupon every six months, send it to the issuer of the bond, and in return receive the interest payments.

In terms of Table 5.4, the first five promissory notes (1 Month, 2 Months, 3 Months, 6 Months, and 1 Year) will be considered Treasury bills. The next five promissory notes (2 Years, 3 Years, 5 Years, 7 Years, and 10 Years) will be referred to as Treasury notes. And finally, the last two promissory notes (20 Years and 30 Years) are called Treasury bonds.

A diagram that plots interest rates on government securities—bills, notes, and bonds—is called a "Yield Curve." Typically, the longer the time period for which loans are made, the higher the interest rate, holding all else constant. This is called the "Term Structure of Interest Rates." Figure 5.2 plots a stylized version of a yield curve.

In Fig. 5.3, I plot the actual interest rate and time to maturity data presented in Table 5.4 that prevailed on January 2, 2014. Notice the positive relationship between interest rates and time to maturity.

Sometimes, however, this is not the case. The interest rates that prevailed on August 2, 2019 are listed in Table 5.5, and plotted in Fig. 5.4, is one such example. This type of yield curve is called an

[62] Treasury bills, notes, and bonds. https://www.treasurydirect.gov/indiv/products/products.htm (Accessed: August 4, 2019).

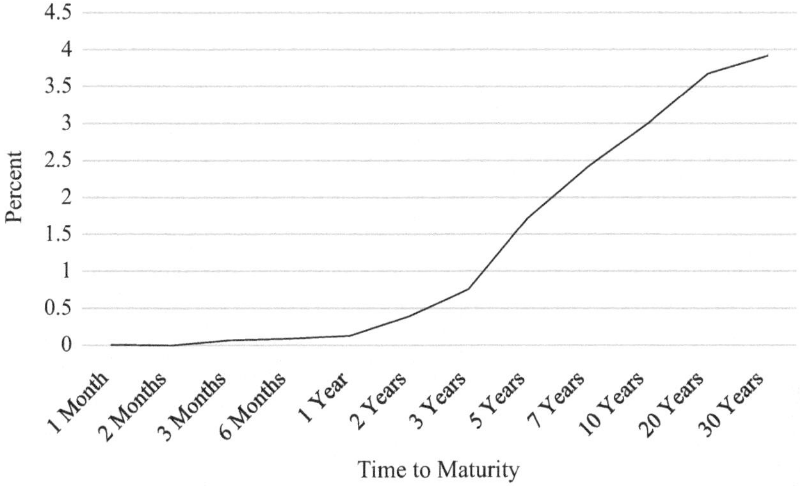

Fig. 5.3 Yield curve (January 2, 2014) (Figure prepared by the author. *Data Source* https://www.treasury.gov/resource-center/data-chart-center/interest-rates/Pages/TextView.aspx?data=yield [Accessed: August 3, 2019])

Table 5.5 US Treasury interest rates

[1] Maturity	*[2] % Yield*
1 Month	2.11
2 Months	2.12
3 Months	2.06
6 Months	2.02
1 Year	1.85
2 Years	1.72
3 Years	1.67
5 Years	1.66
7 Years	1.75
10 Years	1.86
20 Years	2.16
30 Years	2.39

Table prepared by the author. *Data Source* https://www.treasury.gov/resource-center/data-chart-center/interest-rates/Pages/TextView.aspx?data=yield (Accessed: August 3, 2019)

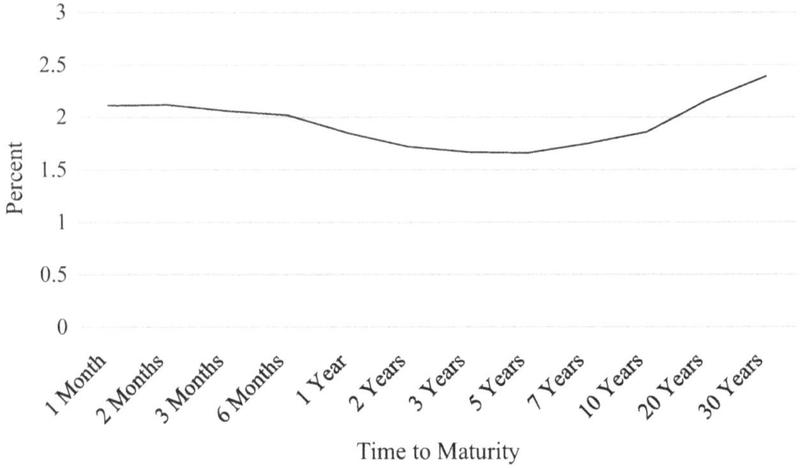

Fig. 5.4 The yield curve (August 2, 2019) (Figure prepared by the author. *Data Source* https://www.treasury.gov/resource-center/data-chart-center/interest-rates/Pages/TextView.aspx?data=yield [Accessed: August 3, 2019])

"Inverted Yield Curve." I will have more to say about the yield curve and its shapes later in this chapter.

Back to open market operations. When the Fed conducts open market operations, it buys and sells already existing government securities—Treasury bills, Treasury notes, and Treasury bonds, but most often Treasury bills—in the open market. It does not buy brand new securities. That is, the Fed does not lend directly to the US Treasury. A purchase of government security is called an open market purchase, and a sale of government security is called an open market sale.

Take the example of a Treasury bill that you bought, say for $97.00. Its maturity date is one month from today. Suppose that you need the funds now. You can resell this Treasury bill to someone else who is willing to lend to the US Treasury. What is actually happening is that you are transferring the right to collect the face value of the Treasury bill to someone else. In return, you are getting the funds today. The price at which you may sell the Treasury bill is determined in the open market. Suppose the buyer of this bill is the Fed. In this case, we will say that the Fed has conducted an open market purchase.

This action by the Fed triggers a series of events. Suppose you sold the Treasury bill for $97.00. The Fed wrote you a check in that amount. You deposited that check in your bank. The bank then deposits the check in its account with the Fed. The Fed increases the amount of reserves that the said bank has. Let's look at the equation from Chapter 4, Eq. 4.1, reproduced here.

$$\Delta D = \left(\frac{1}{rr}\right) \times \Delta R$$

Note that the ΔR has increased by $97.00. Suppose that the required reserve ratio, *rr*, is 10 percent. This means that the value of the money multiplier, $\left(\frac{1}{rr}\right)$, is 10. A change in reserves of $97.00 will lead to a change in demand deposits, ΔD, of $970.00. The Fed has increase money supply by $970.00.

In this example, we are assuming that the bank extends the loans. If the bank, however, does not want to extend loans or does not have any borrower at the time, then the bank has more reserves than it needs. It may lend those reserves to some other bank that has fewer reserves than it needs to meet its reserve requirements. In the second scenario, the lending bank will charge an interest rate. Holding everything else constant, the interest rate that banks charge each other for overnight loans—the federal funds rate—will decrease (more below). Either way, there is an increase in reserves in the banking system. As a result, money supply increases. The M_s curve in Fig. 5.1 shifts to the right. The reverse happens when the Fed sells government securities; money supply decreases and the M_s curve in Fig. 5.1 shifts to the left.

5.3.1.4 Interest Payment on Required and Excess Reserves

Recall that commercial banks are required to hold a percentage of their deposits are reserves—the required reserves. These reserves may be held in vaults of commercial banks or in an account at the Federal Reserve Bank that serves that commercial bank's district. Commercial banks may also hold, and they often do, more reserves than they are required to hold. These are called excess reserves.

Commercial banks argued that the requirement to hold reserves was an implicit tax on depository institutions since they could not lend the amount held as required reserves. In 2006, the US Congress passes the Financial Services Regulatory Relief Act of 2006. This Act allowed the

Federal Reserve Banks to pay interest on total reserves—required reserves plus excess reserves—held at the Federal Reserve Banks.[63] The Act served two purposes. One, it removed the implicit tax on commercial banks on the amount held as required reserves. Two, the payment of interest on excess reserves provided an additional tool of monetary policy to the Federal Reserve System. It allows the Fed to set an effective floor on the federal funds rate target. If the federal funds rate is below where the Fed wants it to be, the Fed can raise the interest rate that it pays on excess reserves. Since banks can earn a higher interest rate by keeping excess reserves at the Federal Reserve Banks, they would not lend those excess reserves in the federal funds market. This would lead to a decline in the quantity of funds available to be borrowed by other banks and raise the federal funds rate to where the Fed wants it to be.

The quantity of money supply alone, however, cannot affect the interest rate. There must also be money demand with which money supply interacts. Let me explain what money demand is. Money demand is the amount of funds that individuals and firms want to hold outside interest-bearing accounts. To keep matters simple, we will divide all forms of holding financial assets into two categories—interest-bearing accounts, which we can call bonds, and non-interest-bearing accounts. The interest-bearing accounts (i.e., bonds) include saving accounts, Certificates of Deposits or CDs, money market accounts, and so on. Accounts that do not pay interest we will call them cash. What about checking accounts? Checking accounts also pay interest, miniscule as it may be. You must have noticed that the more the restrictions on withdrawal of funds, the higher the interest rate that commercial banks pay. For our purposes, we can include checking accounts in cash because as far as back accounts go, checking accounts are the least restricted.

Why would someone want to hold funds outside interest-bearing accounts? Wouldn't one lose interest income by doing so? Yes, they would. The main reason for holding funds outside interest-bearing accounts is to make transactions. In principle, one could convert funds from interest-bearing accounts into cash whenever one wants to make a transaction. This action, however, has costs associated with it. It may be the limit on the amount one can withdraw at one point. There may also be a penalty for an early withdrawal. So basically we make a trade-off

[63] Interest on required and excess reserves. https://www.federalreserve.gov/monetarypolicy/reqresbalances.htm (Accessed: August 5, 2019).

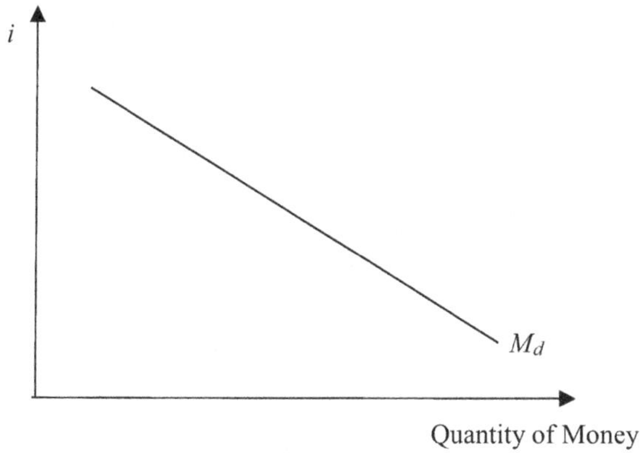

Fig. 5.5 Money demand (Figure prepared by the author)

between the convenience of making transactions with cash and earning interest. The higher the interest rate, the more interest amount we forgo for keeping funds outside interest-bearing accounts, and the lower the amount held in cash. So we can say that there is a negative relationship between the interest rate and the quantity of money demanded. A diagram, again, will be helpful.

As in the case of Fig. 5.1, in Fig. 5.5 we have the Quantity of Money on the horizontal axis and the interest rate, i, on the vertical axis. The negative slope of the money demand curve, M_d, represents the fact that, holding all else constant, when interest rate increases, people hold fewer fund outside interest-bearing accounts, and vice versa.

5.3.2 The Interaction of Money Supply and Money Demand

The forces of demand and supply interact to determine interest rate. When the Fed wants to increase interest rate, it decreases the quantity of money supply, and when the Fed wants to decrease interest rates, it increases the quantity of money supply, all else constant. Figure 5.6 shows this interaction.

In Fig. 5.6, I have combined Fig. 5.1, the money supply curve, and Fig. 5.5, the money demand curve. The interaction of money demand and money supply produces the equilibrium interest rate. It is represented here by i^* in Fig. 5.6.

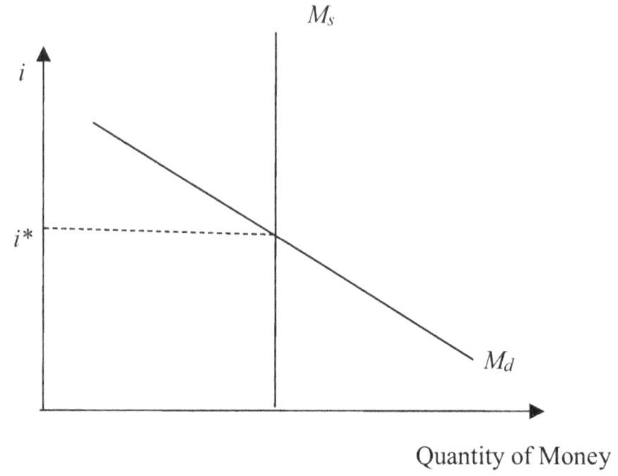

Fig. 5.6 The interaction of money demand and money supply (Figure prepared by the author)

We often hear in the news that the Fed has changed *the* interest rate. In fact, there are several interest rates that prevail in the economy at any given point. As we saw earlier that one reason for these differences is the term to maturity. It is referred to as the "term structure of interest rates." That is, the time period for which the loan is made. Typically the longer the time to maturity, the higher the interest rate.

The differences among the various interest rates also exist because of the riskiness of loans. There are other differences among various bonds as well. Some bonds may be more or less liquid than other bonds. Some may have lower or higher tax rates for the interest income earned on bonds. All these considerations are collectively called the "risk structure of interest rates." Holding all else constant, the riskier the borrower, the higher the interest rate. It makes sense. When someone takes on higher risk, they want to be compensated for taking the higher risk.

Holding all else constant, the more liquid a bond is, the lower the interest rate. Recall that liquidity refers to the ease with which an asset can be converted into another asset. Suppose that you bought a bond at a price of $1000.00. In other words, you lent $1000.00 to a borrower. The borrower is supposed to return the principal and the interest in a year. That is, the maturity date is a year from today. Suppose that you need the funds sooner, say in a month. You are more likely to lend the funds at a lower interest rate if the bond can easily be resold to someone else versus if it was a harder sell.

Finally, holding all else constant, the lower the tax rate on the interest income earned from a bond, the lower the interest rate. The reason is that since the lenders will be paying a lower tax rate on the interest income from these bonds, their after-tax income will be higher. So they are willing to lend funds at a lower interest rate.

While there are differences among various interest rates due to the time to maturity (the term structure of interest rates), and the riskiness, liquidity, and tax considerations of the interest income on these loans (the risk structure of interest rates), they tend to move together. Just as examples, I plot various interest rates in Figs. 5.7 and 5.8.

In Fig. 5.7, the series labeled "GS1" represents interest rates the one-year Treasury bill, "GS5" represents interest rates on the five-year Treasury note, "GS10" represents interest rates on the 10-year Treasury note, "GS20" represents interest rates on the 20-year Treasury bond, and the series labeled "GS30" represents the interest rates on the 30-year Treasury bond.

The data plotted in Fig. 5.7 are monthly data that range from April 1953 to July 2019. Note that all these bonds were not issued for the entire time period. As a result, some data are missing. For example, the series "GS20" which represents Treasury bonds with a 20-year maturity has missing values from January 1987 to September 1993. During this time period, the December 1986 observation and the October 1993 observation are joined by a straight line. Another point to keep in mind while looking at the data plotted in Fig. 5.7 is that the interest rate differences due to differences in the maturity dates are represented by the vertical distance in the lines representing the interest rates on various securities.

As another example, in Fig. 5.8, I have plotted three different interest rate series from December 1, 1954 to June 1, 2019. "FEDFUNDS" is represented by a dotted line, "GS10" is represented by a broken line, and "MPRIME" is represented by a solid line. Note that the direction of changes in these interest rates is the same. When one interest rate increases, so do the other interest rates, and when one interest rate decreases, so do the other interest rates.

At the end of each business day, banks must meet their reserve requirements. Some banks may have more reserves than they need while others may have fewer. It makes sense for the banks that have more reserves than

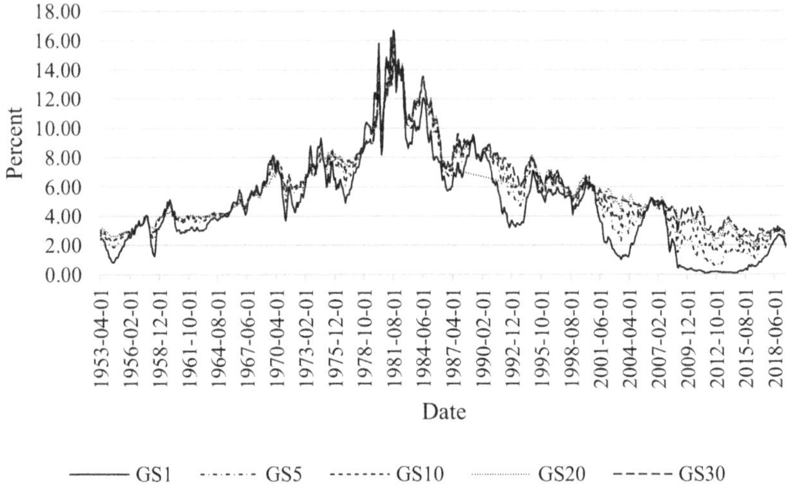

Fig. 5.7 Co-movement of Treasury interest rates (Figure prepared by the author. *Data Source* Federal Reserve Economic Data. Board of Governors of the Federal Reserve System [US], 1-Year Treasury Constant Maturity Rate [GS1]; Board of Governors of the Federal Reserve System [US], 5-Year Treasury Constant Maturity Rate [GS5]; Board of Governors of the Federal Reserve System [US], 10-Year Treasury Constant Maturity Rate [GS10]; Board of Governors of the Federal Reserve System [US], 20-Year Treasury Constant Maturity Rate [GS20]; Board of Governors of the Federal Reserve System [US], 30-Year Treasury Constant Maturity Rate [GS30]; retrieved from FRED, Federal Reserve Bank of St. Louis. https://fred.stlouisfed.org. Monthly observations. Not seasonally adjusted [Accessed: August 12, 2019])

they need to lend the excess reserves to those banks that may have fewer reserves than they need. This lending and borrowing takes place in the federal funds market, and the interest rate that banks charge each other for overnight loans is called the federal funds rate. It is represented by FEDFUNDS in Fig. 5.8.

The second series plotted is "GS10." This is the interest rate that prevailed on 10-year government securities. That is, the interest rate that we charged the US Treasury when we extended loans for ten years—Treasury notes. The third series plotted is Prime Rate (MPRIME). It is the interest that the banks charge their borrowers with an excellent credit history. As mentioned above, while the interest rates differ, the trend of

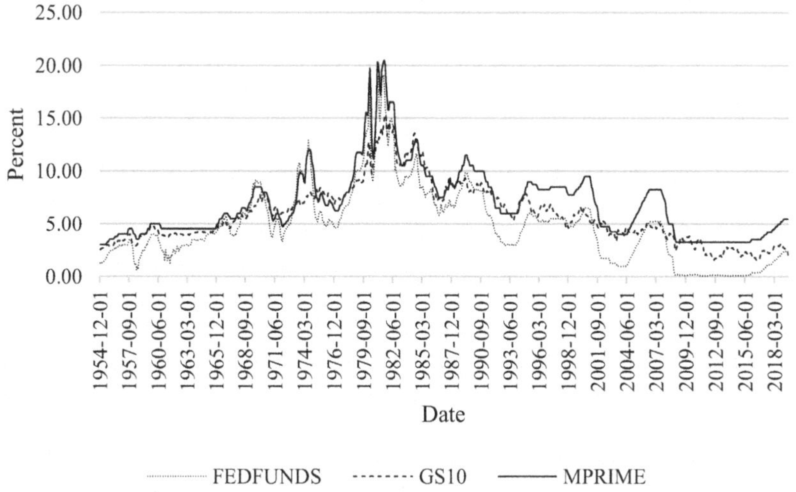

Fig. 5.8 Co-movement of the various interest rates (Figure prepared by the author. *Data Source* Federal Reserve Economic Data. https://fred.stlouisfed.org. Monthly observations. Not seasonally adjusted [Accessed: August 12, 2019])

these interest rates is similar. They all move in the same general direction over time.

The term "federal funds rate" is a bit of a misnomer. The Fed cannot dictate which particular interest banks should charge each other. It is an arrangement between two private parties. What the Fed actually does is that it sets a target for the federal funds rate—the interest rate that banks charge each other for overnight loans.[64] The Fed then changes the money supply such that the target is met. The Fed changes the amount of reserves in the banking system. This leads commercial banks to engage in borrowing and lending, thus changing the federal funds rate.

The point of plotting these rather hard to read various interest rate series is to show that various interest rate in the economy tend to move together.

[64] Federal funds rate target. https://www.federalreserve.gov/monetarypolicy/openmarket.htm. (Accessed: August 4, 2019).

5.4 The Impact of Changes in Money Supply on the Economy

We have learned that the Fed changes the federal funds rate target. We have also learned about the tools the Fed uses to change money supply to meet that target. The question arises: How does this change in the federal funds rate affect the economy? In other words, what is the channel through which monetary policy affects the economy?

First, recall that various interest rates move in the same direction (Figs. 5.7 and 5.8). This means that interest rates that commercial banks charge the borrowers move in the same direction. For instance, when the Fed raises the federal funds rate target, and decreases the money supply to meet that target, other interest rates also increase. This increases the costs of borrowing for all borrowers. As a result of the increase in borrowing costs, some projects are no longer profitable (Table 5.2). The quantity of investment in the economy decreases. At this point, it is helpful to recall that investment is an addition to the existing stock of capital plus changes in inventories. The owners of the firm who wanted to build the plant to produce widgets do not deem the project profitable. They will scratch the plan. They will not buy the machines, build the building, and hire workers to product those widgets. Workers who would have gotten the jobs to produce widgets would no longer get those jobs. They will cut back on their consumption (Chapter 4). A household that wanted to build a bigger house reacts the same way. With an increase in the mortgage rates, the cost of borrowing for the household increases. The plan to build a bigger house is scratched for now. So on and so forth. The overall economic activity in the economy declines. The reverse happens when the Fed lowers the federal funds rate target and increases money supply to meet the target.

We, as consumers, often borrow to buy big-ticket items like cars and appliances. When interest rates increase, our costs of borrowing increase. We hold off purchasing a new car or a new refrigerator. This dampens the demand for consumer goods. The firms that build these consumer goods cannot sell the items they have already produced. Inventories pile up. They cut back on production. In order to cut back on production, they either ask workers to work fewer hours, or fire some workers, or a combination of the two. Workers' incomes decrease. The affected workers cut back their consumption. Again, the overall economic activity declines. The reverse happens when the Fed lowers the federal funds rate targets and increases money supply to meet this new lowered target. The lowering of the federal funds rate target in the aftermath of the 2007–2009 financial crisis and the Great Recession that followed is one such example. These are the main contours of the channel through which monetary policy (i.e., changes in money supply) affect the economy.

5.5 The Yield Curve

As I briefly mentioned earlier that a graph that plots various interest rates on securities against the time to maturity is called a yield curve. The yield curves shown in Figs. 5.2 through 5.4 are for the US Government securities—Treasury bills, Treasury notes, and Treasury bonds. As long as these bonds only differ with regard to maturity date but have similar other characteristics, yield curve may be drawn for any other bond issuing entity. Here I will only focus on the yield curve for the US Treasury.

Because yield curves garner significant attention in the discipline and the media, it is worth explaining the concept in further detail. It is worth reminding ourselves that while we talk about interest rates when discussing bonds, interest rate is what pops out when we solve the interest rate equation that we discussed above, reproduced here, Interest Rate $= \left(\frac{F-P}{P}\right)$. Note also that in discussing the yield curve we take the example of discount bonds. The intuition is the same for coupon bonds as well.

There are three stylized facts about yield curves.

1. Interest rates of bonds that are similar in other aspects but have differing maturity dates tend to move in the same direction. All else constant, when interest rates on short-term bonds increase, so do interest rates on long-term bonds, and vice versa. This can be seen in Fig. 5.7 where I plot interest rates for one-year Treasury bill, five-year Treasury note, 10-year Treasury note, 20-year Treasury bond, and 30-year Treasury bond. Note that the general direction of change of these interest rates is the same.
2. When interest rates on short-term bonds are low, a yield curve is more likely to have a positive slope (Fig. 5.3). On the other hand, when interest rates on short-term bonds are high, yield curve is more likely to have a negative slope (Fig. 5.4).
3. Yield curves almost always have positive slopes. That is, interest rates on short-term bonds are almost always lower than interest rates on

long-term bonds (Figs. 5.2 and 5.3). In fact, this is why when I drew a stylized yield curve in Fig. 5.2 the curve had a positive slope.

There are three theories that try to explain these stylized facts about the yield curve. These are the Expectations Theory, the Segmented Markets Theory, and the Liquidity Premium Theory. In fact, the third theory—the Liquidity Premium Theory—combines the first two theories and adds more structure. There is also the Preferred Habitat Theory. As we will see below, this theory leads to the same conclusion that the Liquidity Premium theory suggests. Here, I will briefly lay out the main features of each of the theories.

5.5.1 *The Expectations Theory*

According to the Expectations Theory, the interest rates on the long-term bonds are the average of the short-term interest rates that are expected to prevail over the life of the bond.

A numerical example is helpful here. Suppose that interest rate on one-year Treasury bill right now is 5 percent per year. Suppose also that you expect that the interest rates over the next five years on one-year Treasury bills will be 5 percent per year. This means that the average (expected) interest rate will be 5 percent per year over the next five years. Suppose you want to lend funds to the US Treasury for five years. You could adopt two strategies and earn the same interest income.

Strategy 1. You could buy a one-year Treasury bill today, keep it until it matures a year from today, take the proceeds and buy another one-year Treasury bill again, and repeat this for five years.

Strategy 2. You could buy a five-year Treasury note today and keep it until it matures in five years.

If you expect that the interest rate is going to stay at 5 percent per year for the next five years, you will be indifferent between the two options. In either case, you will earn 5 percent per year. Both securities are perfect substitutes. Let me use a bit of arithmetic to clarify.

$$\left(\frac{5\% + 5\% + 5\% + 5\% + 5\%}{5}\right) = 5\%$$

In this case, the yield curve will be flat and the interest rate on the five-year note will be 5 percent per year.

Suppose now that you expect the following interest rate profile of one-year Treasury bills for the next five year.
Year 1: 5 percent
Year 2: 6 percent
Year 3: 7 percent
Year 4: 8 percent
Year 5: 9 percent

Calculating the average we get,

$$\left(\frac{5\% + 6\% + 7\% + 8\% + 9\%}{5}\right) = 7\%$$

Now the yield curve will be positively slopped. You will be willing to hold the five-year note only if its expected interest rate is 7 percent per year—the average of one-year bills over the next five years. Analogously, according to the Expectations Theory, when the interest rates are expected to decline, the yield curve will be negatively slopped—an inverted yield curve.

A question arises: How do people form expectations? An answer: In the absence of detailed information, we use simple rules of thumb. If we have seen prices rise in the past, we expect that prices will rise in the future as well. Same goes for interest rates, but with a twist. If the interest rates have been rising in the past, we expect that they will rise in the future as well. The twist is that when the short-term interest rates are low, people expect that short-term interest rates will increase to a "normal" level in the future. On the other hand, when the short-term interest rates are high, people expect that future short-term interest rates will decline to a "normal" level—however that "normal" level is defined, quite likely another rule of thumb based on previous experiences. Since long-term interest rates are the average of the expected short-term future interest rates, the long-term interest rate follows accordingly.

While the Expectations Theory does explain the stylized facts 1 and 2, the third one is left unanswered. Here is why: Suppose that the normal level of short-term interest rates is 5 percent. From this level, interest rates are as likely to rise as to decline. Why is it then that yield curves almost always have a positive slope? This is where the Segmented Markets Theory comes to help.

5.5.2 *The Segmented Markets Theory*

According to this theory, the lenders have strong preference for one type of security versus another. That is, holding all else constant, securities of different maturity dates are not substitutes at all. Here is why: Suppose you are saving to put a down payment on a car. It is likely that your time horizon is short, perhaps a year or so. On the other hand if you are saving to send a child to college, your time horizon is a lot longer, perhaps 15 years or so. And since most people want to save for shorter periods of time, the prices of short-term bonds are higher—interest rates are lower—than the bond prices of long-term bonds, meaning that interest rates on long-term bonds are higher. You may want to review the interest rate equation above to see the inverse relationship between the price of the bond and its interest rate.

While this explains why yield curves are almost always positively slopped—stylized fact 3—it does not explain why the interest rates of different maturities tend to move together—stylized fact 1. This theory also does not explain why when short-term interest rates are low, yield curves are more likely to have a positive slope, and vice versa—stylized fact 2.

5.5.3 *The Liquidity Premium Theory*

The Liquidity Premium Theory comes to the rescue. (Since the Preferred Habitat Theory comes to the same conclusion, I will not discuss it here.) The Liquidity Premium Theory combines the Expectations Theory and the Segmented Markets Theory. It argues that while securities of differing maturities are substitutes, they are not perfect substitutes as suggested by the Expectations Theory. People prefer short-term securities and want a premium to lend for longer terms—they want premium to part with their liquidity. Here again, a numerical example will be helpful.

Just as in our first example, suppose that you expect that short-term interest rates will stay at 5 percent per year for the next five years. However, for you to part with liquidity you want a premium, say 1 percent. That is,

$$\left(\frac{5\% + 5\% + 5\% + 5\% + 5\%}{5}\right) + 1\% = 6\%$$

Notice now that even in this case where you expect the short-term interest rates to stay the same, the interest rate on five-year notes is higher—the yield curve is positively slopped. Adding a liquidity premium this theory explains not only the first two stylized facts but also the third one—yield curves almost always have positive slopes.

In this chapter, we have covered a lot of material. We started with the need to establish a central bank. We briefly went over the history of the Federal Reserve System (the Fed)—central bank of the United States. Then we looked at the tools that the Fed uses to conduct monetary policy. We outlined the channel through which changes in money supply affect the economy. Finally, I also discussed in some detail what a yield curve is. One important lesson that we have learned is that changes in money supply affect the economy.

While we are moving along in this book, it is imperative to remind ourselves what money is. It is a medium of exchange, a unit of account, and a store of value. Anything that has these characteristics can serve as money. Another point we need to keep in mind is that the moment we divorce money from the underlying economy, we run into trouble. There have to be goods and services that people can exchange. There have to be goods and services that people want to evaluate. Finally, there have to purchasing power that people want to store.

Works Cited

Feinman, Joshua N. "Reserve Requirements: History, Current Practice, and Potential Reform." *Federal Reserve Bulletin*. June (1993). Print.

Hammond, Bray. "Jackson, Biddle, and the Bank of the United States." *The Journal of Economic History* 7.1 (1947): 1–23. *JSTOR*. Web.

Ledbetter, James. *One Nation Under Gold: How One Precious Metal Has Dominated the American Imagination for Four Centuries*. London: W. W. Norton, 2017. Print.

Morgan, H. W. "The Origins and Establishment of the First Bank of the United States." *The Business History Review* 30.4 (1956): 472–92. *JSTOR*. Web.

Owen, Robert L. *The Federal Reserve Act*. United State of America, 1919. Print.

Primm, James N. *A Foregone Conclusion: The Founding of the Federal Reserve Bank of St. Louis*. Federal Reserve Bank of St. Louis, 1989. Print.

Sprague, O. M. W. *History of Crises Under the National Banking System*. Washington, DC: Government Printing Office, 1910. Print.

CHAPTER 6

The Financial Crisis of 2007–2009 and the Great Recession

This chapter expands upon the topics covered in the previous chapters and covers some new ground. The chapter starts with the impact of monetary policy on the economy. It presents an overview of the financial crisis that started in 2007. I discuss various factors that led to the financial crisis and how the Fed responded. Then I talk about the so-called Modern Monetary Theory.

6.1 Monetary Policy and the Economy

In the previous chapter, I mentioned that the Fed changes the money supply to affect interest rates in the economy. As interest rates change, the costs of borrowing and the rewards for lending change accordingly. For instance, as interest rates increase, fewer and fewer projects remain profitable, holding all else constant. As a result, firms cut back on investment. Recall that investment refers to an addition to the existing stock of capital plus changes in inventories. Households, who want to buy a new house, add a room or two to the existing house, or buy big-ticket items—cars, appliances, etc.—hold off. The reverse happens when the costs of borrowing decrease. We also saw in the previous chapter how the Fed changes money supply such that its target federal funds rate—the interest rate that banks charge each other for overnight loans—is met.

Aggregates output of an economy fluctuates over time. When the economy is below its potential level of output, the Fed decreases the

M. Ashraf, *Money*,
https://doi.org/10.1007/978-3-030-50378-9_6

target of the federal funds rate. To meet this lower target, it increases money supply. Since various interest rates move in the same direction, all interest rates that prevail in the economy are affected. These are the main contours of how the Fed affects the economic activity.

6.1.1 A Business Cycle

Before we go any further, a better understanding of aggregate fluctuations is in order. Let me start with the definition of business cycles. Short-run ups and downs in output are called business cycles. Figure 6.1 presents a stylized business cycle.

Figure 6.1 has time on the horizontal axis and a measure of aggregate output on the vertical axis. I have drawn this figure using gross domestic product (GDP) on the vertical axis. The solid line represents the actual GDP. Notice the peaks and valleys. Typically, when economy's output is declining for two consecutive quarters the economy is said to be in a recession. On the other hand, when an economy's output is increasing for two consecutive quarters, the economy is said to be in a recovery.

Economists at the National Bureau of Economic Research (NBER), a nonprofit organization of economists, conduct research on numerous economic topics. According to the NBER, "... a recession is a significant decline in economic activity spread across the economy, lasting more than a few months, normally visible in real GDP, real income, employment,

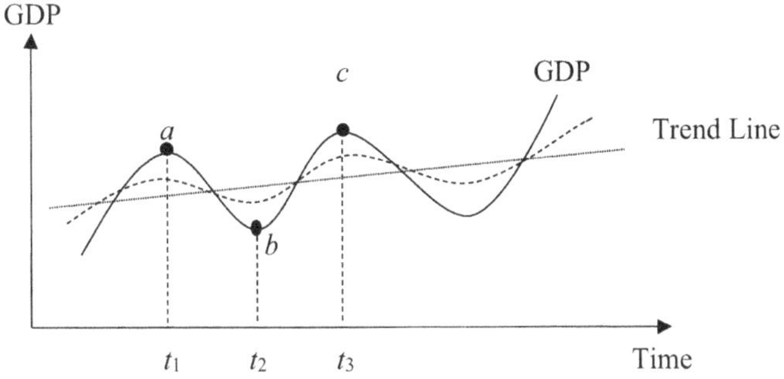

Fig. 6.1 A stylized business cycle (Figure prepared by the author)

industrial production, and wholesale-retail sales."[1] In terms of Fig. 6.1, point *a* will be considered a peak of the business cycle, and past point *a*, all the way to point *b*, we will consider the economy to be in a recession. Point *b* will be a trough, and from point *b* to point *c* will be a recovery.

NBER provides dates of business cycles. While NBER is a private nonprofit organization, the business cycle dates provided by the entity are taken to be semiofficial dates. NBER has calculated business cycle dates all the way going back to the mid-1850s. Table 6.1 lists all these dates.

Note that the previous recession started in December 2007 and ended in June 2009. It lasted for 18 months, making it the longest recession since World War II.[2] Due to the length and severity of this downturn, it has been termed "Great Recession."[3] The length of the Great Recession is the second longest since the Great Depression of the 1920s and 1930s which lasted for 43 months—from August 1929 to March 1933. What distinguishes a "recession" from a "depression." There isn't a hard and fast rule. It depends upon the length and severity of the downturn—low output and widespread high unemployment rate for an extended period of time. A depression is much more severe than a recession in depth and length.

During recessions our incomes are declining so, in terms of Fig. 6.1, we would want to decrease the depths of the valleys. However, why would we want the highs not to be too high? The reason is that when the economy is producing above the trend line, workers and machines are

[1] NBER definition of a recession. https://www.nber.org/cycles/cyclesmain.html (Accessed: August 19, 2019).

[2] The length of the Great Recession. https://admin.nber.org/cycles/sept2010.html (Accessed: August 19, 2019).

[3] The term "Great Recession." Kenneth N. Kuttner. "Outside the Box: Unconventional Monetary Policy in the Great Recession and Beyond." *Journal of Economic Perspectives* 32.4 (2018): 121–46. Print, Laurence Ball. "Long-Term Damage from the Great Recession in OECD Countries." *European Journal of Economics and Economic Policies: Intervention* 11.2 (2014): 149–60. Print, Patricia M. Anderson, Kristin F. Butcher, and Diane Whitmore Schanzenbach. "Changes in Safety Net Use During the Great Recession." *American Economic Review* 105.5 (2015): 161–65. Web, Jesse Rothstein, Stephanie Aaronson, and Lisa B. Kahn. "Unemployment Insurance and Job Search in the Great Recession [with Comments and Discussion]." *Brookings Papers on Economic Activity* (2011): 143–214. Web, Ben S. Bernanke. *The Courage to Act: A Memoir of a Crisis and Its Aftermath.* New York, NY: W. W. Norton, 2015. Web. https://economix.blogs.nytimes.com/2009/03/11/great-recession-a-brief-etymology/?searchResultPosition=3 (Accessed: August 19, 2019).

Table 6.1 Business cycle dates

[1]	[2]	[3]	[4]	[5]	[6]
BUSINESS CYCLE REFERENCE DATES		*DURATION IN MONTHS*			
Peak	*Trough*	*Contraction*	*Expansion*	*Cycle*	
Quarterly dates are in parentheses		Peak to Trough	Previous Trough to this Peak	Trough from Previous Trough	Peak from Previous Peak
	December 1854 (IV)	–	–	–	–
June 1857 (II)	December 1858 (IV)	18	30	48	–
October 1860 (III)	June 1861 (III)	8	22	30	40
April 1865(I)	December 1867 (I)	32	46	78	54
June 1869 (II)	December 1870 (IV)	18	18	36	50
October 1873 (III)	March 1879 (I)	65	34	99	52
March 1882 (I)	May 1885 (II)	38	36	74	101
March 1887 (II)	April 1888 (I)	13	22	35	60
July 1890 (III)	May 1891 (II)	10	27	37	40
January 1893 (I)	June 1894 (II)	17	20	37	30
December 1895 (IV)	June 1897 (II)	18	18	36	35
June 1899 (III)	December 1900 (IV)	18	24	42	42
September 1902 (IV)	August 1904 (III)	23	21	44	39
May 1907 (II)	June 1908 (II)	13	33	46	56
January 1910 (I)	January 1912 (IV)	24	19	43	32
January 1913 (I)	December 1914 (IV)	23	12	35	36
August 1918 (III)	March 1919 (I)	7	44	51	67

(continued)

Table 6.1 (continued)

[1]	*[2]*	*[3]*	*[4]*	*[5]*	*[6]*
BUSINESS CYCLE REFERENCE DATES		*DURATION IN MONTHS*			
Peak	*Trough*	*Contraction*	*Expansion*	*Cycle*	
Quarterly dates are in parentheses		Peak to Trough	Previous Trough to this Peak	Trough from Previous Trough	Peak from Previous Peak
January 1920 (I)	July 1921 (III)	18	10	28	17
May 1923 (II)	July 1924 (III)	14	22	36	40
October 1926 (III)	November 1927 (IV)	13	27	40	41
August 1929 (III)	March 1933 (I)	43	21	64	34
May 1937 (II)	June 1938 (II)	13	50	63	93
February 1945 (I)	October 1945 (IV)	8	80	88	93
November 1948 (IV)	October 1949 (IV)	11	37	48	45
July 1953 (II)	May 1954 (II)	10	45	55	56
August 1957 (III)	April 1958 (II)	8	39	47	49
April 1960 (II)	February 1961 (I)	10	24	34	32
December 1969 (IV)	November 1970 (IV)	11	106	117	116
November 1973 (IV)	March 1975 (I)	16	36	52	47
January 1980 (I)	July 1980 (III)	6	58	64	74
July 1981 (III)	November 1982 (IV)	16	12	28	18
July 1990 (III)	March 1991(I)	8	92	100	108
March 2001 (I)	November 2001 (IV)	8	120	128	128
December 2007 (IV)	June 2009 (II)	18	73	91	81

Table prepared by the author. Data Source: National Bureau of Economic Research. www.nber.org (Accessed: August 19, 2019)

working beyond their normal hours. Take the example of workers first. When workers are working overtime, the employers will have to pay them higher wages. Depending upon the industry, part or all of this increase in wages may be passed on to consumers in the form of higher prices.

The use of machines beyond the normal hours can also lead to an increase in the costs of production and hence prices of goods and services. When machines are being used beyond normal hours, their wear and tear increases and because they are not being serviced on regular intervals, the likelihood of machines breaking down increases. Take the example of your car. The more you drive your car, along with regular maintenance—oil changes, tire rotations, etc.—the more repairs it will need, all else constant. And if maintenance and repairs are put off because you cannot take time off to take your car to the mechanic, the likelihood of your car breaking down increases. Just as in the case of higher wages, higher maintenance costs will be passed on to consumers, in whole or in part, depending upon the industry. Increases in costs of production—higher wages, higher raw material prices, higher maintenance costs—may lead to an increase in price level beyond an optimal level. In terms of Fig. 6.1, we would want to be as close to the curve labeled "Trend Line" as possible. The "broken" curve represents one such path; its valleys are shallower and its peaks are more muted than those of the curve labeled "GDP."

Figure 6.1 may give the impression that changes in aggregate output are smooth. This is not the case, however. These changes are more erratic. Figure 6.2 plots actual real GDP and real potential GDP. I will go into more detail about potential GDP shortly. For now, think of it as the equivalent of trend line in Fig. 6.1.

In Fig. 6.2, real actual GDP is represented by a solid line (GDPC1), and real potential GDP is represented by a dotted line (GDPPOT). These are quarterly data from the first quarter of 1949 to the first quarter of 2019. Both data series are in real terms in billions of chained 2012 US dollars. Recall that when we convert a nominal data series into a real data series we take the impact of changes in prices out. That is, we represent the data series in terms of actual goods and services.

Potential real GDP is an estimate of real GDP that would prevail in an economy when the economy's resources (labor, machines, buildings, etc.) are fully employed. The government agency that is responsible for calculating potential real GDP is the Congressional Budget Office (CBO).

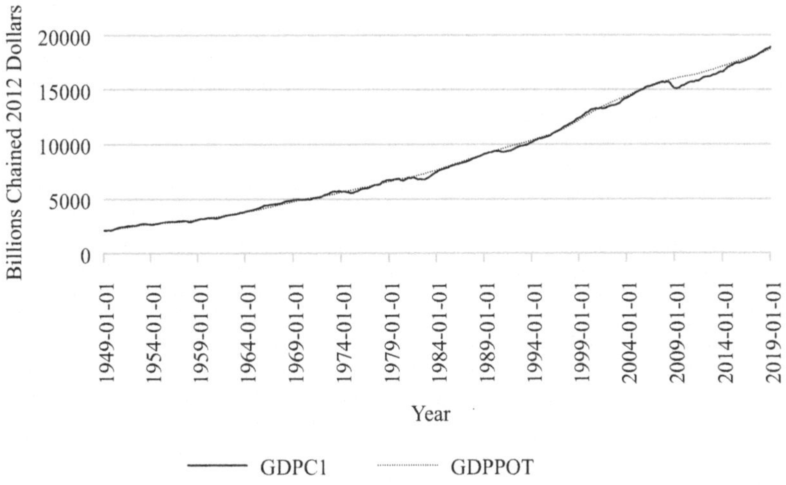

Fig. 6.2 Real actual and potential US GDP, billions of chained 2012 US dollars (Figure prepared by the author. *Data Source* US Bureau of Economic Analysis, Real Gross Domestic Product [GDPC1], retrieved from FRED, Federal Reserve Bank of St. Louis; https://fred.stlouisfed.org/series/GDPC1; US Congressional Budget Office, Real Potential Gross Domestic Product [GDPPOT], retrieved from FRED, Federal Reserve Bank of St. Louis. https://fred.stlouisfed.org/series/GDPPOT [Accessed: August 18, 2019])

The CBO, using statistical models, provides estimates of the potential real GDP of the economy. According to the CBO[4]:

> Potential output—the trend growth in the productive capacity of the economy—is an estimate of the level of GDP attainable when the economy is operating at a high rate of resource use. It is not a technical ceiling on output that cannot be exceeded. Rather, it is a measure of maximum *sustainable* output—the level of real GDP in a given year that is consistent with a stable rate of inflation. If actual output rises above its potential level, then constraints on capacity begin to bind and inflationary pressures build; if output falls below potential, then resources are lying idle and inflationary pressures abate. (Italics original)

[4] Potential real GDP. http://www.cbo.gov/sites/default/files/cbofiles/ftpdocs/30xx/doc3020/potentialoutput.pdf (Accessed: August 20, 2019).

To highlight the point that potential real GDP is not the "technical limit"—it is not the maximum output that an economy can produce—I have plotted actual real GDP (solid line) and real potential GDP (dotted line) data from 1990 (first quarter) to 2019 (first quarter) in Fig. 6.3. The figure also plots the difference between the actual real GDP and the potential real GDP (right scale). These data are represented by a dashed line.

Notice that at times actual real GDP is below the potential real GDP and at other times the former is above the latter. For instance, during the third quarter of 1990, the actual real GDP was \$9398, and the potential real GDP was \$9518 (both figures in billions chained 2012 US dollars). Refer to Table 6.1 and you will see that this is when the US economy was in a recession. The economy's output hit the trough during the first quarter of 1991. At that point, the actual real GDP was \$9269 and the

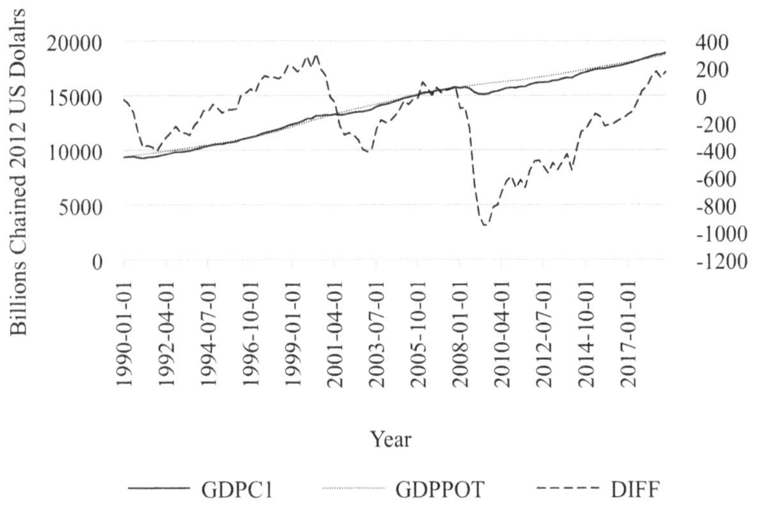

Fig. 6.3 Real actual and potential US GDP, billions of chained US dollars (from 1990 to 2019) (Figure prepared by the author. *Data Source* US Bureau of Economic Analysis, Real Gross Domestic Product [GDPC1], retrieved from FRED, Federal Reserve Bank of St. Louis; https://fred.stlouisfed.org/series/GDPC1; US Congressional Budget Office, Real Potential Gross Domestic Product [GDPPOT], retrieved from FRED, Federal Reserve Bank of St. Louis. https://fred.stlouisfed.org/series/GDPPOT [Accessed: August 18, 2019])

real potential GDP was $9645 (both figures in billions chained 2012 US dollars). Compare these figures with the third quarter of 2000. The actual real GDP during the third quarter of 2000 was $13,178 and the potential real GDP was $12,983 (both figures in billions chained 2012 US dollars). In the latter case, the actual real GDP was higher than the potential real GDP.

The purpose of monetary policy (and fiscal policy) is to moderate these ups and downs. As mentioned above, ideally, we would want to have a smooth straight line labeled Trend Line and represented by a broken line in Fig. 6.1. This, however, we have not been able to achieve given the complexity of the economy. But this does not mean that monetary and fiscal policies are useless. Quite the contrary. When it comes to the economy, muted peaks and shallow valleys are certainly better than steep mountains and deep canyons. In terms of Fig. 6.1, the path of the broken line is better than the path of the solid line. Well-thought out and well-implemented monetary and fiscal policies help alleviate the severity of a business cycle.

6.2 The Financial Crisis of 2007–2009 and the Ensuing Great Recession

Now that we understand what a business cycle is and how monetary policy affects the economy (Chapter 5), let us take a look at a recent example—the Great Recession. There is a wide agreement among economists that the cause of the Great Recession was the financial crisis that started in 2007.[5]

[5] The causes of the Great Recession. Ben S. Bernanke. *The Courage to Act: A Memoir of a Crisis and Its Aftermath*. New York, NY: W. W. Norton, 2015. Web, Atif Mian and Amir Sufi. "Finance and Business Cycles: The Credit-Driven Household Demand Channel." *The Journal of Economic Perspectives* 32.3 (2018): 31–58. Web, Anderson, Butcher, and Schanzenbach: 161–65, Ball: 149–60. See also *The Financial Crisis Inquiry Report: Final Report of the National Commission on the Causes of the Financial and Economic Crisis in the United States*. Washington: Financial Crisis Inquiry Commission, January 27, 2011. https://fraser.stlouisfed.org/title/5034 (Accessed: August 27, 2019); *Wall Street and the Financial Crisis: Anatomy of a Financial Collapse: Majority and Minority Staff Report, Permanent Subcommittee on Investigations, Committee on Homeland Security and Governmental Affairs, United States Senate, April 13, 2011*. https://fraser.stlouisfed.org/title/5094 (Accessed: August 27, 2019).

6.2.1 A Timeline of the 2007–2009 Financial Crisis

Let me start by providing a brief timeline of the financial crisis. I present this timeline in Table 6.2. It lists some of the key events that took place. The table also lists the dates of the start and end of the Great Recession.

The source of this table is the Federal Reserve Bank of St. Louis.[6] I will have more to say in the coming pages. I will refer to this table in this and the following chapters. There are a few terms whose understanding will be helpful.

In this table, the term "subprime" appears often. Subprime loans are those loans that are made to individuals who do not have a good credit history. They may have defaulted on loans, have had bounced checks on their records, or have not made payments on time. Lenders making loans to such individuals will require higher interest rates to be compensated for the higher risk they are taking. I will go into more detail in the coming pages.

"Libor" stands for London interbank offer rate. It is an "index used to determine interest rate changes for certain ARM [Adjustable Rate Mortgage] plans, based on the average interest rate at which international banks lend to or borrow funds in the London interbank market."[7] Note that an ARM is a mortgage for which the lender may adjust the interest rate charged based on specific indices of economic activity. "OIS" stands for Overnight Indexed Swap rate. OIS rate is the "rate on the derivative contract on the overnight rate. In such a contract two parties agree that one will pay the other a rate of interest that is the difference between the term OIS rate and the geometric average of the overnight federal funds rate over the term of the contract," notes Daniel L. Thornton.[8] In the United States, the overnight rate is the effective federal funds rate. Recall that this is the interest rate that banks charge each other for overnight loans. The Libor-OIS spread is a measure of the financial health of banking industry. A higher spread indicates financially unhealthy banking industry.

[6] Source of Table 6.2. Federal Reserve Banks of St. Louis. https://www.stlouisfed.org/annual-report/2017/crisis-to-recovery-timeline (Accessed: August 28, 2019).

[7] Libor. https://www.stlouisfed.org/financial-crisis/glossary (Accessed: August 28, 2019).

[8] Libor-OIS spread. "What the Libor-OIS Spread Say." https://files.stlouisfed.org/files/htdocs/publications/es/09/ES0924.pdf (Accessed: August 28, 2019).

Table 6.2 The 2007–2009 financial crisis, and the great recession and recovery timeline

[1] *Date*	*[2]* *Event*
August 9, 2007	"The Libor-OIS spread rises, escalating fear of bank insolvency. The spread is interpreted as the market's perception of the risk associated with subprime mortgages spreading to the broader mortgage market and overall economy."
September 18, 2007	"The FOMC reduces the target for the federal funds rate from 5.25 to 4.75 percent."
October 31, 2007	"The FOMC reduces the target for the federal funds rate to 4.50 percent."
December 2007	"The Great Recession begins, per the National Bureau of Economic Research."
December 11, 2007	"The FOMC reduces the target for the federal funds rate to 4.25 percent."
December 12, 2007	"To address pressures in short-term funding markets, the Fed establishes a temporary Term Auction Facility—whereby term funds are auctioned to depository institutions against a variety of collateral—and also establishes swap lines with the European and Swiss central banks."
March 18, 2008	"The FOMC reduces the target for the federal funds rate to 2.25 percent."
March 24, 2008	"The New York Fed announces it would provide term financing to facilitate JPMorgan Chase's acquisition of Bear Stearns. This action prevents Bear Stearns from filing for bankruptcy and represents one of the first bank bailouts of the financial crisis."
April 30, 2008	"The FOMC reduces the target for the federal funds rate to 2.00 percent."
September 6, 2008	"Fannie Mae and Freddie Mac—the nation's two largest mortgage finance companies—are placed into conservatorship to prevent further disruption in financial markets.
September 15, 2008	"Lehman Brothers files for Chapter 11 bankruptcy. This announcement spurs concern in financial markets around the world."
September 16, 2008	"The Fed authorizes the New York Fed to lend up to $85 billion to the American International Group (AIG). The deal implies that AIG was 'too big to fail.'"
December 16, 2008	"The FOMC reduces the target range for the federal funds rate to zero to 0.25 percent (the zero lower bound)."

(continued)

Table 6.2 (continued)

[1] *Date*	*[2]* *Event*
March 18, 2009	"The FOMC expands its large-scale asset purchase program under QE1. In total, the FOMC says it will purchase up to $1.25 trillion of mortgage-backed securities, up to $200 billion of agency debt and up to $300 billion of longer-term Treasury securities."
September 21, 2011	"The FOMC votes to extend the average maturity of its Treasury securities ('Operation Twist'). To put downward pressure on longer-term interest rates, the Fed will purchase longer-term Treasuries using proceeds from selling or redeeming shorter-term Treasuries."
June 24, 2013	"Financial markets experience significant turmoil due to uncertainty about the Fed's timing of scaling back bond purchases, a reaction known as the 'taper tantrum.'"
December 18, 2013	"The FOMC announces that it will begin 'tapering,' or reducing the pace of asset purchases, in further measured steps at future meetings, depending on underlying economic data."
October 29, 2014	"The FOMC announces that it will conclude QE3."
December 16, 2015	"The FOMC raises the target range for the federal funds rate to 0.25 to 0.50 percent—the so-called "liftoff." This is the first step in the FOMC's process of normalizing monetary policy."
June 14, 2017	"The FOMC raises the target range for the federal funds rate to 1.00 to 1.25 percent and announces plans to gradually reduce the Fed's balance sheet. This reduction would occur once normalization of the level of the federal funds rate is well underway. The announcement is interpreted as a move by the Fed to increase transparency around a future policy action in an effort to avoid another taper tantrum."
December 13, 2017	"The FOMC raises the target range for the federal funds rate to 1.25 to 1.50 percent, representing the third rate hike in 2017."

Table prepared by the author. *Data Source* Federal Reserve Banks of St. Louis. https://www.stlouisfed.org/annual-report/2017/crisis-to-recovery-timeline (Accessed: August 28, 2019). Libor: London interbank offer rate. OIS: Overnight Indexed Swap. FOMC: Federal Open Market Committee. QE: Quantitative Easing

"FOMC" is the Federal Open Market Committee of the Federal Reserve System. As we saw in Chapter 5, this is the entity that sets the federal funds rate target. "QE" stands for Quantitative Easing. It is essentially an increase in the money supply.

Back to the financial crisis of 2007–2009. What started this financial crisis? Economists agree that subprime lending was a major culprit. What is subprime lending?

6.2.2 *Subprime Lending*

Homeownership has a special appeal for many. Indeed, homeownership is the only form of wealth for many. As Souphala Chomsisengphet and Anthony Pennington-Cross (2006) note, in 1995, "a typical household held no corporate equity" (p. 31).[9] Often households that either do not have a credit history or have a poor credit history—defaulted loans, bounced checks, late payments, etc.—are more likely to get subprime loans. These loans tend to have higher interest rates as compared with loans that are offered to borrowers with good credit history, i.e., prime loans. Some of the features of subprime loans are "limited or no documentation about income or assets, high loan-to-value ratios or high payment-to-income ratios."[10] The lenders want to be compensated for taking on the extra risk. This compensation comes in the form of a higher interest rate.

It is instructive to recall that interest rate is what pops out of when we compare the difference between the price of a bond and its face value with the price of a bond. A higher interest rate implies lower price of a bond and vice versa. And the price of a bond is the amount of funds that the lender is willing to lend (see Chapter 5).

While the term "subprime loan" gained widespread popularity in the aftermath of the 2007–2009 financial crisis, subprime loans are nothing new. As early as the early 1980s lenders like Household Finance Corp. and Long Beach Savings and Loan made loans to households with less than sterling credit history. These loans were often in the form of second mortgages.[11] The borrowers benefited from such loans because the interest payment on mortgage was tax deductible. Borrowers who had been

[9] Homeownership as the main form of wealth. Souphala Chomsisengphet and Anthony Pennington-Cross. "The Evolution of the Subprime Mortgage Market." *Review* 88.1 (2006): 31–56. Print.

[10] Characteristics of sub-prime loans. https://www.stlouisfed.org/financial-crisis/glossary (Accessed: August 26, 2019).

[11] Subprime loans in the early 1980s. https://fraser.stlouisfed.org/files/docs/historical/fct/fcic_report_final_20110127.pdf (Accessed: August 26, 2019).

subjected to discrimination due to ethnicity or economic conditions also benefitted. Chomsisengphet and Pennington-Cross (2006) note, citing a 1999 study by Daniel Immergluck and Marti Wiles, that "more than half of subprime refinances originated in predominately African-American census tracts, whereas only one tenth of prime refinances originated in predominately African-American census tracts" (pp. 36–37). Numerous other studies have found similar evidence.[12]

There were perils of subprime loans as well. Chomsisengphet and Pennington-Cross (2006) note that subprime borrowers are six times more likely to default than prime borrowers, they are less sensitive to interest rate changes because they are less likely to get loans than the prime borrowers, and the initiation of the foreclosure process is 10 times as high as those with prime loans.

6.2.3 Housing Boom and Bust

Increased access to loans allowed many borrowers to get loans. This led to an increased demand for houses. While the quantity supplied of houses increased, the quantity demanded of houses increased even more. As the textbook model would predict, this led to an increase in housing prices. Figure 6.4 plots housing index.

Figure 6.4 plots annual data for three indices—US level (CSUSH-PINSA) represented by a solid line, 10-city composite (SPCS10RNSA) represented by a dashed line, and for the city of San Francisco (SFXRNSA) represented by a dotted line. The value of all three indices is set to 100 for the year 2000.

Note the increase in the values of the indices. The indices peaked in 2006 before declining. These index values reached 183 for the overall US, 225 for the 10-citiy composite, and 216 for San Francisco. The overall US index and the 10-city composite index reached their lows in 2011, 139 and 153, respectively. For San Francisco, the decline was even faster and bumpier; the index value declined to 128 in 2009, increased in 2010 to 139, and declined again to 132 in 2011.

[12] Subprime lending to minorities. Daniel Immergluck and Marti Wiles. *Two Steps Back: The Dual Mortgage Market, Predatory Lending, and the Undoing of Community Development*. Chicago: The Woodstock Institute, 1999. Print, Marvin M. Smith and Christy Chung Hevener. "Subprime Lending Over Time: The Role of Race." *Journal of Economics and Finance* 38.2 (2014): 321–44. Web.

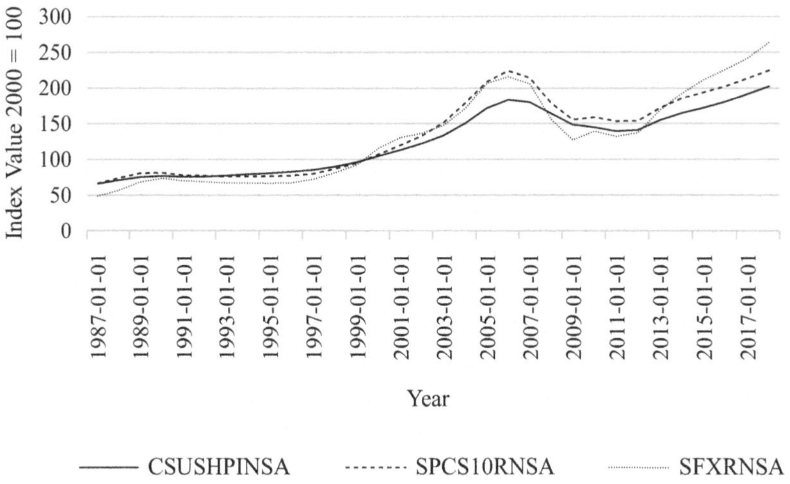

Fig. 6.4 Case-Shiller house price indices (1987–2018) (Figure prepared by the author. *Data Source* S&P Dow Jones Indices LLC, S&P/Case-Shiller US National Home Price Index [CSUSHPINSA]; S&P Dow Jones Indices LLC, S&P/Case-Shiller 10-City Composite Home Price Index [SPCS10RNSA]; S&P Dow Jones Indices LLC, S&P/Case-Shiller CA-San Francisco Home Price Index [SFXRNSA], retrieved from FRED, Federal Reserve Bank of St. Louis. https://fred.stlouisfed.org/series/SFXRNSA [Accessed: August 29, 2019])

Due to easy access to credit, homeownership increased, and so did the household debt. Figure 6.5 plots three data series from 1987 to 2018. These are total household debt as a percentage of disposable income, household mortgage debt as a percentage of disposable income, and homeownership rate.

In Fig. 6.5, total household debt as a percentage of disposable income (TDSP) is represented by a solid line, mortgage debt as a percent of disposable income (MDSP) is represented by a dashed line, and homeownership rates (RHORUSQ156N) are presented by a dotted line. Both TDSP and MDSP figures are plotted on the left-hand-side vertical axis, while RHORUSQ156N figures are plotted on the right-hand-side vertical axis. The horizontal axis plots the year. All three series are annual data. A few points are worth noting in Fig. 6.5.

One, homeownership rate peaked at 69 percent during 2004, and stayed high during 2005 (68.9 percent) and 2006 (68.8 percent). The

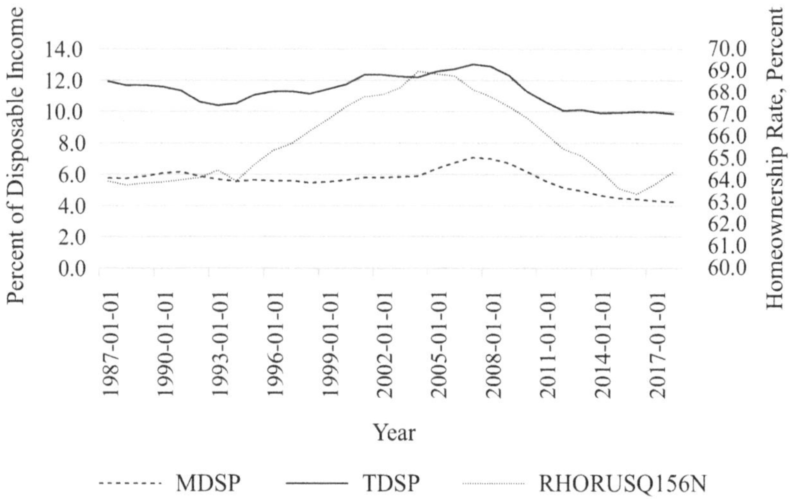

Fig. 6.5 Household debt as a percent of disposable income and homeownership rate (1987–2018) (Figure prepared by the author. *Data Source* Board of Governors of the Federal Reserve System [US], Mortgage Debt Service Payments as a Percent of Disposable Personal Income [MDSP]; Board of Governors of the Federal Reserve System [US], Household Debt Service Payments as a Percent of Disposable Personal Income [TDSP]; US Census Bureau, Homeownership Rate for the United States [RHORUSQ156N], retrieved from FRED, Federal Reserve Bank of St. Louis. https://fred.stlouisfed.org/series/RHORUSQ156N [Accessed: August 29, 2019])

average homeownership rate from 1987 to 2018 was about 65.81 percent. The homeownership rates during 2004–2006 were statistically significantly different from the series mean. (The 95 percent confidence interval around the mean is [65.146—66.474].) Indeed, the homeownership rates started increasing around 1999 and stayed high until 2010; the homeownership rates stayed outside the 95 percent confidence interval band. They hit their lowest levels during 2016 at 63.4 percent before increasing again.

Mortgage debt as well as total debt as a percentage of disposable income hit their highs during 2007 (7.1 percent and 13.0 percent, respectively). By 2007, the housing bubble had already burst and home prices had started declining (Fig. 6.4). There are a couple of reasons for the debt to remain high. Remember that usually subprime mortgages are offered to individuals with "limited or no documentation about income or assets, high loan-to-value ratios or high payment-to-income ratios."[13] Other features, as noted by Ben Bernanke who was the Fed Chair from February 1, 2006 to January 31, 2014, of subprime loans include[14]:

- Interest-only (IO) adjustable-rate mortgages (ARMs);
- Option ARMs (which permit borrowers to vary the size of monthly payments);
- Long amortizations (payment periods greater than thirty years);
- Negative amortization ARMs (initial payments do not even cover interest costs); and
- No-documentation loans.

A common feature of these mortgage loans was that "they reduced monthly payments early in the mortgage but allowed mortgage payments to rise over time."[15] This is why the mortgage debt as a percentage of disposable income kept on increasing even after homeownership rate started to decrease. It may also be the case that some homeowners' disposable income started declining as well with the onset of the ensuing Great Recession; some homeowners might have lost jobs.

As it turned out subprime lending was just the beginning. In fact, subprime lending, in and of itself, was not a big problem. As Bernanke points out:

> If you put together all the subprime mortgages in the United States and assumed they were all worthless, the total losses to the financial system would be about equivalent to one bad day in the stock market: they were not very big. The problem was that they were distributed throughout different securities and different places and nobody know where they were and who was going to bear the losses.[16] (pp. 71–72)

[13] Characteristics of subprime loans. https://www.stlouisfed.org/financial-crisis/glossary (Accessed: August 26, 2019).

[14] Other characteristics of subprime loans. Ben S. Bernanke. *The Federal Reserve and the Financial Crisis*. Princeton: Princeton University Press, 2013. Web.

[15] Shared features of subprime loans. Ben S. Bernanke. *The Federal Reserve and the Financial Crisis*. Princeton: Princeton University Press, 2013. Web.

[16] The size of subprime loans. Ben S. Bernanke. *The Federal Reserve and the Financial Crisis*. Princeton: Princeton University Press, 2013. Web.

Ordinarily financial innovations that allow savers and borrowers to hedge their bets are desirable and, indeed, needed. They allow for a stronger and much broader financial foundation. Money is a prime example of one such financial innovation. The problem arises when the underlying structure of these financial innovations is not transparent. What started as quite a manageable problem of subprime lending led to a full-blown worldwide crisis was securitization. Securitization is the process of combining various loans and reselling, either in parts or as a whole, to other savers. Here is how this works.

First, the term "security" in financial parlance refers to a financial asset—a bond, for instance—that the original lender can resell it to other lenders. We used the term "government securities" to refer to the bonds issued by the US Treasury in Chapter 5. As another example, suppose I lend to the US Treasury $100 on, say, January 1, 2019. It is maturing in 20 years. That is, I buy a $100 bond with a maturity date of January 1, 2039. Suppose that I need the money before the bond matures. I can resell it to someone else who is willing to buy it. Put another way, I can resell the bond to someone who is willing to lend to the US Treasury. For how much will the bond resell? That depends upon the price of the bond at the time of the resale. The price of a bond will depend upon the supply and demand of the bond. Recall again, that the price of a bond is the amount of funds that one is willing to lend.

Back to securitization. Imagine that a bank has issued loans to various borrowers. These loans may be mortgages, car loans, credit card loans, home-equity loans, business loans, or whatever. Each loan carries a certain degree of risk. Spreading the risk is, indeed, a good practice. Financial experts stress upon the value of diversification. As a lender, i.e., a buyer of bonds, I would like to know the risk associated with the loan. For this, I would rely on bond rating agencies. The three most popular rating agencies are Moody's, Standard & Poor's, and Fitch. These rating agencies rate the creditworthiness of borrowers. For instance, Moody's[17] rating agency rates bonds as Aaa, Aa, A, Baa, Ba, B, Caa, Ca, and C, from

[17] Moody's credit ratings. https://www.moodys.com/Pages/amr002002.aspx (Accessed: September 4, 2019).

the most creditworthy to the least. Standard & Poor's[18] and Fitch[19] rate bonds as AAA, AA, A, BBB, BB, B, CCC, CC, C, and D, from the most creditworthy to the least. These rating agencies are paid by the bond issuers—the borrowers.

There is a problem in this model, however. Since the bond-issuing firms are the ones who pay these rating agencies to rate their bonds, it is not hard to imagine then that bargaining takes place. Suppose I am issuing a bond. It is in my interest to have the highest rating, say, AAA or Aaa. Suppose Moody's evaluates my financial health and gives me a Baa rating. This means that I will not be able to borrow at the lowest interest rate possible. Since I am the one paying Moody's to evaluate my financial health, I can always tell it that my bond better be rated the highest. Otherwise, I will take my business to, say, Standard & Poor's rating agency. This raises a conflict of interest for the rating agencies.

Ideally the lenders—the bond buyers—will pay to evaluate the financial health of bond issuers—the borrowers. This, however, raises another issue: free rider problem. Suppose you paid a rating agency to evaluate the creditworthiness of a borrower. Unless you are able to keep the information secret, I can keep an eye on which bonds you buy and buy the same ones. This way, I do not have to pay for the rating agency's fees. I get the information without having to pay for it. That is, I can free ride. Since you are the one who is incurring the cost of information gathering, your net return is definitely lower than mine. This creates a disincentive for you to hire a rating agency and incur the costs. As of now, there really is not any way out of these dilemmas in the bond market, except that various government regulations require disclosure and transparency.[20]

The government regulations work well, except when they do not. Indeed, the events that led to the financial crisis of 2007–2009 are one such example. These regulations and the agencies that implement these regulations were not able to keep up with the changes that were taking place in the financial industry.

[18] Standard & Poor's credit ratings. https://www.standardandpoors.com/en_US/web/guest/article/-/view/sourceId/504352 (Accessed: September 4, 2019).

[19] Fitch credit ratings. https://www.fitchratings.com/site/home (Accessed: September 4, 2019).

[20] House Committee on Financial Services. https://financialservices.house.gov/ (Accessed: September 4, 2019).

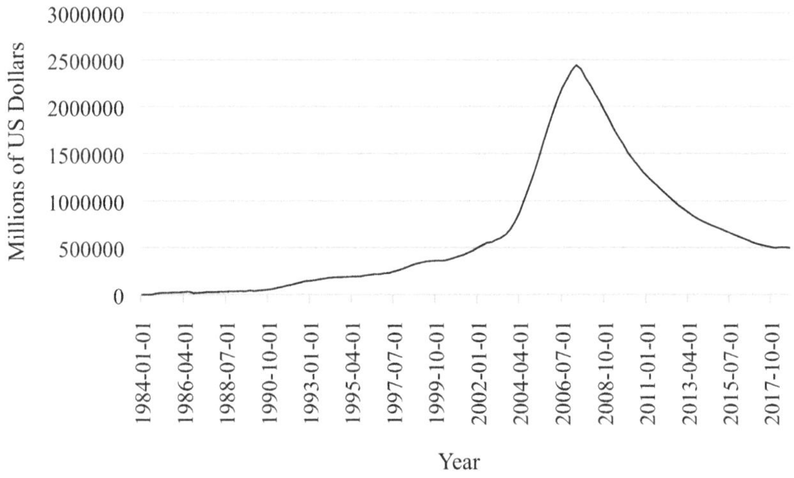

Fig. 6.6 Mortgage-backed securities (1984–2018) (Figure prepared by the author. *Data Source* Board of Governors of the Federal Reserve System [US], Issuers of asset-backed securities; home mortgages, including REIT securitized home mortgages; asset, Level [BOGZ1FL673065103Q]. https://fred.stlouisfed.org [Accessed: September 4, 2019]. *Note* REIT stands for Real Estate Investment Trust [REIT and its history (Steinhauser and Koch 1981)])

The financial industry was creating securities that lacked transparency and the rating agencies were providing credit ratings that did not reflect the underlying risks associated with these securities. The savers, basing their trust in the ratings provided by the rating agencies, were buying these securities. However, once they became aware of the opacity of the securities, they tried to withdraw their funds. It was a classic example of a bank run.

In Fig. 6.6, I plot data on mortgage-backed securities.[21] Note the rise and fall of the amount of funds that poured in. At its peak, during the

[21] Asset-backed securities. Board of Governors of the Federal Reserve System [US], Issuers of asset-backed securities; home mortgages, including REIT securitized home mortgages; asset, Level [BOGZ1FL673065103Q], retrieved from FRED, Federal Reserve Bank of St. Louis; https://fred.stlouisfed.org/series/BOGZ1FL673065103Q (Accessed: September 4, 2019).

fourth quarter of 2007, these securities were worth 2,445,705 million US dollars. Then the funds started to dry up.

Firms, both industrial and commercial, borrow for short-term needs. These may include payroll and purchases of other assets. These short-term promissory notes are called commercial paper. Foreign governments also issue commercial paper to meet their short-term obligations. There are two types of commercial papers—unsecured and asset backed. As the terms imply, unsecured commercial paper is not backed by any assets, whereas asset-backed commercial paper is backed by some asset. Another difference is the maturity dates. Typically an unsecured commercial paper has maturity date between 90 and 180 days, whereas and asset-backed commercial paper is issued from one day to 170 days.[22] These loans are crucial for borrowers.

Take the example of industrial firms. When the financial system is functioning smoothly, the borrowing and lending in the commercial paper market goes on without a hitch. Workers and suppliers of raw materials are paid on time, firms meet their production schedules, and the economy is humming along. When funding stops, firms cannot make the payrolls and pay the raw material suppliers. Workers and raw material suppliers rely on their paychecks and receivables. They cannot pay their bills in turn. So on and so forth. The output declines and unemployment rises.

In Fig. 6.7, I plot commercial paper outstanding, asset-backed commercial paper outstanding (left-hand side vertical axis), and commercial paper interest rate (right-hand-side vertical axis).

Note the increase and then decrease in the amount lent and borrowed via commercial paper, both unsecured and asset-backed. The rise, fall, and then again rise of the financial commercial paper interest rate are also noticeable.

A rule worth remembering is that whenever someone is hiding something, the one doing the hiding is getting some benefit, either actual or perceived. Here is the reason why: There is marginal cost to every act of hiding. The marginal benefit, actual or perceived, of hiding has to be at least as high as the marginal cost for the act of hiding to be worth it.

[22] Commercial paper and asset-backed commercial paper. https://www.stlouisfed.org/financial-crisis/glossary (Accessed: September 4, 2019).

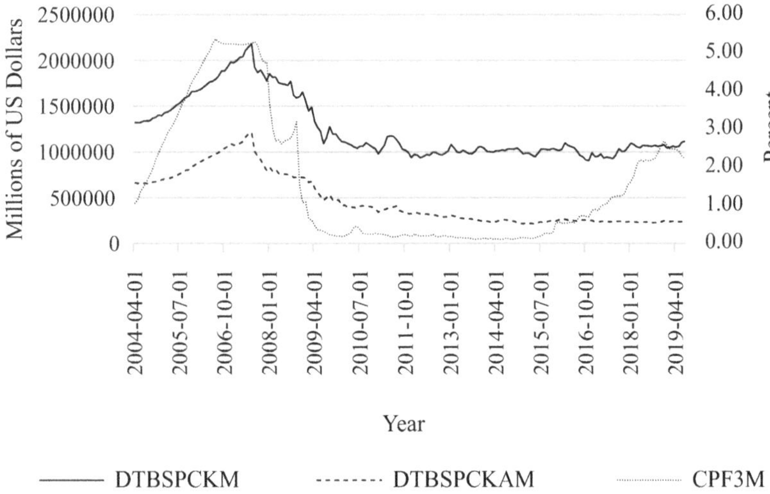

Fig. 6.7 Commercial paper, asset-backed commercial paper, and 3-month financial commercial paper rate (Figure prepared by the author. *Data Source* Board of Governors of the Federal Reserve System [US], Commercial Paper Outstanding [DTBSPCKM]; Board of Governors of the Federal Reserve System [US], Asset-backed Commercial Paper Outstanding [DTBSPCKAM]; Board of Governors of the Federal Reserve System [US], 3-Month AA Financial Commercial Paper Rate [CPF3M], retrieved from FRED, Federal Reserve Bank of St. Louis. https://fred.stlouisfed.org [Accessed: September 4, 2019])

6.2.4 *Findings of the Studies by the Congress and the Senate*

To understand the causes of the 2007–2009 financial crisis in depth, the US Congress created the National Commission on the Causes of the Financial and Economic Crisis in the United States. It was part of the Fraud Enforcement and Recovery Act (Public Law 111–21). This independent Commission had 10 members, composed of "private citizens with experience in areas such as housing, economics, finance, market regulation, banking, and consumer protection. Six members of the Commission were appointed by the Democratic leadership of Congress and four members by the Republican leadership" (p. xi).[23] They were Phil

[23] Membership of the National Commission on the Causes of the Financial and Economic Crisis in the United States. *The Financial Crisis Inquiry Report: Final Report of*

Angelides, Brooksley Born, Byron Georgiou, Keith Hennessey, Douglas Holtz-Eakin, Bob Graham, Heather H. Murren, Bill Thomas, John W. Thompson, Peter J. Wallison. After eighteen months of in-depth research that included a review of "millions of pages of documents" and interviews of "more than 700 witnesses," the Commission released its final 662-page report on January 27, 2011.

In summarizing the report, the Commission concluded as follows: (pp. xvii–xxv)[24]

1. We conclude this financial crisis was avoidable.
2. We conclude widespread failures in financial regulation and supervision proved devastating to the stability of the nation's financial markets.
3. We conclude dramatic failures of corporate governance and risk management at many systemically important financial institutions were a key cause of this crisis.
4. We conclude a combination of excessive borrowing, risky investments, and lack of transparency put the financial system on a collision course with crisis.
5. We conclude the government was ill prepared for the crisis, and its inconsistent response added to the uncertainty and panic in the financial markets.
6. We conclude there was a systemic breakdown in accountability and ethics.
7. We conclude collapsing mortgage-lending standards and the mortgage securitization pipeline lit and spread the flame of contagion and crisis.
8. We conclude over-the-counter derivatives contributed significantly to this crisis.
9. We conclude the failures of credit rating agencies were essential cogs in the wheel of financial destruction.

the National Commission on the Causes of the Financial and Economic Crisis in the United States. Washington: Financial Crisis Inquiry Commission, January 27, 2011. https://fraser.stlouisfed.org/title/5034 (Accessed: August 27, 2019).

[24] Main conclusions of the National Commission on the Causes of the Financial and Economic Crisis in the United States. *The Financial Crisis Inquiry Report: Final Report of the National Commission on the Causes of the Financial and Economic Crisis in the United States*. Washington: Financial Crisis Inquiry Commission, January 27, 2011. https://fraser.stlouisfed.org/title/5034 (Accessed: August 27, 2019).

The Commissioners Phil Angelides, Brooksley Born, Byron Georgiou, Bob Graham, Heather H. Murren, John W. Thompson voted to adopt the report, while the Commissioners Keith Hennessey, Douglas Holtz-Eakin, Bill Thomas, Peter J. Wallison voted against the adoption.

The United State Senate also investigated the matter. The US Senate Permanent Subcommittee on Investigations released its 646-page report on April 13, 2011. It was titled *Wall Street and the Financial Crisis: Anatomy of a Financial Collapse.*[25] The Senate report reached similar conclusions to those of the National Commission. The Subcommittee identified four main areas of concern. These were, "High Risk Lending, Regulatory Failure, Inflated Credit Ratings, and Investment Bank Abuses" (pp. 2–8). The Subcommittee made the following recommendations in each are of concern: (pp. 12–14).

<u>Recommendations on High Risk Lending</u>

1. Ensure "Qualified Mortgages" Are Low Risk.
2. Require Meaningful Risk Retention.
3. Safeguard Against High Risk Products.
4. Require Greater Reserves for Negative Amortization Loans. [In negative amortization loans the mortgage balance keeps on increasing. This happens because, "initial payments do not even cover interest costs"(p. 67).[26]]
5. Safeguard Bank Investment Portfolios.

<u>Recommendations on Regulatory Failures</u>

1. Complete OTS [Office of Thrift Supervision] Dismantling.
2. Strengthen Enforcement. Federal banking regulators should conduct a review of their major financial institutions to identify those with ongoing, serious deficiencies, and review their enforcement approach to those institutions to eliminate any policy of deference to bank management, inflated CAMELS ratings, or use of short-term profits to excuse high risk activities.
3. Strengthen CAMELS Ratings. [CAMELS, an acronym, stands for Capital adequacy, Asset quality, Management, Earnings, Liquidity, Sensitivity to market. It is a measure of a bank's financial health. Banks are

[25] The U.S. Senate report on the 2007–2009 financial crisis. *Wall Street and the Financial Crisis: Anatomy of a Financial Collapse: Majority and Minority Staff Report, Permanent Subcommittee on Investigations, Committee on Homeland Security and Governmental Affairs, United States Senate, April 13, 2011* (Accessed: August 27, 2019).

[26] Negative amortization loans. Ben S. Bernanke. *The Federal Reserve and the Financial Crisis.* Princeton: Princeton University Press, 2013. Web.

rated from 1 through 5, where 1 is "strong," 2 is "satisfactory," 3 is "less than satisfactory," 4 is "deficient," and 5 is "critically deficient."][27]

4. Evaluate Impacts of High Risk Lending.

Recommendations on Inflated Credit Ratings

1. Rank Credit Rating Agencies by Accuracy.
2. Help Investors Hold CRAs [Credit Rating Agencies] Accountable.
3. Strengthen CRA [Credit Rating Agency] Operations.
4. Ensure CRAs Recognize Risk.
5. Strengthen Disclosure.
6. Reduce Ratings Reliance [by the federal regulators].

Recommendations on Investment Bank Abuses

1. Review Structured Finance Transactions.
2. Narrow Proprietary Trading Exceptions.
3. Design Strong Conflict of Interest Prohibitions.
4. Study Bank Use of Structured Finance.

The findings of the Financial Crisis Inquiry Commission and the findings of the US Senate Permanent Subcommittee on Investigations have been supported by the subsequent research conducted by various academic researchers.[28]

As we saw, the housing bubble had burst and housing pricing had started to decline (Fig. 6.4). As is usually the case with bubbles, the decline in housing prices was steeper than the incline. Housing market has an especially large impact on the economy. It is not only the construction industry that is affected with the boom and bust, but also related industries—the furniture industry, the appliance industry, the trucking industry, and of course the banking industry.[29] Just as an example, Fig. 6.8 plots the unemployment rate at the US level along with the unemployment rates of the financial, construction, and transportation industries.

The thick solid line plots the unemployment rate at the US level (UNRATENSA), thin solid line plots the unemployment rate for the

[27] CAMELS rating system. https://www.stlouisfed.org/on-the-economy/2018/july/abcs-camels (Accessed: August 28, 2019).

[28] Research on the 2007–2009 financial crisis. See for instance, Atif Mian, Amir Sufi, and Francesco Trebbi. "The Political Economy of the US Mortgage Default Crisis." *The American Economic Review* 100.5 (2010): 1967–98. Web, Mian and Sufi: 31–58, Atif R. Mian and Amir Sufi. "The Consequences of Mortgage Credit Expansion: Evidence from the 2007 Mortgage Default Crisis." *NBER Working Paper No. w13936* April (2008). Print, Bernanke, Bernanke.

[29] The impact of the housing market on the economy. Bernanke.

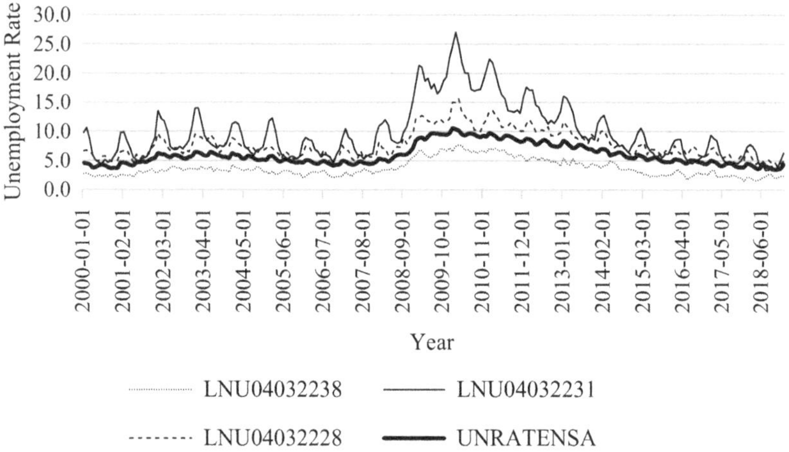

Fig. 6.8 Unemployment rates: US, financial services, construction, and transportation (Figure prepared by the author. *Data Source* US Bureau of Labor Statistics, Unemployment Rate: [LNU04032238]) Financial Activities Industry, Private Wage and Salary Workers; [LNU04032231] Construction Industry, Private Wage and Salary Workers; [LNU04032228] Transportation and Material Moving Occupations; [UNRATENSA] Civilian Unemployment Rate. Retrieved from FRED, Federal Reserve Bank of St. Louis. https://fred.stlouisfed.org [Accessed: September 6, 2019])

construction industry (LNU04032231), the dotted line plots the unemployment rate for the transportation industry (LNU04032228), and the dashed line plots the unemployment rate for the financial services industry (LNU04032238). Note that while there are differences between the unemployment rates—the unemployment rate for the construction industry peaked at 27.1 percent (February 2010), and the unemployment rate for the financial industry it peaked at 7.7 percent (March 2010)—the unemployment rates of these industries did move in the same direction.

What accounts for the differences in unemployment rates? Education seems to be the main culprit. On average, the higher the level of education, the more likely is the individual to be employed. For instance, according to the Bureau of Labor Statistics, a typical worker in "business and financial occupations" is at least a college graduate. Whereas a typical worker in "construction and extraction occupations" has earned only a high school diploma (or no formal education),[30] Wages also differ according to education significantly. A typical worker in "business and financial occupations" had a median wage of $68,350 during May 2018.[31] The unemployment rate of workers with a college degree (a bachelor's degree or higher) during May 2018 was 1.8 percent. On the other hand, the median wage of a typical worker in "construction and extraction occupations" was $46,010 during May 2018, and the unemployment rate of workers in construction and extraction occupations during May 2018 was 3.6 percent (Fig. 6.8).

Curious readers may be wondering about the lag in the peak of unemployment rate and the end of recession. As it turns out, unemployment rate almost always starts to rise after the recession has hit, and peaks sometime after the end of the recession. The reason is that firms want to hold on to workers as long as they can. Firing workers creates morale issues among the remaining workers. Not only that, hiring suitable workers is an expensive proposition, and smart firm managers try to avoid unnecessary expenses. Figure 6.9 plots US unemployment rate along with recessions from January 1948 to August 2019.

Shaded areas in Fig. 6.9 represent recessions. The width of the vertical shaded bars represents the length of a given recession—the wider the bar the longer the recession lasted. Note that unemployment rate tends to peak after the recession has ended. Note that between 1948 and 2019 the United States has had ten recessions. In each case the unemployment rate peaked after the recession had ended.

6.3 The Response of the Federal Reserve System

Ben Bernanke, a well-known scholar of the Great Depression of the 1920s and 1930s, was the Fed chair when the financial crisis hit in 2007.[32] Before becoming the Fed Chair, Dr. Bernanke had taught economics and conducted research in economics for over 27 years. He had held academic positions at Stanford (Assistant Professor: 1979–1983; Associate

[30] Median wage of workers in construction and extraction occupations. https://www.bls.gov/ooh/construction-and-extraction/home.htm (Accessed: September 6, 2019).

[31] Median wage of workers in business and financial occupations. https://www.bls.gov/ooh/business-and-financial/home.htm (Accessed: September 6, 2019).

[32] The Fed Chair during the financial crisis. https://www.federalreservehistory.org/people/ben_s_bernanke (Accessed: September 6, 2019).

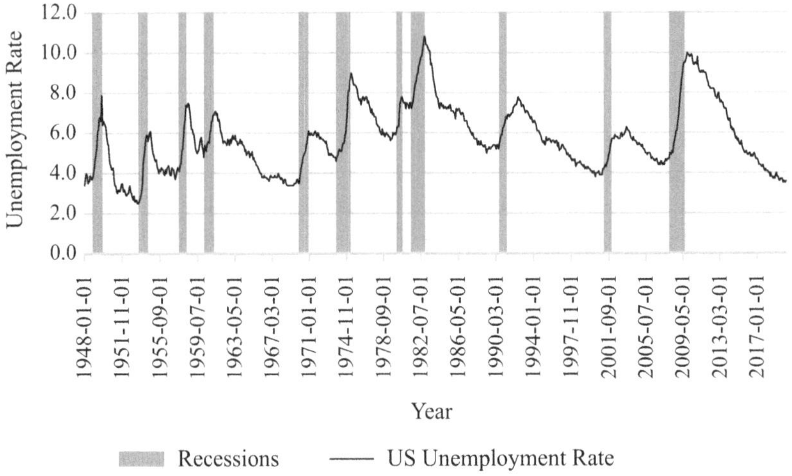

Fig. 6.9 US civilian unemployment rate and recessions (Figure prepared by the author. Shaded areas represent recessions. Recession dates. *Data Source* National Bureau of Economic Research. www.nber.org [Accessed: August 19, 2019]. Unemployment Rate *Data Source* US Bureau of Labor Statistics, Unemployment Rate [UNRATE], retrieved from FRED, Federal Reserve Bank of St. Louis. https://fred.stlouisfed.org/series/UNRATE [Accessed: May 13, 2020])

Professor: 1983–1985), and Princeton (Professor 1985–2002). He had also taught at New York University (1993) and at Massachusetts Institute of Technology (1989–1990) as a visiting professor of economics. Bernanke had also served at the Fed in various capacities over the years. He served as a member of the Board of Governors from 2002 to 2005. He was a visiting scholar at the Federal Reserve Bank of Philadelphia from 1987 to 1989, at the Federal Reserve Bank of Boston from 1989 to 1990, and at the Federal Reserve Bank of New York from 1990 to 1991 and from 1994 to 1996. He also served as a member of the Academic Advisory Panel at the Federal Reserve Bank of New York from 1990 to 2002.[33] Given his extensive experience, he knew well how to tackle the problems arising from the housing bust and the ensuing financial crisis.

[33] Bernanke's career. https://www.federalreservehistory.org/people/ben_s_bernanke (Accessed: September 6, 2019).

We learned in Chapter 5 that the Fed has two mandates—high employment and a stable price level. At the risk of repeating, let me mention that costs of borrowing decrease when interest rates decrease, and vice versa. As costs of borrowing decrease, more and more projects become profitable and firms are more likely to invest—build new buildings, plants and equipment—and households are more likely to buy new houses, new furniture, appliances, and other big-ticket items like cars, all else constant. These acts on the parts of firms and households increase the aggregate demand for various goods and services. In turn, increased demand leads firms to increase output and hire more workers. The Fed increases money supply in order to lower interest rates. It decreases money supply when it wants to increase interest rates. These changes in money supply are called monetary policy.

The Fed applied the tools at its disposal once the house prices plummeted, leading to a widespread financial panic, and the signs of economic slowdown appeared. On September 18, 2007, the Fed reduced the federal funds rate target from 5.25 percent to 4.75 percent, and then again on October 31, 2007 to 4.50 percent. As it turned out, this was just the beginning of a number of federal funds rate target reductions. Over the next year, the Fed reduced the target federal funds rate to between zero percent and 0.25 percent. We had hit the, so-called, zero-lower-bound—the nominal interest rates could not be lowered any further. The federal funds rate target would remain between zero percent and 0.25 percent until December 12, 2015. On December 16, 2015, the Fed raised its target federal funds rate to between 0.25 percent and 0.5 percent. The Fed also took several steps to make sure that the financial system and the economy were on secure footings (see Table 6.2).

6.3.1 The Zero-Lower-Bound

What does a zero-lower-bound (ZLB) mean and how does it affect the economy? Let us revisit Fig. 5.6—the money demand and money supply diagram—and modify to reflect ZLB. In Chapter 5, we saw that the Fed sets a target for the federal funds rate and changes money supply such that the target is met. Figure 5.6 provided a graphical depiction. We noticed in Fig. 5.6 that the money supply curve was a vertical line and the money demand curve had a negative slope. When we have hit the ZLB the money demand curve becomes horizontal when it hits the horizontal axis. That is, when interest rate becomes zero. Figure 6.10 shows this case.

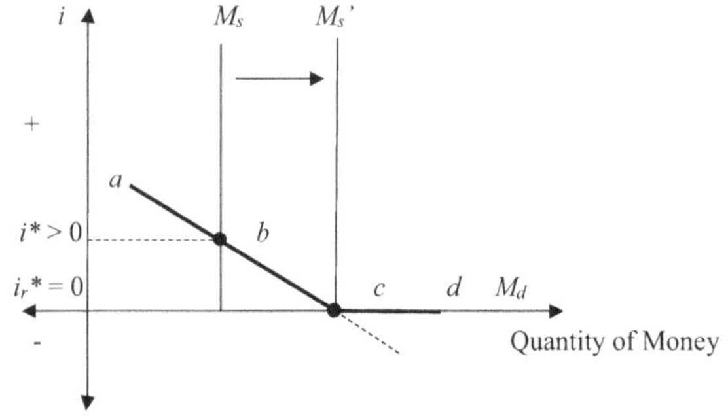

Fig. 6.10 Money demand, money supply, and the zero-lower-bound (Figure drawn by the author)

Notice the differences between Fig. 5.6 and Fig. 6.10. In Fig. 6.10, the vertical axis extends below zero—it goes into the negative territory and a negative sign (−) represents that range. Above zero the range is positive and it is represented by a positive sign (+). The horizontal axis also extends to the left of zero. This figure draws the money demand curve that is kinked. It looks like a "laid-back" L shape. It has two segments—from *a* to *c*, and from *c* to *d*, with a kink at point *c*. The segment *a*–*c* has a negative slope just as we saw in Chapter 5. The segment *c*–*d* has a slope of zero; it is horizontal. For visual ease, I have drawn the money demand curve using a thicker line. At this point, it is useful to recall that money demand is the amount of funds that people want to hold outside interest-bearing accounts. The segment of the money demand curve that is below the horizontal axis is represented by a dashed line. I will come back to this shortly. (It may not be a bad idea to review Sect. 5.3 to further solidify the concept of money demand and why does it have a negative slope?)

Suppose that before the recession hit the money supply curve was represented by M_s. When the quantities of money supplied and money demanded are equal, the equilibrium interest rate is i^*. This is represented by point *b* at the intersection of the money demand curve and money supply curve. Note that it is at some positive level ($i^* > 0$). Once the recession hit and the Fed, following its Constitutional mandate, increased money supply so that it could lower the cost of borrowing which, in turn, would increase investment in machines and building, and households would buy more big-ticket items. (I would suggest reviewing Sect. 5.3

if you are not clear about what is meant by changes in money supply or how the Fed changes money supply.)

Suppose that the Fed increases money supply and the money supply curve shifts to M_s'. Now the money supply and money demand curves intersect at point *b* and the new equilibrium interest rate is $i_r{}^*$. At that point interest rate is equal to zero ($i_r{}^* = 0$). This is the point where the Fed has hit the zero-lower-bound and conventional monetary policy tools are no longer useful. Notice that the money demand curve beyond this point, represented by point *c*, is horizontal. The money demand curve no longer has a negative slope beyond point *c*. To the right of point *c* the slope of the money demand curve is zero. This is why I drew the money demand curve below the horizontal axis with a dashed line. In plain English what this means is that once we hit the zero-lower-bound the quantity demanded of money is not affected by the changes in interest rate. This makes sense. Nominal interest rates (i.e., interest rate unadjusted for inflation rate) cannot be negative. To have a negative nominal interest rate would mean paying the borrowers to borrow. The lenders would rather keep their funds "under the mattress" as opposed to lending.

This, however, does not mean that a central bank cannot set a policy rate below zero.[34] When that happens the lenders are basically paying the banks safe-keeping fees. One example is that of Japan. Figure 6.11 plots annual nominal and real interest rate data for the 10-year Japanese government bond from 1990 to 2018. It also plots the inflation rate data.

To highlight the point about negative policy rate, I provide part of the data (from 1995 to 2018) used in Fig. 6.11, in Table 6.3. Column [1] in Table 6.3 lists the year, Column [2] lists inflation rate calculated from the Japanese Consumer Price Index (CPI), and Columns [3] and [4] provide nominal and real yields for the 10-year government bonds. I follow the methodology of the Bank of Japan (BOJ) in calculating real yield and use CPI to calculate inflation rate.

The real yield in Column [4] is calculated by deducting inflation rate—Column [2]—from the nominal yield—Column [3]. Recall also that yield and interest rate are used interchangeably in economics and finance. Furthermore, since real interest rate is the nominal interest rate minus the inflation rate, whenever inflation rate is negative (i.e., deflation rate) real interest rate is higher than the nominal interest rate. For example,

[34] Negative policy rate. See Marco Bassetto. "Negative Nominal Interest Rates." *American Economic Review* 94.2 (2004): 104–8. Web. for a theoretical exposition.

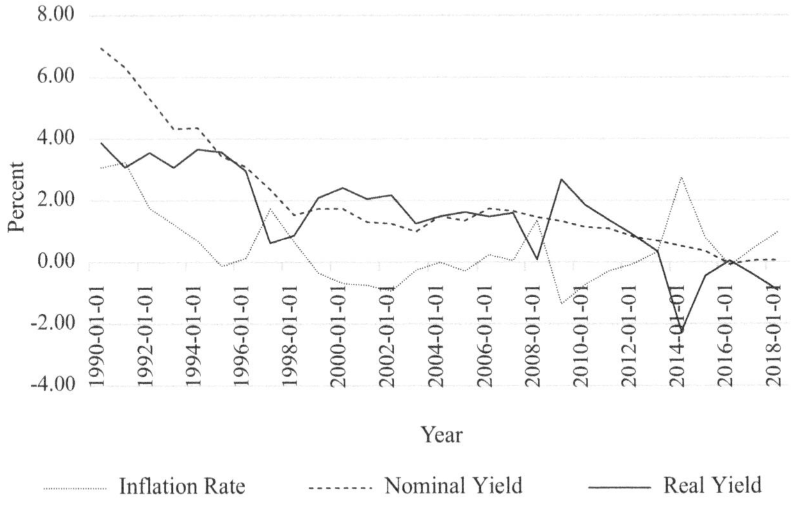

Fig. 6.11 Inflation rate, nominal, and real yields rates on Japanese government 10-year bond (Figure prepared by the author. *Data Source* Organization for Economic Co-operation and Development, Long-Term Government Bond Yields: 10-year: Main [Including Benchmark] for Japan [IRLTLT01JPM156N], retrieved from FRED, Federal Reserve Bank of St. Louis. https://fred.stlouisfed.org/series/IRLTLT01JPM156N. World Bank, Inflation, consumer prices for Japan [FPCPITOTLZGJPN], retrieved from FRED, Federal Reserve Bank of St. Louis. https://fred.stlouisfed.org/series/FPCPITOTLZGJPN [September 10, 2019])

during 2002 the nominal interest rate was 1.26 percent and inflation rate was –0.92, making the real interest rate 2.19 [$\approx 1.26 - (-0.92)$]. (The exact value is 2.19. The difference between what is listed in the table, 2.19, and in the example—$2.18 = 1.26 - [-0.92]$—is due to rounding.)

Note that the nominal policy interest rate was negative during 2016. This was no accident. The BOJ adopted a negative policy rate—Japanese equivalent of the federal funds rate—to meet the inflation rate target of 2 percent. This was not the first time that a central bank had set the policy rate below zero either. As Jens Christensen and Mark Spiegel (2019) note, "Denmark's policy rates fell below zero in July 2012, rapidly followed by

Table 6.3 Inflation rate, nominal and real yields

[1] *Year*	[2] *Inflation rate*	[3] *Nominal yield*	[4] *Real yield*
1995	−0.13	3.44	3.57
1996	0.14	3.10	2.96
1997	1.75	2.37	0.63
1998	0.66	1.54	0.88
1999	−0.34	1.75	2.09
2000	−0.68	1.74	2.42
2001	−0.74	1.32	2.06
2002	−0.92	1.26	2.19
2003	−0.26	1.00	1.26
2004	−0.01	1.49	1.50
2005	−0.28	1.35	1.64
2006	0.25	1.74	1.49
2007	0.06	1.67	1.61
2008	1.38	1.47	0.09
2009	−1.35	1.33	2.69
2010	−0.72	1.15	1.87
2011	−0.27	1.10	1.37
2012	−0.05	0.84	0.89
2013	0.35	0.69	0.34
2014	2.76	0.52	−2.24
2015	0.79	0.35	−0.44
2016	−0.12	−0.07	0.05
2017	0.47	0.05	−0.42
2018	0.98	0.07	−0.91

Table prepared by the author. *Data Source* Organization for Economic Co-operation and Development, Long-Term Government Bond Yields: 10-year: Main (Including Benchmark) for Japan [IRLTLT01JPM156N], retrieved from FRED, Federal Reserve Bank of St. Louis; https://fred.stlouisfed.org/series/IRLTLT01JPM156N. World Bank, Inflation, consumer prices for Japan [FPCPITOTLZGJPN], retrieved from FRED, Federal Reserve Bank of St. Louis; https://fred.stlouisfed.org/series/FPCPITOTLZGJPN (September 10, 2019)

a number of other central banks, including the European Central Bank, the Swedish Riksbank, and the Swiss National Bank."[35]

[35] Negative policy interest rates set by the various central banks. Jens H. E. Christensen and Mark M. Spiegel. "Negative Interest Rates and Inflation Expectations in Japan." *FRBSF Economic Letter*, August 26 (2019). Print.

As we saw in Chapter 4, while a decreasing price level may sound like a good idea, it has negative consequences for the economy. The idea behind having a negative policy rate is to induce banks to lend more. Recall that, all else constant, as banks lend more the money supply increases leading to a lower cost of borrowing. This, in turn, makes more project profitable, investment in machines and buildings increases, as does the demand for big-ticket items like appliances and cars, by households, which leads to an increase in output. When the policy rate is negative the banks are paying the central bank to hold their reserves. Banks are better off lending even if the interest rates they charge are extremely low—a zero percent interest rate is better than a negative interest rate.

Japan has had low inflation and deflation ever since the mid-1990s (Fig. 6.11). When Shinzo Abe became Japan's Prime Minister, he introduced numerous economic reforms, including expansionary monetary policy. Inflation rate is a combination of past inflation and future inflation expectations, which, in turn, are based on the expected future monetary policy and the economy, among other factors. In 2013, the BOJ announced an inflation rate target of 2 percent. The BOJ wanted to increase inflation and inflation expectations. This, however, did not work as intended. People's inflation expectations adjusted to a still lower inflation rate. Results of the Christensen and Spiegel study indicate that, instead of increasing, the expected inflation decreased. The authors suggest caution in interpreting their results. They write that, "the BOJ['s] move toward negative rates may itself have reflected deteriorating economic conditions." Furthermore, "the changes in the market's expectations could have been responses to that deterioration rather than to the policy change." They go on to write that, "it is possible that the decline in medium- and long-term inflation expectations in the data might have been even steeper if the BOJ had not moved into negative policy rates."[36]

Back to zero-lower-bound and continuing the example of the Fed. Once the Fed hit the zero-lower-bound it ran out of its conventional monetary policy tool. The Fed hit the zero-lower-bound on December

[36] Possible reasons for lower expected inflation after negative policy rate by BOJ. Jens H. E. Christensen and Mark M. Spiegel. "Negative Interest Rates and Inflation Expectations in Japan." *FRBSF Economic Letter*, August 26 (2019). Print.

10, 2008.[37] The FOMC formally set the target federal funds rate between 0.00 percent and 0.25 percent on December 16, 2008 (See Table 6.2). This did not, however, mean that the Fed was out of monetary policy tools. It had "unconventional" policy tools at its disposal. It turned to purchasing promissory notes with longer maturities.

6.3.2 *The Yield Curve Again*

As you know, when the demand for a financial asset increases, its price increases and the interest rate decreases. In Chapter 5 we learned that a Treasury yield curve plots the interest rates of various Treasury securities along the vertical axis and the time to maturity along the horizontal axis. We also learned that the various interest rates that prevail in the economy tend to move together (Figs. 5.7 and 5.8). When the Fed conducts monetary policy to meet its targeted federal funds rate—the interest rate that banks charge each other for overnight loans—it also affects the interest rates charged for promissory notes of other maturities. That is, the yields tend to shift up or down in tandem, all else constant. Here is what the yield curves looked like on December 15, 2008 and December 16, 2008.

The dashed line in Fig. 6.12 is the yield curve on the eve of the Fed's announcement, December 15, 2008, to set the federal funds rate target between 0.00 percent and 0.25 percent. The solid line represents the yield curve on December 16, 2008 when the Fed announced its new target for the federal funds rate. Note the parallel shift downward. Except for the one-month and the three-month Treasury bills, the rest of the interest rates decreased. That is, the yield curve shifted downward. I present these yield data in Table 6.4 to highlight the point.

A clarificatory note is in order here. While talking about the yield curve I mentioned that the interest rates on promissory notes of various maturities tended to move in the same direction; when short-term interest rates decreased, so did the long-term interest rates, and vice versa. The key word is *tend*. This is a generally observed behavior of interest rates. It in no way implies that there are not any deviations. In fact, we saw such deviations in Figs. 5.7 and 5.8, and again in Fig. 6.12. In Fig. 6.12 and Table 6.4, we saw that the interest rates on the one-month and

[37]The Fed hits the zero-lower-bound. https://www.treasury.gov/resource-center/data-chart-center/interest-rates/Pages/TextView.aspx?data=yieldYear&year=2008 (Accessed: September 10, 2019).

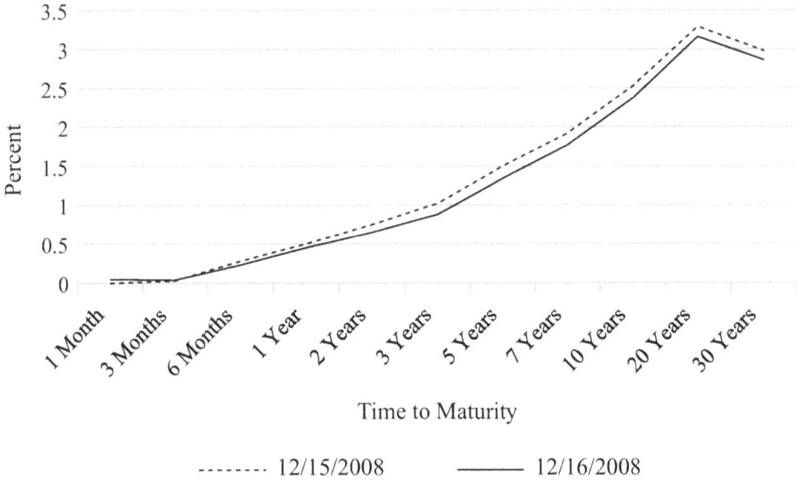

Fig. 6.12 Yield curves (December 15, 2008 and December 16, 2008) (Figure prepared by the author. *Data Source* US Treasury. https://www.treasury.gov/resource-center/data-chart-center/interest-rates/Pages/TextView.aspx?data=yieldYear&year=2008 [Accessed: September 10, 2019]. *Note* The Treasury did not offer 2-month Treasury bills during 2008)

Table 6.4 Treasury yields (December 15, 2008 and December 16, 2008)

[1] *Maturity*	*[2]* *12/15/2008*	*[3]* *12/16/2008*
1 Month	0	0.05
3 Months	0.03	0.04
6 Months	0.28	0.23
1 Year	0.5	0.45
2 Years	0.75	0.65
3 Years	1.02	0.88
5 Years	1.5	1.34
7 Years	1.92	1.77
10 Years	2.53	2.37
20 Years	3.29	3.16
30 Years	2.98	2.86

Table prepared by the author. *Data Source* US Treasury. https://www.treasury.gov/resource-center/data-chart-center/interest-rates/Pages/TextView.aspx?data=yieldYear&year=2008 (Accessed: September 10, 2019). *Note* The Treasury did not offer 2-month Treasury bills during 2008

the three-month Treasury bills increased a bit when the Fed lowered its target for the federal funds rate. Not only that, an inverted yield curve exists because long-term and short-term interest rates start moving in the opposite direction (Fig. 5.4).

6.3.3 *Quantitative Easing (QE)*

Before digging deeper, it is worth mentioning that Quantitative Easing is hardly a new tool. The Fed used it during the 1930s, the Bank of Japan during 2001, and more recently the Bank of England during 2016.[38] The popular media and even economics literature made the Fed's actions sound like it was something brand new. Perhaps to capture the audience attention and convey the sense of urgency the adjective "unconventional" became in vogue.

While the interest rates on short-term loans—the Fed's main monetary policy tool—had hit the zero-lower-bound, the economy was still in recession. The Fed was not completely helpless however. It still had room to affect the long-term interest rates. On March 18, 2009, the Fed announced that it would purchase long-term Treasury bonds and mortgage-backed securities worth up to $1.25 trillion (Table 6.2).[39] A mortgage-backed security is a pool of various mortgage loans issued by banks that "comply with standards set by Fannie Mae and Freddie Mac" and then sold to savers.[40] Fannie Mae, Freddie Mac, and Ginnie Mae are the government-sponsored enterprises created to increase homeownership. The mortgage-backed securities that the Fed purchased were backed by Fannie Mae, Freddie Mac, and Ginnie Mae.[41] For these asset purchases to have impact on the long-term interest rates the purchases have to be

[38] Quantitative Easing by the Fed and by the Bank of Japan. https://files.stlouisfed.org/files/htdocs/pageone-economics/uploads/newsletter/2011/201102.pdf (Accessed: September 12, 2019). Quantitative Easing by Bank of England. https://www.bankofengland.co.uk/monetary-policy/quantitative-easing (Accessed: September 12, 2019).

[39] Mortgage-backed securities purchase program. https://www.federalreserve.gov/regreform/reform-mbs.htm (Accessed: September 12, 2019).

[40] Definition of mortgage-backed security. https://files.stlouisfed.org/files/htdocs/pageone-economics/uploads/newsletter/2011/201104.pdf. See also https://www.federalreserve.gov/regreform/reform-mbs.htm (Accessed: September 12, 2019).

[41] Mortgage-backed securities are guaranteed by Fannie Mae, Freddie Mac, or Ginnie Mae. Bernanke. See also https://www.federalreserve.gov/aboutthefed/files/combinedfinstmt2018.pdf (Accessed: September 11, 2019).

at a large scale. The term "Quantitative Easing" is used when the Fed, or any other central bank, makes large-scale asset purchases.[42] Later on, it became known as QE1. The addendum "1" refers to the fact that the Fed conducted three rounds of Quantitative Easing—QE1, QE2, and QE3.

Along with QE1, QE2, and QE3, the Fed also enacted the Maturity Extension Program on September 21, 2011. It was nicknamed "Operation Twist." The purpose of Operation Twist was to "put downward pressure on longer-term interest rates" (see Table 6.2). To this end, the Fed started by purchasing "$400 billion of 6- to 30-year Treasuries, accompanied by the sale of the same quantity of 1- to 3-year securities."[43] The Fed continued this program till December 2012, and purchased a total of $667 billion of 6- to 30-year securities from the proceeds of equal amount of sale of the 1- to 3-year securities.[44] The process in which the Fed purchases long-term securities from the proceeds of selling the short-term securities is called "sterilization."[45] Note that in this case the Fed's total value of assets on its balance sheet does not change. The only change is in the composition of assets. Figure 6.13 shows the amount of long-term assets purchased by the Fed.

In Fig. 6.13, the amount of the US Treasury bonds and the mortgage-backed securities purchased (in millions of US dollars) is listed on the left-hand-side vertical axis, and the interest rates on the 10-year, 20-year, and 30-year government securities on the right-hand-side vertical axis.

As Kenneth Kuttner (2018) notes, "[a] common misconception is that the purpose of quantitative easing was to increase bank reserves and the money supply" (p. 124). While, it is true that quantitative easing did increase bank reserves and money supply, the main motive was to stabilize the financial system and the economy. While there were similarities among the actions of the Fed during 2008, and those that it took during the

[42] The term "Quantitative Easing" used to refer to large-scale asset purchases. Ben S. Bernanke. *The Federal Reserve and the Financial Crisis*. Princeton: Princeton University Press, 2013. Web, Kuttner: 121–46.

[43] "Operation Twist". Kenneth N. Kuttner. "Outside the Box: Unconventional Monetary Policy in the Great Recession and Beyond." *Journal of Economic Perspectives* 32.4 (2018): 121–46. Print.

[44] The length and amount of Operation Twist. https://www.federalreserve.gov/monetarypolicy/maturityextensionprogram.htm (Accessed: September 16, 2019).

[45] "Sterilization". Kenneth N. Kuttner. "Outside the Box: Unconventional Monetary Policy in the Great Recession and Beyond." *Journal of Economic Perspectives* 32.4 (2018): 121–46. Print.

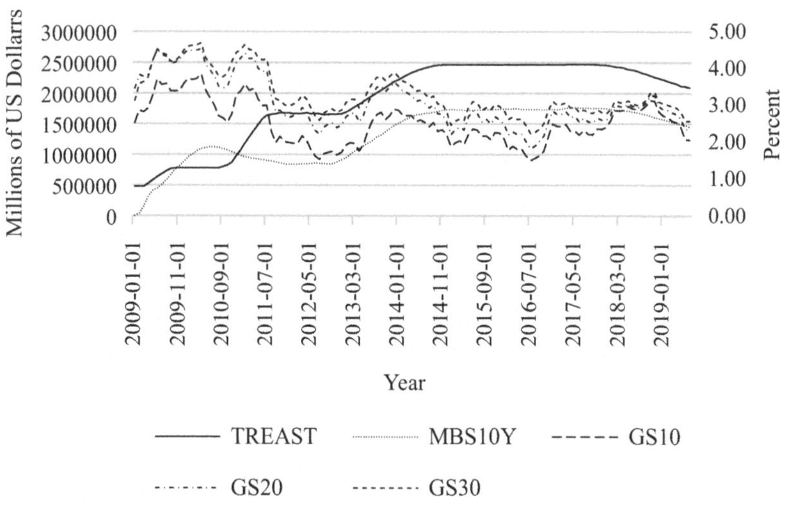

Fig. 6.13 US Treasuries, mortgage-backed securities, and yields (Figure prepared by the author. *Data Source* Board of Governors of the Federal Reserve System [US], Assets: Securities Held Outright: Mortgage-Backed Securities: Maturing in Over 10 Years: Wednesday Level [MBS10Y]; Assets: Securities Held Outright: US Treasury Securities: All: Wednesday Level [TREAST]; Federal Reserve Economic Data. Board of Governors of the Federal Reserve System [US], 10-Year Treasury Constant Maturity Rate [GS10]; Board of Governors of the Federal Reserve System [US], 20-Year Treasury Constant Maturity Rate [GS20]; Board of Governors of the Federal Reserve System [US], 30-Year Treasury Constant Maturity Rate [GS30]; retrieved from FRED, Federal Reserve Bank of St. Louis. https://fred.stlouisfed.org. Monthly observations. Not seasonally adjusted [Accessed: August 12, 2019])

1930s, and those of other central banks, there were notable differences. In the December 15–16, 2008 meeting of the Federal Open Market Operations (FOMC), the then Chair of the Fed, Ben Bernanke clarified the objectives of Quantitative Easing and highlighted the differences between the Fed's actions and those of the Bank of Japan.[46]

[46] Differences in the objectives of Quantitative Easing. https://www.federalreserve.gov/monetarypolicy/files/FOMC20081216meeting.pdf (Accessed: September 16, 2019).

> In some respects our policies are similar to the quantitative easing of the Japanese, but I would argue that, when you look at it more carefully, what we're doing is fundamentally different from the Japanese approach. ... The Japanese approach...was focused on the liability side of the balance sheet—specifically the quantity of bank reserves, the monetary base..... The theory behind quantitative easing was that providing enormous amounts of very cheap liquidity to banks, ..., would encourage them to lend and that lending, in turn, would increase the broader measures of the money supply, which in turn would raise prices and stimulate asset prices, and so on, and that would suffice to stimulate the economy. ... [T]he focus of the quantitative easing was on the liability side, and indeed, there were targets ... for the amount of excess reserves or reserves in the system. ... [W]hat we are doing is different...because, unlike the Japanese focus on the liability side of the balance sheet, we are focused on the asset side of the balance sheet. ... [W]e have adopted a series of programs, all of which involve some type of lending or asset purchase, which has brought onto our balance sheet securities other than the typical Treasuries that we usually transact in. ... In this case, rather than being a target of policy, the quantity of excess reserves in the system is a byproduct of the decisions to make these various types of credit available.

What impact did Quantitative Easing have on the various sectors of the economy? I start by plotting excess reserves, monetary base, and bank loans data in Fig. 6.14.

Excess reserves are represented by a solid line in Fig. 6.14. Recall from Chapter 5 that depository institutions—commercial banks, saving associations, credit unions, and so on[47]—are required to hold reserves, called required reserves. Banks may hold excess reserves as well. The total reserves are the sum of required reserves and excess reserves. All else equal, it will not be in a bank's financial interest to hold excess reserves. This is because the bank will forgo interest revenue. A clarification is in order here.

Traditionally the Fed did not pay interest on the total reserve balances that depository institutions held at the Fed. As we saw in Chapter 5, the Financial Services Regulatory Relief Act of 2006 allowed the Fed to start paying interest on total reserves held at the Fed by the depository institutions. According to the Act, "Balances maintained at a Federal Reserve

[47] Depository institutions. https://www.federalreserve.gov/monetarypolicy/reservereq.htm. (Accessed: July 27, 2019).

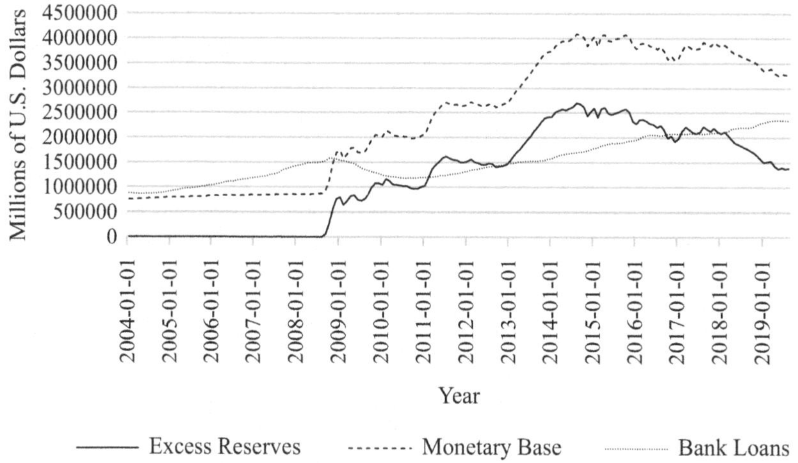

Fig. 6.14 Excess reserves, monetary base, and bank lending (Figure prepared by the author. *Data Source* Federal Reserve Bank of St. Louis, Excess Reserves of Depository Institutions [EXCSRESNS], retrieved from FRED, Federal Reserve Bank of St. Louis. https://fred.stlouisfed.org/series/EXCSRESNS. Federal Reserve Bank of St. Louis, St. Louis Adjusted Monetary Base [AMBNS], retrieved from FRED, Federal Reserve Bank of St. Louis. https://fred.stlouisfed.org/series/AMBNS. Board of Governors of the Federal Reserve System (US), Commercial and Industrial Loans, All Commercial Banks [BUSLOANSNSA], retrieved from FRED, Federal Reserve Bank of St. Louis. https://fred.stlouisfed.org/series/BUSLOANSNSA [Accessed: September 16, 2019]. *Note* Data on monetary base and bank loans are provided in billions of US Dollars. I converted these data into millions by multiplying these series by 1000 so that the scale of all three series would be the same)

bank by or on behalf of a depository institution may receive earnings to be paid by the Federal Reserve bank at least once each calendar quarter, at a rate or rates not to exceed the general level of short-term interest rates."[48]

This tool allowed the Fed more flexibility to reach and maintain the federal funds rate target. Originally the Act allowed the Fed to start paying interest on October 1, 2011. The 2007–2009 financial crisis necessitated

[48]The Financial Services Regulatory Relief Act of 2006. https://fraser.stlouisfed.org/title/1035 (Accessed: September 20, 2019).

that the effective date be moved to October 1, 2008. This modification was part of the Emergency Economic Stabilization Act of 2008.[49] Along with the federal funds rate target range, interest rate on required and excess reserves balance puts a tighter band around the effective federal funds rate. Furthermore, from the point of view of the depository institutions, required (and excess) reserves balances that do not earn interest represent an implicit tax. This tool effectively removed that implicit tax.

The interest rate on required and excess reserves balances is set by the Board of Governors of the Federal Reserve System. At the time of this writing, the interest rate on required reserve and excess reserve balances was 0.10 percent,[50] and the federal funds rate target was set between 0.0 percent and 0.25 percent.[51] Ever since the implementation of the policy, interest rates on both excess reserve balances and required reserve balances have been the same except for a brief period from October 10, 2008 to November 5, 2008. During that time period the interest rate on required reserve balances was slightly higher than interest rate on excess reserves.[52]

Let me now talk about "monetary base." This will help us develop a deeper understanding of the impact of the Fed's actions in the aftermath of the 2007–2009 financial crisis. What is monetary base and why is it important? Monetary base is the sum of currency in circulation and reserves held by the depository institutions at the Federal Reserve Banks. By "currency in circulation" we mean bills and coins outside the Federal Reserve Banks and the US Treasury. It is represented by a dashed line in Fig. 6.14.

Remember from Chapters 4 and 5 that we defined money multiplier as $\left(\frac{1}{rr}\right)$, where *rr*, the required reserve ratio, is the percentage of deposits that banks are required to keep as reserves. In Chapter 4, we learned that

[49] The Emergency Economic Stabilization Act of 2008. https://fraser.stlouisfed.org/title/1036 (Accessed: September 20, 2019).

[50] Interest rates on required and excess reserves balances. https://www.federalreserve.gov/monetarypolicy/reqresbalances.htm(Accessed: April 14, 2020).

[51] Federal funds rate target. https://www.federalreserve.gov/monetarypolicy/openmarket.htm (Accessed: April 14, 2020).

[52] Interest rates on required and excess reserves balances. Board of Governors of the Federal Reserve System [US], Interest Rate on Required Reserves [IORR]. https://fred.stlouisfed.org/series/IORR. Interest Rate on Excess Reserves [IOER]. https://fred.stlouisfed.org/series/IOER. Retrieved from FRED, Federal Reserve Bank of St. Louis (Accessed: September 20, 2019).

a bank's ability to extend loans is inversely related to the required reserve ratio: The lower the required reserve ratio, the higher the amount that a bank has at its disposal to extend loans, all else constant. Using Eq. 4.1—reproduced here, $\Delta D = \left(\frac{1}{rr}\right) \times \Delta R$—we were able to find out exactly how much money will be created. We multiplied the change in reserve, ΔR, with the money multiplier to get the change in deposits, ΔD, which are a part of money supply. In that discussion, we made two simplifying assumptions. One, no one uses cash (either to make transactions or as a financial asset), and two, depository institutions do not keep excess reserves. Note also that because of the assumption that no one uses cash, the total money supply was equal to the amount of demand deposits. So the total amount of reserves multiplied by the money multiplier gave us the total amount of money.

This may not be the case, however. People may use cash to buy and sell goods and services, and banks may hold more reserves than are required; they may hold excess reserves. Individuals may also hold cash as an asset. Indeed, as Fig. 6.14 shows, depository institutions have been holding large amounts of excess reserves ever since the middle of 2008. In order to account for excess reserves held by banks and cash by households and firms we need to modify our money multiplier. Equation 6.1 includes these modifications.

$$\Delta M = \left[\frac{1 + \frac{C}{D}}{rr + \frac{ER}{D} + \frac{C}{D}}\right] \times \Delta MB \tag{6.1}$$

In Eq. 6.1, C represents the amount of cash held by households and firms to make transactions and/or as a financial asset. More precisely, it is "[t]he currency … in circulation outside the U.S. Treasury and Federal Reserve Banks."[53] D is the amount held in demand deposits. Money supply is represented by M and MB is the monetary base. The Greek letter Δ represents the change in a given variable. The term rr represents the amount of required reserves, and ER represents the amount of excess reserves. The term $\frac{C}{D}$ represents the cash as a percentage of demand deposits, and the $\frac{ER}{D}$ represents the amount of excess reserves as a percentage of demand deposits.

[53] Definition of currency. Board of Governors of the Federal Reserve System (US), Currency Component of M1 [CURRNS], retrieved from FRED, Federal Reserve Bank of St. Louis; https://fred.stlouisfed.org/series/CURRNS (Accessed: September 23, 2019).

In Eq. 6.1, the quantity $\left[\frac{1+\frac{C}{D}}{rr+\frac{ER}{D}+\frac{C}{D}}\right]$ is the money multiplier after we take into account the amount of cash held by firms and households and the amount of excess reserves. I will not go into the derivation of the money multiplier here. Curious reader may find the derivation in any money and banking textbook. Frederic Mishkin's *The Economics of Money, Banking, and Financial Markets* is one such example.[54]

Let us take a look at the modified money multiplier, Eq. 6.1. First, note that the required reserve ration, *rr*, appears in the denominator just as it did in the earlier case, Eq. 4.1. All else constant, the higher the required reserve ratio, the lower the value of the money multiplier, and vice versa. Next, note that the quantity $\frac{C}{D}$, which represents cash held as a percentage of demand deposits, appears both in the numerator and in the denominator. In the numerator a 1 is added to this quantity. As long as the term $rr+\frac{ER}{D}$, which appears in the denominator is less than 1, the numerator will be greater than 1 and the value of the money multiplier will be greater than 1. This means that a given change in monetary base, ΔMB, will lead to a greater than proportionate change in money supply, ΔM. If, on the other hand, when the terms $rr+\frac{ER}{D}$ are greater than 1, then the value of the money multiplier will be less than 1 and a given change in monetary base, ΔMB, will lead to a less than proportionate change in money supply, ΔM.

What have been the values of $\frac{C}{D}$ and $\frac{ER}{D}$ over the course of the 2007–2009 financial crisis? Figure 6.15 plots these values. For comparison, I have plotted data since 2004.

We notice in Fig. 6.15 that the currency to deposits ratio, $\frac{C}{D}$, declined somewhat around mid-2008. It is represented by the dashed line. The mean of $\frac{C}{D}$ is 1.604 and standard error is 0.04. Its maximum value is 2.568 and minimum value is 0.981. The excess reserves to deposits ratio, $\frac{ER}{D}$, however, jumped significantly around that time. This is represented by the solid line in Fig. 6.15. The mean of $\frac{ER}{D}$ is 1.276 and standard error is 0.067. It has maximum value of 2.719 and minimum value of 0.003. The value of *rr* had not changed during this time period (see Table 5.3). These data tell us that the denominator in the money multiplier—$\left[\frac{1+\frac{C}{D}}{rr+\frac{ER}{D}+\frac{C}{D}}\right]$—increased significantly around this time leading to a

[54] Derivation of the money multiplier. Frederic S. Mishkin. *The Economics of Money, Banking, and Financial Markets*. New York: Pearson, 2019. Print.

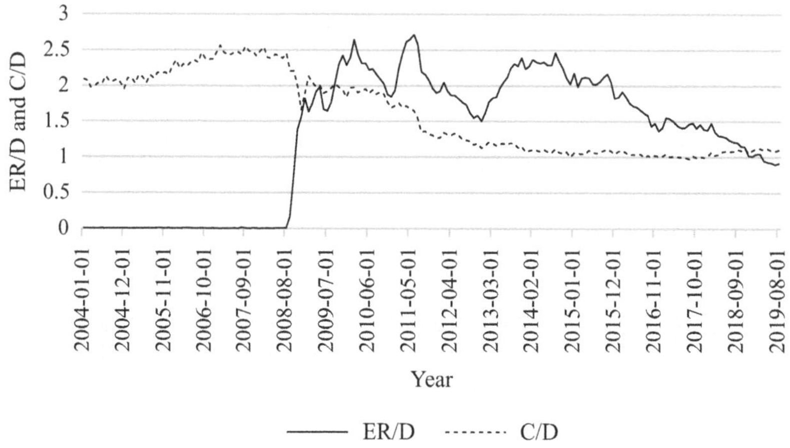

Fig. 6.15 Excess reserves to demand deposits and currency to demand deposits ratios (Figure prepared by the author. *Data Source* Federal Reserve Bank of St. Louis, Excess Reserves of Depository Institutions [EXCSRESNS], retrieved from FRED, Federal Reserve Bank of St. Louis. https://fred.stlouisfed.org/series/EXCSRESNS. Board of Governors of the Federal Reserve System [US], Currency Component of M1 [CURRNS], retrieved from FRED, Federal Reserve Bank of St. Louis. https://fred.stlouisfed.org/series/CURRNS. Board of Governors of the Federal Reserve System [US], Demand Deposits: Total [DEMDEPNS], retrieved from FRED, Federal Reserve Bank of St. Louis. https://fred.stlouisfed.org/series/DEMDEPNS [Accessed: September 23, 2019]. *Note* Data on excess reserves are in millions of US dollars. Whereas data on demand deposits and currency are reported in billions of US dollars. For scale consistency I converted the demand deposit and currency data into millions)

decline in the value. I plot the money multiplier value during this time period in Fig. 6.16.

Notice the precipitous decline in the money multiplier value in January 2009. It fell below 1 and stayed below 1 till the beginning of 2018. During 2009 the value briefly reached 1 twice but did not cross the threshold. All this means that even though the Fed was increasing monetary base, most of it was going into excess reserves (Fig. 6.14). Banks were not lending the increased reserves, at least not proportionately.

What led to this change in the amount of excess reserves held by depository institutions? The 2007–2009 financial crisis was the trigger.

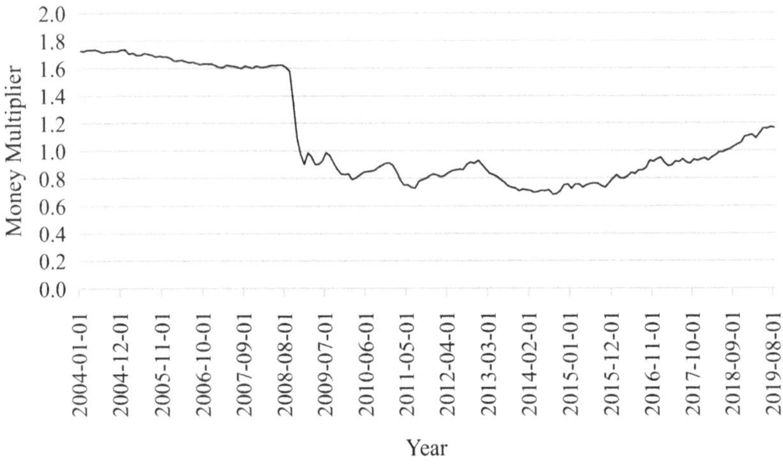

Fig. 6.16 Money multiplier (Figure prepared by the author. *Data Source* Federal Reserve Bank of St. Louis, M1 Money Multiplier [MULT], retrieved from FRED, Federal Reserve Bank of St. Louis. https://fred.stlouisfed.org/series/MULT [Accessed: September 21, 2019])

As we saw earlier in this chapter, while before the financial crisis banks were lending too liberally, ignoring all rules of responsible lending, they became too risk averse once the crisis hit. While before the financial crisis, one did not need even a proof of income, a rather high credit score became the minimum standard after the financial crisis. Bank lending dropped significantly (Fig. 6.14). Credit markets froze. Pendulum had swung the other way, to use the cliché.

6.4 Did the Unconventional Monetary Policy Work?

The short answer is "yes." Quantitative Easing has been successful in achieving its objectives. Remember why did the Fed need the unconventional monetary policy—QE1, QE2, QE3, and Maturity Extension Program? The US economy was in a recession and the interest rate on short-term securities had hit the zero-lower-bound. Fed's conventional tools of conducting monetary policy had become ineffective. While the interest rates were extremely low by historical standards, borrowing and lending activities had shrunk significantly. One may evaluate the efficacy of Quantitative Easing and the Maturity Extension Program by looking at the effects that these policies had on long-term interest rates, borrowing and lending activities, and more importantly on the economy—unemployment rate and output. Kenneth Kuttner (2018) provides a comprehensive review of economic studies that looked at these variables.[55] These studies show that the policy stance adopted by the Fed in the aftermath of the 2007 financial crisis and the Great Recession was successful. The Fed's policy was able to lower the long-term interest rates by about 1.5 percent. (Interest rate on 10-year Treasury notes is used as benchmark of long-term interest rates.) "Taken together, the studies suggest that the policies collectively reduced the 10-year term premium by as much as 150 basis points," writes Kuttner (2018, pp. 133–134). Note, by the way, 100 basis points are equal to 1 percent. When the Fed announces, for instance, that it has lowered the federal funds rate target by 25 basis points, it translates into lowering the federal funds rate target by 0.25 percent. And that the Fed changes money supply such that the target is met.

Lowering of the long-term interest rate is not an end in and of itself. As Kuttner (2018) notes, "in an environment of financial stress, uncertainty, and scarce investment opportunities, it is not a foregone conclusion that interest rate reductions will have the same effects on spending as at other times. Perhaps in a time of economic stress, the cost of funds is of second-order importance for potential borrowers" (p. 136). What matters is the economic decisions of firms and banks—borrowing and lending, respectively. Studies show that the Fed's policies were successful on both accounts. Banks increased their lending and firms increased their borrowing to build plants and equipment. At the macroeconomic level, these decisions, in turn, led to an increase in output and an estimated decline in the unemployment rate "by 1.2 percentage points relative to what it would have been in the absence of quantitative easing" (p. 138).[56]

When the Fed adopted the Quantitative Easing policy not everyone was in favor of such a policy. Pundits argued that Quantitative Easing will debase the US dollar and lead to hyperinflation, which the Fed

[55] A review of the impact of the unconventional monetary policy. Kuttner: 121–46.

[56] An estimate of decline in unemployment rate. Kenneth N. Kuttner. "Outside the Box: Unconventional Monetary Policy in the Great Recession and Beyond." *Journal of Economic Perspectives* 32.4 (2018): 121–46. Print.

would have hard time controlling. Indeed, on November 15, 2010, an open letter appeared on the Hoover Institution's Website whose signatories included journalists as well as well-known academic and professional economists, 23 in total. Here is what the letter said[57]:

> We believe the Federal Reserve's large-scale asset purchase plan (so-called "quantitative easing") should be reconsidered and discontinued. We do not believe such a plan is necessary or advisable under current circumstances. The planned asset purchases risk currency debasement and inflation, and we do not think they will achieve the Fed's objective of promoting employment.
>
> We subscribe to your statement in the Washington Post on November 4 that "the Federal Reserve cannot solve all the economy's problems on its own." In this case, we think improvements in tax, spending and regulatory policies must take precedence in a national growth program, not further monetary stimulus.
>
> We disagree with the view that inflation needs to be pushed higher, and worry that another round of asset purchases, with interest rates still near zero over a year into the recovery, will distort financial markets and greatly complicate future Fed efforts to normalize monetary policy.
>
> The Fed's purchase program has also met broad opposition from other central banks and we share their concerns that quantitative easing by the Fed is neither warranted nor helpful in addressing either U.S. or global economic problems.

The concerns raised in this letter and other media reports have not realized. The inflation rate has not increased beyond control. Quite the opposite has been the case. Indeed, central banks are having hard time meeting the inflation rate targets around the developed world. One reason is that inflation depends upon, among other factors, inflation expectations which, in turn, partly depend upon the previous inflation. As we saw in Chapter 4, when one has observed prices to decrease yesterday, one expects the prices to decrease today as well, all else constant.

[57] Open Letter to Ben Bernanke. https://www.hoover.org/research/open-letter-ben-bernanke (Accessed: September 25, 2019).

There were also concerns about the Fed's ability to normalize monetary policy. The Fed was, however, able to raise short-term interest rates once the Great Recession abated. Yet another concern was that with such low interest rates, firms might engage in excessive risk taking. Empirical evidence provides little support for this either. As Kuttner (2018) notes, "There is nothing to indicate that the risk-taking was excessive" (p. 139). Concluding the review of studies Kuttner (2018) writes:

> A preponderance of evidence nonetheless suggests that forward guidance and quantitative easing succeeded in lowering long-term interest rates. Studies using micro data have documented tangible effects of quantitative easing on firms and financial intermediaries. Macro models suggest that the interest rate reductions are likely to have had a meaningful impact. The adverse side effects appear to have been mild, and are dwarfed by the costs of the more protracted recession in the United States that likely would have occurred in the absence of the unconventional policies. The benefits of unconventional policy therefore probably outweighed the costs. (p. 142)

6.5 Modern Monetary Theory

One could misinterpret the success of a policy in a particular set of circumstances to be applicable regardless of circumstances. Indeed, this has been the case with the Modern Monetary Theory (MMT). MMT has had a resurgence of late. L. Randall Wray, now Professor Emeritus at the University of Missouri, Kansas City and Stephanie Kelton (nee Bell), Professor of Public Policy and Economics at Stoney Brook University, are perhaps the most visible promoters of MMT.[58] Professor Kelton has also served as chief economist for the Senate Budget Committee Democratic staff, and an advisor to Senator Bernie Sanders in his 2016 presidential

[58] Stephanie Kelton and L. Randall Wary as the main promoters of MMT. https://www.nytimes.com/2019/03/29/business/modern-monetary-theory-shiller.html (Accessed: October 4, 2019), L. R. Wray. *Understanding Modern Money: The Key to Full Employment and Price Stability*. Cheltenham, UK: Edward Elgar, 1998. Print, L. R. Wray. *Modern Money Theory: A Primer on Macroeconomics for Sovereign Money Systems*. Basingstoke, UK: Palgrave Macmillan, 2012. Print, Thomas I. Palley. "Money, Fiscal Policy, and Interest Rates: A Critique of Modern Monetary Theory." *Review of Political Economy* 27.1 (2015b): 1–23. Web, Thomas I. Palley. "The Critics of Modern Money Theory (MMT) Are Right." *Review of Political Economy* 27.1 (2015a): 45–61. Web.

campaign. As a result, she is prominent in the media. Other promoters include Mathew Forstater and Warren Mosler.[59]

One of the tents of MMT is that deficits do not matter.[60] As odd as it may sound, and it should, the adherents of this tenet include the former Vice President Dick Cheney as well as the Democrat, Representative Alexandria Ocasio-Cortez of New York. It is not that often that one can find an example of polar opposites like these agreeing on such an extreme idea and so that agreement is notable.

The MMT seems to rest on the Functional Finance doctrine of Abba P. Lerner.[61] I say "seems" because there remain some confusions. As Paul Krugman, in his distinct style, put it, "I think this critique [of the Functional Finance doctrine] applies to MMT as well, although if past debates are any indication, I will promptly be told that I don't understand, am a corrupt tool of the oligarchy, or something."[62]

Before I go any further on MMT, let me provide a brief outline of the Functional Finance doctrine.

6.5.1 Functional Finance Doctrine

In his 1943 article "Functional Finance and the Public Debt" Abba Lerner wrote[63]:

[59] Other promoters of MMT. Mathew Forstater and Warren Mosler. "The Natural Rate of Interest Is Zero." *Journal of Economic Issues* 39.2 (2005): 535–42. *JSTOR*. Web.

[60] Deficits do not matter. Stephanie Kelton. https://www.nytimes.com/2017/10/05/opinion/deficit-tax-cuts-trump.html?module=inline (Accessed: October 4, 2019).

[61] Functional Finance doctrine. Abba P. Lerner. "Functional Finance and the Federal Debt." *Social Research* 10.1 (1943): 38–51. *JSTOR*. Web, Abba P. Lerner. "From Pre-Keynes to Post-Keynes." *Social Research* 44.3 (1977): 387–415. *JSTOR*. Web. See also Louisa Connors and William Mitchell. "Framing Modern Monetary Theory." *Journal of Post Keynesian Economics* 40.2 (2017): 239–59. Web, Andrés Álvarez and Vincent Bignon. "L. Walras and C. Menger: Two Ways on the Path of Modern Monetary Theory." *The European Journal of the History of Economic Thought* 20.1 (2013): 89–124. Web.

[62] Krugman's critique of MMT. https://www.nytimes.com/2019/02/12/opinion/whats-wrong-with-functional-finance-wonkish.html (Accessed: October 3, 2019). See also Robert Shiller. https://www.nytimes.com/2019/03/29/business/modern-monetary-theory-shiller.html (Accessed: October 4, 2019).

[63] Definition of Functional Finance. Lerner: 38–51.

> The central idea is that government fiscal policy, taxing, its borrowing and repayment of loans, its issue of new money and its withdrawal of money, shall all be undertaken with an eye only to the *results* of these actions on the economy and not to any established traditional doctrine about what is sound or unsound. ... The principle of judging fiscal measures by the way they work or function in the economy we may call *Functional Finance*. (p. 39, Italics original)

Lerner (1943) argues that the main focus of the government should be to maintain full employment. A government can achieve this objective by managing aggregate demand. As such, the government should not worry about the level of public debt. In summarizing the doctrine he wrote[64]:

> Functional Finance rejects completely the traditional doctrines of "sound finance" and the principle of trying to balance the budget over a solar year or any other arbitrary period. In their place it prescribes: first, the adjustment of total spending (by everybody in the economy, including the government) in order to eliminate both unemployment and inflation, using government spending when total spending is too low and taxation when total spending is too high; second, the adjustment of public holdings of money and of government bonds, by government borrowing or debt repayment, in order to achieve the rate of interest which results in the most desirable level of investment; and, third, the printing, hoarding or destruction of money as needed for carrying out the first two parts of the program. (p. 41)

Wouldn't the effort to maintain full employment by deficit financing lead to an ever increasing public debt? Lerner's answer was a resounding no. He gave five reasons why it would not happen.[65]

> First, full employment *can* be maintained by printing the money needed for it, and this does not increase the debt at all. It is probably advisable, however, to allow debt and money to increase together in a certain balance, as long as one or the other has to increase. (Italics original)

[64] In summarizing Functional Finance. Abba P. Lerner. "Functional Finance and the Federal Debt." *Social Research* 10.1 (1943): 38–51. *JSTOR*. Web.

[65] Lerner's arguments about why would the public debt not keep on increasing. Abba P. Lerner. "Functional Finance and the Federal Debt." *Social Research* 10.1 (1943): 38–51. *JSTOR*. Web.

> Second, since one of the greatest deterrents to private investment is the fear that the depression will come before the investment has paid for itself, the guarantee of permanent full employment will make private investment much more attractive, ... The greater private investment will diminish the need for deficit spending.
>
> Third, as the national debt increases, and with it the sum of private wealth, there will be an increasingly [*sic*] yield from taxes on higher incomes and inheritances, even if the tax rates are unchanged. ... the government ... can devote them to paying the interest on the national debt.
>
> Fourth, as the national debt increases it acts as a self-equilibrating force, gradually diminishing the further and finally reaching an equilibrium level where its tendency to grow comes completely to an end. The greater the national debt the greater is the quantity of private wealth. The reason for this is simply that for every dollar of debt owed by the government there is a private creditor who owns the government obligation.
>
> Fifth, if for any reason the government does not want to see private property grow too much (whether in form of government bonds or otherwise) it can check this by taxing the rich instead of borrowing from them, in its program of financing government spending to maintain full employment. (pp. 48–49)

6.6 Back to the Modern Monetary Theory

When two Democrats, Representative Alexandria Ocasio-Cortez of New York and Senator Edward J. Markey of Massachusetts, introduced the Green New Deal they relied on MMT.[66] Under the Green New Deal, the government will embark on extensive and expensive infrastructure and

[66] The Green New Deal. https://apps.npr.org/documents/document.html?id=5729033-Green-New-Deal-FINAL (Accessed: October 4, 2019). https://www.npr.org/2019/07/17/742255158/this-economic-theory-could-be-used-to-pay-for-the-green-new-deal (Accessed: October 4, 2019). https://www.nytimes.com/2019/03/29/business/modern-monetary-theory-shiller.html (Accessed: October 4, 2019). See also. https://www.project-syndicate.org/commentary/federal-reserve-modern-monetary-theory-dangers-by-kenneth-rogoff-2019-03 (Accessed: October 4, 2019).

social projects to be paid for by public borrowing.[67] The proposed Green New Deal did not have much details about how to pay for these project. It still does not, as of this writing. Steve Inskeep of the National Public Radio, in an interview that aired on February 7, 2019, asked Representative Ocasio-Cortez about the sources of funds. Below is a part of the transcript of the interview[68]:

Inskeep: You're talking about things that obviously would cost a lot of money. I know you'd rather think of it as an investment rather than a cost, but it is ... certainly a lot of money. You don't specify where it's going to come from, other than saying it will all pay for itself.

Ocasio-Cortez: Yeah. I think the first thing that we need to do is kind of break the mistaken idea that taxes pay for a hundred percent of government expenditure. It's just not how government expenditure works. We can recoup costs, but oftentimes you look at, for example, the GOP tax cut, which I think was an irresponsible use of government expenditure. But government projects are often financed by a combination of taxes, deficit spending and other kinds of investments - you know, bonds and so on.

Inskeep: Well, I get that. But deficit spending is borrowing money that has to be paid back eventually through taxes.

Ocasio-Cortez: Yeah. And I think it - I think that is always the crux of it. So when we decide to go into the realm of deficit spending, we have to do so responsibly. We ask, is this an investment or is this actually going to pay for itself?

Inskeep: So you're saying borrow the money, make the investment. The economy will grow. It will pay off the debt.

[67] NPR interview of Representative Alexandria Ocasio-Cortez. https://www.npr.org/2019/02/07/692259103/ocasio-cortez-to-unveil-ambitious-plan-to-combat-climate-change (Accessed: October 4, 2019).

[68] NPR transcript of the Representative Ocasio-Cortez. https://www.npr.org/2019/02/07/692259103/ocasio-cortez-to-unveil-ambitious-plan-to-combat-climate-change (Accessed: October 4, 2019).

Ocasio-Cortez: Absolutely. Because we're creating jobs.

Inskeep: Although, I do have to say, you mentioned the Republican tax cut. They said the same thing about the tax cut – let's do this tax cut. The economy will grow. It's going to be great. It's going to pay for itself. Hasn't turned out to be true at all.

Ocasio-Cortez: Absolutely. And I think that that is an important distinction to make because when they were advancing that cause, they had no evidence to say that these things were going to happen. But we actually do have the evidence. For every $1 invested in infrastructure, we get $6 back.

There is a reason for the Representative Ocasio-Cortez's confusion and perhaps equivocation: MMT's arguments have not been fleshed out properly.

MMT has received a lot of criticism from mainstream economists. It is one thing to state that when the economy is in a recession, increased government spending financed by borrowing does help bring the economy out of recessions. In such situations, worrying about deficits and holding back government spending would be considered an irresponsible economic policy. There is a lot of empirical evidence to support this.[69] It is completely another thing, however, to say that deficits do not matter, regardless of how the economy is behaving. "The idea that deficits don't matter for countries that can borrow in their own currency I think is just wrong," emphasized Jerome Powel, the Federal Reserve Chairman, in a Congressional testimony.[70]

Careless thinking is prone to making errors. An idea may very well be correct in one situation and completely wrong in another.

> During the late 1970s, this was the story of supply-side, Laffer-curve economics. It began with the valid idea that taxes had important incentive effects and that, in conceivable circumstances, tax cuts could raise

[69] Benefits of deficit spending during economic downturns. See, for instance, Paul Krugman. *End This Depression Now!* New York, NY: W. W. Norton, 2012. Print.

[70] The Fed Chair on "deficits do not matter." https://www.cnbc.com/2019/02/26/fed-chief-says-economic-theory-of-unlimited-borrowing-supported-by-ocasio-cortez-is-just-wrong.html (Accessed: October 4, 2019).

> revenue. It grew into the ludicrous idea that tax cuts would always pay for themselves, ... MMT, is the supply-side economics of our time. A valid idea — that traditional fiscal-policy taboos need to be rethought in an era of low real interest rates — has been stretched by fringe economists into ludicrous claims that massive spending on job guarantees can be financed by central banks without any burden on the economy.

So wrote Lawrence H. Summers, a professor at Harvard and a US Treasury Secretary from 1999–2001, in an op-ed which appeared in the *Washington Post*. "But for neither the right nor the left is there any such thing as a free lunch. It's the responsibility of serious economists, whatever their political party, to make this clear," he urged.[71]

Robert Shiller, a Yale economics professor and a Nobel laureate, put it this way in an op-ed in the *New York Times*[72]:

> M.M.T. is sometimes invoked to justify reckless government borrowing for marginally good causes, without raising taxes. Well, here's a spoiler alert: Though increased spending on infrastructure, education, social welfare and the environment may be wise, and rising deficits may make sense some of the time, we really cannot borrow ceaselessly without risking real harm.

Kenneth Rogoff, Professor of Economics and Public Policy at Harvard, was not this kind when critiquing MMT. The title of his column, "Modern Monetary Nonsense," which appeared in *Project Syndicate* on March 4, 2019, says it all.[73] Thomas Palley, an independent economist, has provided a more formal critique of MMT.[74] There is agreement among mainstream economists that a lot more work needs to done before MMT can be taken seriously.

In this chapter, we have covered the 2007–2009 financial crisis and the Great Recession that followed. We looked at the role that the Fed played

[71] Op-ed by Summers. https://www.washingtonpost.com/opinions/the-lefts-embrace-of-modern-monetary-theory-is-a-recipe-for-disaster/2019/03/04/6ad88eec-3ea4-11e9-9361-301ffb5bd5e6_story.html (Accessed: October 4, 2019).

[72] Shiller on MMT. https://www.nytimes.com/2019/03/29/business/modern-monetary-theory-shiller.html (Accessed: April 14, 2020).

[73] "Modern Monetary Nonsense" by Rogoff. https://www.project-syndicate.org/commentary/federal-reserve-modern-monetary-theory-dangers-by-kenneth-rogoff-2019-03?barrier=accesspaylog (Accessed: October 4, 2019).

[74] Thomas Palley's formal critique of MMT. Palley: 1–23, Palley: 45–61.

in reviving the economy. Along the way we took a glimpse at the need for careful and precise thinking. In the next chapter, I pick up the topic of economic growth and the role that money has played in this regard.

Works Cited

Álvarez, Andrés, and Vincent Bignon. "L. Walras and C. Menger: Two Ways on the Path of Modern Monetary Theory." *The European Journal of the History of Economic Thought* 20.1 (2013): 89–124. Web.

Anderson, Patricia M., Kristin F. Butcher, and Diane Whitmore Schanzenbach. "Changes in Safety Net Use During the Great Recession." *American Economic Review* 105.5 (2015): 161–65. Web.

Ball, Laurence. "Long-Term Damage from the Great Recession in OECD Countries." *European Journal of Economics and Economic Policies: Intervention* 11.2 (2014): 149–60. Print.

Bassetto, Marco. "Negative Nominal Interest Rates." *American Economic Review* 94.2 (2004): 104–8. Web.

Bernanke, Ben S. *The Courage to Act: A Memoir of a Crisis and Its Aftermath*. New York, NY: W. W. Norton, 2015. Web.

———. *The Federal Reserve and the Financial Crisis*. Princeton: Princeton University Press, 2013. Web.

Chomsisengphet, Souphala, and Anthony Pennington-Cross. "The Evolution of the Subprime Mortgage Market." *Review* 88.1 (2006): 31–56. Print.

Christensen, Jens H. E., and Mark M. Spiegel. "Negative Interest Rates and Inflation Expectations in Japan." *FRBSF Economic Letter*, August 26 (2019). Print.

Connors, Louisa, and William Mitchell. "Framing Modern Monetary Theory." *Journal of Post Keynesian Economics* 40.2 (2017): 239–59. Web.

Forstater, Mathew, and Warren Mosler. "The Natural Rate of Interest Is Zero." *Journal of Economic Issues* 39.2 (2005): 535–42. *JSTOR*. Web.

Immergluck, Daniel, and Marti Wiles. *Two Steps Back: The Dual Mortgage Market, Predatory Lending, and the Undoing of Community Development*. Chicago: The Woodstock Institute, 1999. Print.

Krugman, Paul. *End This Depression Now!* New York, NY: W. W. Norton, 2012. Print.

Kuttner, Kenneth N. "Outside the Box: Unconventional Monetary Policy in the Great Recession and Beyond." *Journal of Economic Perspectives* 32.4 (2018): 121–46. Print.

Lerner, Abba P. "From Pre-Keynes to Post-Keynes." *Social Research* 44.3 (1977): 387–415. *JSTOR*. Web.

———. "Functional Finance and the Federal Debt." *Social Research* 10.1 (1943): 38–51. *JSTOR*. Web.

Mian, Atif R., and Amir Sufi. "The Consequences of Mortgage Credit Expansion: Evidence from the 2007 Mortgage Default Crisis." *NBER Working Paper No. w13936*, April (2008). Print.

Mian, Atif, and Amir Sufi. "Finance and Business Cycles: The Credit-Driven Household Demand Channel." *The Journal of Economic Perspectives* 32.3 (2018): 31–58. Web.

Mian, Atif, Amir Sufi, and Francesco Trebbi. "The Political Economy of the US Mortgage Default Crisis." *The American Economic Review* 100.5 (2010): 1967–98. Web.

Mishkin, Frederic S. *The Economics of Money, Banking, and Financial Markets*. New York: Pearson, 2019. Print.

Palley, Thomas I. "The Critics of Modern Money Theory (MMT) are Right." *Review of Political Economy* 27.1 (2015a): 45–61. Web.

———. "Money, Fiscal Policy, and Interest Rates: A Critique of Modern Monetary Theory." *Review of Political Economy* 27.1 (2015b): 1–23. Web.

Rothstein, Jesse, Stephanie Aaronson, and Lisa B. Kahn. "Unemployment Insurance and Job Search in the Great Recession [with Comments and Discussion]." *Brookings Papers on Economic Activity* (2011): 143–214. Web.

Smith, Marvin M., and Christy Chung Hevener. "Subprime Lending Over Time: The Role of Race." *Journal of Economics and Finance* 38.2 (2014): 321–44. Web.

Wray, L. R. *Modern Money Theory: A Primer on Macroeconomics for Sovereign Money Systems*. Basingstoke, UK: Palgrave Macmillan, 2012. Print.

———. *Understanding Modern Money: The Key to Full Employment and Price Stability*. Cheltenham, UK: Edward Elgar, 1998. Print.

CHAPTER 7

Economic Growth and the Role of Money

In this chapter, I talk about how money facilitated the division of labor and specialization, which in turn led to economic growth. Before we dig deeper into the role that money played, it is instructive to remind ourselves what money is. Recall that for something to serve as money, it has to have three characteristics: a medium of exchange; a unit of account; and a store of value. As a medium of exchange, this thing, i.e., money, allows us to exchange what we produce in excess of what we want to consume with what we want but either do not produce ourselves or do not produce enough. As a unit of account, money allows us to evaluate what we want to sell and what we want to buy. And as a store of value money allows us to save now and consume later.

7.1 What Is Economic Growth?

Simply put, economic growth refers to an increase in the total output of an economy. This means having more of goods and services that an economy did before. Economic growth is often conflated with economic development. While related, these are two distinct concepts. Economic growth, as mentioned, refers to having a higher output level, whereas economic development refers to masses having more and better goods and services—better living conditions, better education, better roads, and so on. In this respect, economic development is more focused on distributional issues.

M. Ashraf, *Money*,
https://doi.org/10.1007/978-3-030-50378-9_7

Amartya Sen, in his book *Development as Freedom*, defines economic development more broadly. "Development can be seen... as a process of expanding real freedoms that people enjoy. Focusing on human freedoms contrasts with narrower views of development, such as identifying development with the growth of gross national product, or with the rise of personal incomes, or with industrialization, or with technological advance, or with social modernization" (p. 3). Sen names five types of freedoms, which he calls "instrumental freedoms." These are "(1) political freedoms, (2) economic facilities, (3) social opportunities, (4) transparency guarantees and (5) protective security" (p. 38).[1] While there is no guarantee that masses will have these freedoms as the national income of an economy rises—wealth could be concentrated in a few hands—these freedoms are certainly not possible without an economy having higher levels of incomes. Economic growth serves as means of achieving these freedoms. Economic growth serves as means to economic development.[2] Here, I will focus on the means.

While defining economic growth is easy, measuring it is not. For one thing, in order to measure economic growth, we need a reliable measure of output. One measure of the total output of an economy is its gross domestic product (GDP). We saw a plot of real GDP for the United States in Fig. 1.1. While there are ups and downs, i.e., business cycles, there is a clear upward trend in the total output of the United States We came across the concepts of GDP and measures of the overall price level—GDP deflator and Consumer Price Index (CPI)—in Chapter 4. Another commonly used measure of the total output of an economy is gross national product (GNP). There are a few differences between GDP and GNP. Let me go into more details about GDP, GNP, GDP deflator, and CPI before moving on. As before, I will use the United States as an example.

[1] Amartya Sen's "instrumental freedoms." Amartya Sen. *Development as Freedom*. Westminster, MD, USA: Alfred A. Knopf Incorporated, 1999. Print.

[2] Economic growth to achieve economic development. Amartya Sen. *Development as Freedom*. Westminster, MD, USA: Alfred A. Knopf Incorporated, 1999. Print, Steven Pinker. *Enlightenment Now: The Case for Reason, Science, Humanism, and Progress*. New York: Penguin Books, 2018. Print.

7.1.1 *What Is Gross Domestic Product?*

In the United States, the Bureau of Economic Analysis (BEA) provides estimates of the various economic activities in the National Income and Product Accounts (NIPAs). "The NIPAs present the value and composition of national output and the types of incomes generated in its production."[3] In order to measure the output of the United States economy, the NIPAs provide estimates of the GDP. GDP may be defined more formally as the market value of all the final goods and services produced within the geographic boundaries of the United States in a given year.[4] As noted in the *NIPA Handbook: Concepts and Methods of the U.S. National Income and Product Accounts*, the GDP "measure can be arrived at by three separate means: as the sum of goods and services sold to final users, as the sum of income payments and other costs incurred in the production of goods and services, and as the sum of the value added at each stage of production."[5] Furthermore, it is worth noting that while "…these three ways of measuring GDP are conceptually the same, their calculation may not result in identical estimates of GDP because of differences in data sources, timing, and estimation techniques."[6] In the following pages, I will briefly go over these three measures.

Going back to the definition of GDP, a few questions arise. Why market value? Why final goods and services? What is geographic boundary and why the geographic boundary restriction? Why a given time period?

Let's start with the question of market value. First, note that market value is the price of a good multiplied by its quantity. For instance, if an economy produces, say, 100,000 units of a particular kind of chair and each chair sells for \$200, then the market value of these chairs is \$20,000,000 (= \$200 × 100,000).

Remember what we are trying to do here. We are trying to figure out the total output of the economy. Countries produce a large number of goods and services. In Chapter 1, we talked about the North American

[3] What are NIPAs? https://www.bea.gov/system/files/2019-05/Chapter-1.pdf (Accessed: October 31, 2019).

[4] Definition of GDP. https://www.bea.gov/sites/default/files/2018-04/GDP-Education-by-BEA.pdf (Accessed: October 23, 2019).

[5] Three measures of GDP. https://www.bea.gov/system/files/2019-05/Chapter-2.pdf (Accessed: October 31, 2019).

[6] Three measures of GDP. https://www.bea.gov/system/files/2019-05/Chapter-2.pdf (Accessed: October 31, 2019).

Product Classification System (NAPCS) which categorizes the various goods and services produced in an hierarchical manner. There are over 2100 main categories of goods and services produced. According to the Census Website, "The 2017 NAPCS structure is a six-level hierarchical structure consisting of 24 sections, 61 subsections, 172 divisions, 276 groups, 497 subgroups, and 1167 trilateral products."[7] According to the United States Census Website[8]:

> The North American Product Classification System (NAPCS) is a comprehensive, market- or demand-based, hierarchical classification system for products (goods and services) that (a) is not industry-of-origin based but can be linked to the NAICS industry structure, (b) is consistent across the three North American countries, and (c) promotes improvements in the identification and classification of service products across international classification systems, such as the Central Product Classification System of the United Nations.

Table 1.1 provided a brief introduction to the subcategories of fresh vegetables.

A country's economic activity may also be divided by sector and industry. While the NAPCS divides the economy according to the products produced, the North American Industry Classification System (NAICS) divides the economy by sector and industry. According to the Census Website, "The North American Industry Classification System ... is the standard used by Federal statistical agencies in classifying business establishments for the purpose of collecting, analyzing, and publishing statistical data related to the U.S. business economy." The NAICS also has a hierarchical structure. It is organized as follows[9]:

- Sector: 2-digit code
    - Subsector: 3-digit code
        - Industry Group: 4-digit code

[7] NAPCS structure. https://www.census.gov/eos/www/napcs/structure.html (Accessed: October 23, 2019).

[8] NAPCS versus NAICS. https://www.census.gov/programs-surveys/economic-census/guidance/understanding-napcs.html (Accessed: October 23, 2019).

[9] NAICS structure. https://www.census.gov/programs-surveys/economic-census/guidance/understanding-naics.html#par_textimage_0 (Accessed: October 23, 2019).

- NAICS Industry: 5-digit code
    - National Industry: 6-digit code.

Back to the question of why we use market value of these goods and services to calculate GDP. Why do we not just add up all the various goods and services produced? Take a simple example. Suppose that a fictional country produces only two goods—picnic benches and airplanes. Of course, there can be numerous kinds of planes and picnic benches. For the sake of simplicity, I will abstract here from the details of the kinds of picnic benches and the kinds of airplanes. Suppose that during 2010 this country produced ten picnic benches and ten airplanes. If we just add these two goods, we see that the economy produced 20 goods—10 picnic benches and 10 airplanes. Suppose now that during 2011 this country produced 11 picnic benches and nine airplanes. Adding the two again gives us a total of 20. This tells us that country's output has stayed the same. We know, however, that it takes a lot more resources to produce an airplane than it does to produce a picnic table. Just think about the person-hours that can go into the production of an airplane versus the production of a picnic bench. It may take years for highly skilled aero engineers to design an airplane that can fly safely. To design a picnic bench on which people can sit? Not so many. How do we deal with situation?

Prices of goods and services come to rescue. They provide us estimates of what goes into the production of one good versus the other. Yes, price of the same product can vary from time to time and place to place, but on average, prices are a pretty good indicator of what a good is worth. This is why I used the word "estimate."

I just checked the price of a picnic bench on Amazon. A 72-inch rectangle metal picnic table is about \$650 plus taxes.[10] The delivery is free. The price of a Boeing 737 ranges between \$89.1 million and \$134.9 million depending upon the configuration, according to the Boeing Website.[11] One could purchase about 155,000 picnic benches for the price of a Boeing 737—\$100,000,000/\$645 $\approx$ 155,000. Quite a bit of difference. This difference reflects the differences in the wages of workers, the differences in the material, the differences in machinery,

[10] Price of a picnic table. www.amazon.com (Accessed: October 28, 2019).

[11] Price of Boeing 737. http://www.boeing.com/company/about-bca/ (Accessed: October 28, 2019).

and so on, that is used to produce an airplane versus a picnic bench. There are millions of distinct parts that go into the production of airplanes and picnic benches, produced by millions of individuals across the globe. Comparing the value of picnic benches in terms of airplanes, and vice versa will be extremely difficult. Now think of all the various goods and services that a modern economy produces. It will almost be impossible to compare the value of one good in terms of another without the help of prices. Money helps us calculate the relative values of goods and services. So when we want to find out the output that an economy produces, we look at the market value, which is just the price of the product multiplied by its quantity.

Why do we only look at the market value of the final goods and services? Final good or service is the one that the end-consumer consumes. This is as opposed to the intermediate good or service—a good or service that is used in the production of the final good or service. The reason we use the values of only the final goods and services is that the value of the intermediate goods and services has already been accounted for in the value of the final goods and services. An example helps. Suppose you bought a new car, say a Ford, that was made in the United States during 2019 for $30,000. This car has numerous parts that have been built and put together by numerous workers. Suppose the price of the four tires that this car has is $700, and that these tires were also made in the United States during 2019. Should we add the price of tires and the price of car to the total value of goods and services produced in the United States during 2019? The answer is no. The price of tire, $700, has already been accounted for in the price of the car. If we were to add the price of the car *and* the price of tires, it would turn out to be $30,700 (= $30,000 + $700). If we were to do that, we would be double-counting the price of tires.

How do we define geographic boundary? According to the Bureau of Economic Analysis, geographic boundary "…cover[s] the 50 states, the District of Columbia, and U.S. military installations, embassies, and consulates abroad… [T]he U.S. territories, Puerto Rico, and the Northern Mariana Islands are also treated as part of the domestic economy."[12]

[12] Geographic boundary of the U.S. economy. https://www.bea.gov/system/files/2019-05/Chapter-2.pdf (Accessed: October 31, 2019).

Why do we have this restriction? This is because we are calculating the output of an economy. Using this method, we do not care who produced those goods and services. All we care about is whether or not those goods and services were produced within the United States. You could have bought a Toyota for $30,000 that was produced in a factory located in the United States and its value would have been included in the GDP of the United States for 2019.

And finally, why a given year? This is because we want to measure the amount of output in a given time period. While quarterly estimates are produced, usually it is a year over which estimates are produced. Here, the distinction between a stock variable and flow variable comes in handy. A stock variable is a variable that is measured at a point in time, whereas a flow variable is a variable that is measured over a period of time. A variable, by the way, is a measure that changes value from observation to observation. Your height is a stock variable. It is measured at a point in time. When someone asks you about your height and you answer it's 6 feet, you are done. You do not need to add more to the explanation for this answer to make sense. On the other hand, suppose someone asks you about your income and you say it's $2000, you are not done. For this answer to make sense, you have to add the time period over which it is measured. An income of $2000 per hour is not the same as an income of $2000 per year. (In case you were wondering, the median weekly earnings of a worker, 16 years of age or older and working full-time, in the United States during the third quarter of 2019 were $923.[13] Using these numbers and assuming that such a worker worked 52 weeks during the year, annual earnings of such a worker would be $47,996.)

GDP is a flow variable. During 2018, the GDP of the United States was $20,580.223 billion.[14] You have to attach a time period for this number to make sense.

There is another measure of the total output of an economy. It is called gross national product (GNP). It is defined as the market value of all the final goods and services produced by the factors of production owned by the residents of a country during a given time period. When we are calculating GNP, we do not care about where that output is produced.

[13] Median earnings. https://fred.stlouisfed.org/series/LES1252881500Q (Accessed: October 29, 2019).

[14] Nominal GDP of the US. https://fred.stlouisfed.org/series/GDPA (Accessed: October 29, 2019).

As long as the output is produced by the factors of production owned by the residents of a country, it is added to the GNP of that country. The Bureau of Economic Analysis defines US residents as[15]:

> ...individuals, governments, business enterprises, trusts, associations, nonprofit institutions, and similar organizations that have the center of their economic interest in the United States and that reside or expect to reside in the United States for 1 year or more. (For example, business enterprises residing in the United States include U.S. affiliates of foreign companies.) In addition, U.S. residents include all U.S. citizens who reside outside the United States for less than 1 year and U.S. citizens residing abroad for 1 year or more who meet one of the following criteria: owners or employees of U.S. business enterprises who reside abroad to further the enterprises' business and who intend to return within a reasonable period; U.S. government civilian and military employees and members of their immediate families; and students who attend foreign educational institutions.

Continuing with the example of Ford and Toyota. Suppose that Ford Motor Company has a plant in Japan. All the machines are owned by the US residents and all the workers are US residents. Suppose that during 2019 Ford produces $15,000,000 worth of cars. This amount will be added to the GNP of the United States. The same amount will be added to the GDP of Japan. Why? This is because when we are calculating GDP we do not care who produces the output. As long as it is produced within the geographic boundaries of a country, its market value is added to that country's GDP. By way of further clarifying the distinction between GDP and GNP, suppose Toyota Motor Company has a plant in the United States. Analogous to the Ford Motor Company, all the machines are owned by the Japanese residents and all the workers are Japanese residents. Suppose during 2019 it produces $14,000,000 worth of cars. This amount will be added to the GDP of the United States and the GNP of Japan.

Prior to 1991, GNP was the main measure of the total output of the US economy. Afterward, GNP was replaced by GDP to estimate the total output of the US economy. Because of this change, I will focus on GDP.

[15] The BEA definition of US resident. https://www.bea.gov/system/files/2019-05/Chapter-2.pdf (Accessed: October 31, 2019).

As mentioned above, in order to measure GDP we can use three approaches: We can sum up all the expenditures made by the end users on the purchases of goods and services; we can sum up all the incomes of the producers of these goods and services; or we can sum up the values added at each stage of production. Let me go over these three measures.

7.1.1.1 The Expenditure Approach

When we measure GDP by adding up all the expenditures made by end users on the goods and services purchased, we call this the expenditure approach. In the NIPAs, the Bureau of Economic Analysis divides the various expenditures into five main categories (Italics original).[16]

- *Personal consumption expenditures*, which measures the value of the goods and services purchased by, or on the behalf of, persons—that is, households, nonprofit institutions that primarily serve households, private noninsured welfare funds, and private trust funds.
- *Gross private fixed investment*, which measures additions and replacements to the stock of private fixed assets without deduction of depreciation. Nonresidential fixed investment measures investment by businesses and nonprofit institutions in nonresidential structures, equipment, and intellectual property products. Residential fixed investment measures investment by businesses and households in residential structures and equipment, primarily new construction of single-family and multifamily units.
- *Change in private inventories*, which measures the value of the change in the physical volume of inventories owned by private business over a specified period, valued in the average prices of that period.
- *Net exports of goods and services*, which is calculated as exports less imports. Exports consist of goods and services that are sold, given away, or otherwise transferred by US residents to foreign residents. Imports consist of goods and services that are sold, given away, or otherwise transferred by foreign residents to US residents.
- *Government consumption expenditures and gross investment*, which comprises two components. Current consumption expenditures consist of the spending by general government in order to produce and provide goods and services to the public. Gross investment consists of spending by both general government and government enterprises for fixed assets (structures, equipment, and intellectual

[16] Four main categories of expenditure in the NIPAs. https://www.bea.gov/system/files/2019-05/Chapter-2.pdf (Accessed: October 31, 2019).

property products) that benefit the public or that assist government agencies in their productive activities.

Take a look at net exports. These are exports minus imports. Why do we add exports and deduct imports? Recall that the purpose of calculating GDP is to figure out how much output was produced in an economy. The value of exports was not represented in the other categories—personal consumption expenditures, gross private fixed investment, change in private inventories, and government consumption expenditures and gross investment. So adding exports makes sense because these goods and services were produced in the domestic economy and sold to foreigners. Imports, by definition, are not produced in the domestic economy. But the expenditure on imported goods and services was added in these four categories. For instance, the expenditure on clothes is included in the personal consumption expenditure when we buy clothes that are made in other countries. When a rental car company purchases a car, say, made in Japan, the expenditure on this car is included in the gross private domestic investment. Similarly, when a state university purchases computers that are, say made in Singapore, the expenditure goes into the government expenditures and gross investment category. So we deduct imports from the total expenditure.

7.1.1.2 The Income Approach

A main lesson of economics is that expenditure on the part of one economic agent is income for another economic agent. Except for the statistical discrepancy that arises during the data collection, whether we add up all the expenditures or the incomes, the end result should be the same. This means that in calculating GDP we can either add up all the expenditures on the part of various economic agents or all the incomes of various economic agents, the result will be same. Measuring a country's output by adding up all the incomes of various economic agents is referred to as the income approach. This measure is also called the Gross Domestic Income (GDI).

As an example, when you purchased a $30,000 Ford in the above example, it is expenditure on your part and it is revenue on the part of the Ford Motor Company. A part of this $30,000 goes to workers as incomes, a part goes to the suppliers of the various parts that went into the production of the car, a part goes in the payment of taxes, a part goes to the shareholders as dividend, and so on.

The "GDI is equal to compensation of employees, plus taxes on production and imports less subsidies, plus net operating surplus, plus consumption of fixed capital."[17] It has the following components (Italics original).[18]

- *Compensation of employees*, which is the total remuneration of employees in return for their work. It consists of wages and salaries (primarily the monetary remuneration of employees) and supplements (employer contributions for employee pension and insurance funds and employer contributions for government social insurance).
- *Taxes on production and imports*, which consist of taxes payable on products when they are produced, delivered, sold, transferred, or otherwise disposed of by their producers (including federal excise taxes, customs duties, and state and local sales taxes) and of other taxes on production, such as taxes on ownership of assets used in production (including local real estate taxes). These taxes do not include taxes on income.
- *Subsidies*, which are subtracted in the calculation of GDI, are payments by government agencies to private business (for example, federal subsidies to farmers) and to government enterprises (for example, federal subsidies to state and local public housing authorities) to support their current operations.
- *Net operating surplus*, which is a profits-like measure that shows the incomes earned by private and government enterprises from current production before deducting any explicit or implicit interest charges, rent, or other property incomes payable on financial assets, land, or other natural resources required to carry out production. Net operating surplus plus consumption of fixed capital is equal to gross operating surplus.
- *Consumption of fixed capital*, which is the NIPA measure of economic depreciation—that is, the decline in the value of the stock of assets due to physical deterioration, normal obsolescence, and accidental damage except that caused by a catastrophic event.

[17] GDI. https://www.bea.gov/system/files/2019-05/Chapter-2.pdf (Accessed: October 31, 2019).

[18] GDI and its components in detail. https://www.bea.gov/system/files/2019-05/Chapter-2.pdf (Accessed: October 31, 2019).

The income approach in other words measures "the purchasing power of households and the financial status businesses."[19]

7.1.1.3 The Value-Added Approach

A third way to measure GDP is to add up the differences between the market values of all the intermediate goods and services—various engine parts, seats, body, tires, labor of workers, etc.—when they enter a stage of production and when they leave that stage of production. According to the Bureau of Economic Analysis, "the difference between an industry's gross output (sales or receipts plus other operating income and inventory change) and its intermediate inputs (goods and services that are used in production) [is value added by that industry]. When value added is aggregated across all industries in the economy, industry sales to and purchases from each other cancel out, and the remainder is industry sales to final users, or GDP."[20]

7.1.2 Nominal Versus Real GDP

When we talk about economic growth, we are talking about comparing current level of output with output levels of the yesteryears. However, when we calculated GDP, we used the market value, which meant using prices. We multiplied the quantity of the product produced during that year with the price of the product that prevailed during that year. As you know, prices change from year to year as do quantities of the goods and services produced. What matters for output growth comparisons over the years (and across countries) is how the quantities produced have changed. In calculating GDP when we take the effects of changes in prices of goods and services produced out, we get real GDP. In other words, real GDP is calculated in terms of goods and services, as opposed to in terms of the prices of goods and services. In the next subsection, I go into more detail about how to take the effects of changes in prices out of these calculations. Readers who are not interested in these details may skip this subsection.

[19] What the income approach measures. https://www.bea.gov/system/files/2019-05/Chapter-2.pdf (Accessed: October 31, 2019).

[20] The value-added approach. https://www.bea.gov/system/files/2019-05/Chapter-2.pdf (Accessed: October 31, 2019).

7.1.2.1 *Calculating Nominal and Real GDP*

Over the years, I have used this example in my Principles of Macroeconomics classes. It is simple but it gets the job done.

Suppose an economy is producing only two goods. Call them *Good A* and *Good B*. Suppose also that we are comparing the GDP of two years, *Year* 1 and *Year* 2. Recall that GDP is the market value of all the final goods and services produced in an economy during a given year. So the GDP of this economy in *Year* 1 will be $P_1 \times Q_1$, where P represents the price of a good at which it was sold, Q represents the quantity of the good that was produced in this economy, and the subscripts resent the year. Analogously, for *Year* 2 the GDP will be $P_2 \times Q_2$. In Table 7.1, I provide some numbers to make the example more concrete.

Table 7.1 has five rows and nine columns. The top row of Table 7.1 lists the column number. Column 1 has the goods produced, Column 2 lists the prices and quantities of each good produced during *Year* 1, Column 3 provides the market value of each good during *Year* 1, and the last row provides the sum of these market values. That is, the nominal GDP for *Year* 1. Columns 4 and 5 repeat this for *Year* 2. I will get back to Columns 6 through 9 shortly.

Our hypothetical economy produced five units of *Good A* and 11 units of *Good B* during *Year* 1. They were sold at $1 and $2, respectively. The market value of *Good A* is $5 and the market value of *Good B* is $22. When we add these market values, we get $27—Column 3, last row. This is ***nominal*** GDP of this economy during *Year* 1. We follow the same procedure and calculate nominal GDP for *Year* 2. These data are presented in Columns 4 and 5. The last row of Column 5 presents the nominal GDP for *Year* 2. It is $28.5.

Why do we call it ***nominal*** GDP? This is because we used that year's prices, i.e., current year's prices, to calculate the total market value.

Table 7.1 Calculating nominal and real GDP

[1]	*[2]* $P_1 \times Q_1$	*[3]*	*[4]* $P_2 \times Q_2$	*[5]*	*[6]* $P_1 \times Q_2$	*[7]*	*[8]* $P_2 \times Q_1$	*[9]*
Good A	$1 × 5	$5	$2 × 6	$12	$1 × 6	$6	$2 × 5	$10
Good B	$2 × 11	$22	$1.5 × 11	$16.5	$2 × 11	$22	$1.5 × 11	$16.5
Total		$27		$28.5		$28		$26.5

Table prepared by the author

Whenever we are calculating market value using current year's prices, the resulting GDP is in nominal terms. Calculating GDP using current year's prices and comparing the values across years may present a misleading picture. Take a look at Table 7.1, Columns 3 and 5. Notice that the values increased from \$27 in *Year* 1 to \$28.5 in *Year* 2. This increase of \$1.5, however, is a combination of changes in prices and changes in quantities—Columns 2 and 4. Note that the price as well as the quantity of *Good A* increased from *Year* 1 to *Year* 2. The price increased from \$1 per unit to \$2 per unit and the quantity increased from 5 units to 6 units. For *Good B* while the price decreased from \$2 per unit during *Year* 1 to \$1.5 during *Year* 2, the quantity of *Good B* stayed the same—11 units. The resulting increase in nominal GDP from *Year* 1 to *Year* 2 is about 5.56 percent $\left(\left[\frac{28.5-27}{27}\right] \times 100 \cong 5.56\right)$. This 5.56 percent increase from *Year* 1 to *Year* 2, however, is a combination of changes in quantities and changes in prices. In this situation, what we are concerned about is the changes in quantities, and not changes in prices. We want to take the effect of changes in prices out of this combined effect. How do we accomplish this?

One way to do this is to evaluate the quantities of both years in a given year's prices. This way the resulting changes in values, if any, will only reflect the changes in quantities. The year that we pick to evaluate quantities of various years is called the "base year," and this procedure of removing the effects of price changes is called the "fixed-weight procedure." Note that "weight" is the importance assigned to a variable. Using, again, the example that I have used in my classes, if an exam is worth 100 points and a homework assignment is worth 10 points, then the weight of a homework assignment is (1/10)th the weight of an exam. Put another way, an exam is ten times more important than a homework assignment when it comes to course grades. Prices serve as weights in a market economy. Prices tell us how much importance we assign to one product versus the other. If consumers are willing to pay \$10 for a unit of product A and \$20 for a unit of product B, then they are assigning twice as much weight to a unit of product B than to a unit of product A.

Suppose that we use *Year* 1 as base year. That is, we evaluate the quantities of *Good A* and *Good B* of both years—*Year* 1 and *Year* 2—using *Year* 1's prices. We have already evaluated *Year* 1's quantities using *Year* 1's prices—Column 2. The resulting total market value is \$27—Column 3, last row. This is our real GDP for *Year* 1. Curious reader may be wondering that this value was called nominal GDP earlier. What made it real GDP now? The answer lies in the fact that when we pick a year as base year—in this case *Year* 1—the resulting value becomes real GDP for that year. The rationale will become clear shortly.

Now let us evaluate the quantities of both goods—*Good A* and *Good B*—of *Year* 2 in *Year* 1's prices. Column 6 presents these calculations and Column 7, last row, presents the total market value of both goods evaluated in *Year* 1's prices, i.e., in base year's prices. It is \$28. This is the real GDP of *Year* 2. Note that subscripts on P and Q. The subscript on P is "1" and the subscript on Q is "2," indicating that the prices are those of *Year* 1, while the quantities are those of *Year* 2. Now compare \$27—Column 3, last row—with \$28—Column 7, last row. The resulting change of \$1 represents only the change in quantities. In percentage terms, the real GDP has increased from *Year* 1 to *Year* 2 by about 3.7 percent $\left(\left[\frac{28-27}{27}\right] \times 100 \cong 3.7\right)$. Why? Because while the quantities have changed, the prices have been kept the same. We have taken the effects of price changes out. This is also called real GDP in constant prices—in this case *Year* 1—in economic news and elsewhere.

There is nothing sacred about picking *Year* 1 as the base year. What if we were to pick *Year* 2 as the base year? Let us do just that. We have already evaluated Year 2's quantities using Year 2's prices—Columns 4 and 5. Using Year 2 as the base year, the real GDP of Year 2 is \$28.5. Recall that this was the value of nominal GDP of Year 2 earlier. How did it become the real GDP of Year 2? The rationale stays the same as when we picked *Year* 1 our base year and \$27 became the real GDP of *Year* 1—Column 3. Once we pick a year as our base year—in this case *Year* 2—the resulting value becomes the real GDP. Now we evaluate *Year* 1's quantities using *Year* 2's prices. I present these calculations in Column 8 and the total market value of both goods in Column 9, last row. The resulting value is \$26.5. This is the real GDP of *Year* 1 using *Year* 2 as the base year. Notice again the subscripts in Columns 4 and 8: Subscripts on P stay the same, while the subscripts on Q change. This indicates that we have evaluated the quantities of both years in *Year* 2's prices.

Let us now calculate the percentage change in real GDP between *Year* 1 and *Year* 2, using *Year* 2 as our base year. When we perform these calculations, we see that the real GDP has increased from *Year* 1 to *Year* 2 by about 7.55 percent $\left(\left[\frac{28.5-26.5}{26.5}\right] \times 100 \cong 7.55\right)$. This is a larger increase as compared with when we used *Year* 1 as our base year—3.7 percent.

In performing these calculations while we have taken the effects of price changes out, another issue has presented itself: Just by changing the base year, one can get a different result of the percentage change. Economists have a solution. It is called "Chain-Type Index." Here is the formula of the chain-type index.

$$Q_t^F = \sqrt{\frac{\sum_i^n p_{i,t-1}q_{i,t}}{\sum_i^n p_{i,t-1}q_{i,t-1}} \times \frac{\sum_i^n p_{i,t}q_{i,t}}{\sum_i^n p_{i,t}q_{i,t-1}}}$$

where
Q_t^F is Fisher Quantity Index.
$p_{i,t}$ is the price of the ith good/service at time t.
$q_{i,t}$ is the quantity if the ith good/service at time t.

The first quantity under the root sign is called Laspeyres Index and the second quantity is called the Paasche Index. The Bureau of Economic Analysis (BEA) provides a detailed discussion along with examples of a chain-type quantity index.[21] I abstract from these details here and I refer the curious reader to the BEA's website.

I have used the term "index" in the previous discussion. What is an index? An index is a value assigned to a variable or a group of variables. Usually, the value assigned is either 1 or 100. One can, however, assign any value one pleases. The year to whose total market value of the final goods and services we assign a value of 1 or 100 is called the index year. Again, an example may be helpful. To this end, let us use the values of Table 7.1 and calculate a quantity index for real GDP. We continue to assume that the base year is *Year* 1. Furthermore, assume that *Year* 1 is also the index year. That is, we assign the value of 100 to *Year* 1's total market value of final goods and services. Here are the calculations.

Nominal GDP Year 1 = 27
Real GDP Year 1 = 27
Nominal GDP Year 2 = 28.5
Real GDP Year 2 = 28

$$\text{Real GDP Quantity Index for } Year\ 1 = \left(\frac{\text{Total Market Value } Year\,1}{\text{Total Market Value Index Year}}\right)$$

[21] Chain-type quantity index. https://www.bea.gov/system/files/2019-05/Chapter-4.pdf (Accessed: November 6, 2019).

$$\times 100 = \left(\frac{27}{27}\right) \times 100 = 100$$

$$\text{Real GDP Quantity Index for } Year\ 2 = \left(\frac{\text{Total Market Value } Year\ 2}{\text{Total Market Value Index Year}}\right)$$

$$\times 100 = \left(\frac{28}{27}\right) \times 100 \cong 103.7$$

One benefit of creating an index is that it makes comparing values over the years a lot easier. While in this case the calculations are easy to remember, 27, 28, etc., it becomes hard rather quickly when we are dealing with trillions of dollars. To cite just one example, the nominal GDP of the United States during the 3rd quarter of 2019 was 21,525.8 billion dollars.[22]

Note that the index value of *Year* 1 is 100. It turned out so because we multiplied the quantity (27/27) by 100. I could have multiplied it by any number, or not multiplied it by any number at all. This procedure, however, makes it easier to compare across years. Note also that the index value of *Year* 2 is 103.7. Subtract *Year* 1's value from Year 2's value and we get 3.7 (= 103 – 100). This represents the percentage change in real GDP from *Year* 1 to *Year* 2. It is the same value that we arrived at earlier, repeated here for the ease of the reader $\left(\left[\frac{28-27}{27}\right] \times 100 \cong 3.7\right)$. This, however, is a lot easier than calculating percentage change.

Just as an example, in Table 7.2 I present real GDP Index and real GDP data. Real GDP data are 2012 chained-dollars. The value of the index has been set to 100 for 2012. The data source is the Bureau of Economic Analysis.[23]

Notice the ease with which one can calculate percentage change between two values using the index values versus using the actual data.

7.1.3 *GDP Deflator and Consumer Price Index: Measures of Aggregate Price Level*

Now that we have an understanding of nominal and real GDP, calculating a measure of aggregate price level follows directly. Two measures

[22] Nominal GDP of the United States during the 3rd quarter of 2019. https://apps.bea.gov/iTable/iTable.cfm?reqid=19&step=2#reqid=19&step=2&isuri=1&1921=survey (Accessed: November 6, 2019).

[23] GDP Index and GDP data source. www.bea.gov (Accessed: November 7, 2019).

Table 7.2 Real GDP Index and Real GDP

[1] *Year*	*[2]* *Real GDP Index*	*[3]* *Real GDP*
2000	81.07	13131
2001	81.88	13262.1
2002	83.306	13493.1
2003	85.689	13879.1
2004	88.945	14406.4
2005	92.07	14912.5
2006	94.698	15338.3
2007	96.475	15626
2008	96.343	15604.7
2009	93.899	15208.8
2010	96.306	15598.8
2011	97.8	15840.7
2012	100	16197
2013	101.842	16495.4
2014	104.415	16912
2015	107.451	17403.8
2016	109.211	17688.9
2017	111.799	18108.1
2018	115.072	18638.2

Table prepared by the author. Data: Real GDP Index (2012 = 100). Real GDP is in billions of 2012 chained US dollars. *Data Source* US Bureau of Economic Analysis. www.bea.gov (Accessed: November 7, 2019)

of aggregate price level are the most common. One is the GDP deflator and the other is Consumer Price Index (CPI).

In order to calculate GDP deflator, all one needs is to divide the nominal GDP by the real GDP. The following equation presents the GDP deflator:

$$GDPDeflator = \left(\frac{NominalGDP}{RealGDP}\right) \times 100$$

I have multiplied the ratio of nominal and real GDP by 100 to get rid of decimal places.

GDP deflator gets its name from the fact that one can get real GDP by dividing the nominal GDP by the GDP deflator—it "deflates" the nominal GDP. One can see this by bringing real GDP to the left side of this equation and GDP deflator to the right side of the equation.

Consumer Price Index (CPI) provides similar information with a few exceptions. It is defined as the value of the market basket of goods and services that a typical urban consumer consumes. Since it deals with a typical urban consumer, the CPI will include expenditure on dog food but not on horse feed. CPI will include expenditure on a car but not on a tractor, just to cite a couple of examples.

Recall that GDP is the market value of all the final goods and services produced within the geographic boundaries of an economy. As we know, however, any modern economy buys goods and services from other countries and sells goods and services to other countries. In fact, when we used the expenditure approach to calculate GDP, we deducted expenditures on imported goods and services. Since a typical urban consumer spends on goods and services made in other countries, the CPI includes expenditure on foreign-made goods and services, whereas GDP deflator does not.

The agency that prepares this measure and publishes is the Bureau of Labor Statistics (BLS). The Bureau publishes these data on a monthly basis.

There are three measures of consumer expenditure that the BLS prepares and publishes. The main one is CPI-U. The CPI-U measures the expenditures made by urban consumers—"U" stands for urban. According to the BLS[24]:

> [T]he CPI-U (all-urban) population consists of all urban households in Metropolitan Statistical Areas (MSAs) and in urban places of 2,500 inhabitants or more. Nonfarm consumers living in rural areas within MSAs are included, but the index excludes rural nonmetropolitan consumers and the military and the institutional population.

Then, there is the CPI-W. This is the "CPI for Urban Wage Earners and Clerical Workers," and according to the BLS[25]:

> The urban wage earner and clerical worker (CPI-W) population consists of consumer units with clerical workers, sales workers, protective and other service workers, laborers, or construction workers. More than one-half of

[24] CPI-U definition. https://www.bls.gov/opub/hom/pdf/cpihom.pdf (Accessed: November 8, 2019).

[25] CPI-W definition. https://www.bls.gov/opub/hom/pdf/cpihom.pdf (Accessed: November 8, 2019).

> the consumer unit's income has to be earned from these occupations, and at least one of the members must be employed for 37 weeks or more in an eligible occupation.

Note that in constructing these CPIs, we pick quantities of the various goods and services and see how much they cost and how much the cost changes from one time period to the next. In other words, quantities serve as weights. These measures of price level use a fixed-weight procedure. The items and their quantities that go into the basket of goods and services that a typical urban consumer consumes change only periodically—every five years. This creates similar issues to those that we encountered when we constructed the GDP quantity index using the fixed-weight procedure. To overcome those issues, we used the chain-type index. To overcome these issues, the BLS has created "Chained CPI for All Urban Consumers (C-CPI-U)." The BLS notes that the Bureau[26]:

> began publishing this series in August 2002 with data beginning in January 2000. The prices used in the C-CPI-U are the same as those used to produce the CPI-U and CPI-W, but the C-CPI-U uses a different formula and different weights to combine basic indexes. The formula used in the C-CPI-U accounts for consumers' ability to achieve the same standard of living from alternative sets of consumer goods and services. This formula requires consumer spending data that are not immediately available.

The Bureau further creates finer subcategories of the market basket of goods and services consumed by urban consumers and publishes those measures. Some examples include dividing consumer expenditure by region, by goods, by services, and so on.[27] The price level data collected and published by the BLS are not limited only to those of consumer goods and services. BLS published data on the prices that producers pay for their inputs. These indices are called, you guessed it, producer price indices (PPIs). I will not go further into details about PPIs. Going into more detail about the numerous PPIs that the Bureau constructs will lead us too far from the main topic.

[26] Chained CPI definition. https://www.bls.gov/opub/hom/pdf/cpihom.pdf (Accessed: November 8, 2019).

[27] Categories of CPI. www.bls.gov (Accessed: November 8, 2019).

7.1.4 Some Concerns About GDP Calculations

GDP by no means perfectly captures the economic activity of the economy. By definition, GDP measures the market value of goods and services. It leaves out goods and services that are not traded in the market and if traded, are not legally traded. These include household production and illegal activities—illegal drug trades, illegal prostitution, activities undertaken to avoid taxes, etc.

Nor is it a measure of happiness. Here is an example. Suppose someone is working long hours and is earning $200,000 per year. The person, however, does not have much time left family, friends, and other leisurely activities. The long hours are causing the person a lot of stress. She/he decides to cut back on hours. This leads the annual income to drop to $150,000. Now, however, she/he can spend more time with family and friends, and is feeling happier. Earlier, the person was eating out and now they are preparing meals at home. Expenditures on restaurant meals were included in the calculation of GDP, and the value of time and effort spent on preparing meals at home is not included. While the happiness level of the person has likely increased, the GDP of the country has decreased.

There have been efforts to measure happiness and include these measures in the calculations of GDP. Joseph E. Stiglitz, Joseph E., Amartya Sen, and Jean-Paul Fitoussi, in their 2010 book, *Mismeasuring Our Lives: Why GDP Doesn't Add Up*,[28] take a look at the issues involved, present examples of the few countries that have tried to incorporate happiness measures into the calculation of GDP, and suggest solutions. These methods of calculating GDP, however, have not become mainstream.

Flawed GDP as a measure of an economy's output may be, it remains extremely useful. Almost every country, certainly every country that has a functional government, utilizes this measure to estimate its aggregate output and income. We have Simon Kuznets and Richard Stone to thank for their work. Their meticulous efforts to conceptualize, and accumulate and compile data on national income and output—Kuznets for the United States and Stone for the United Kingdom—in the early 1930s led to the

[28] Including happiness measures into the calculation of GDP. Joseph E. Stiglitz, Amartya Sen, and Jean-Paul Fitoussi. *Mismeasuring Our Lives: Why GDP Doesn't Add Up*. New York, NY: The New Press, 2010. Print.

creation of aggregate measures of national output.[29] Both Simon Kuznets and Richard Stone were awarded the Nobel Memorial Prize in Economic Sciences—Kuznets in 1971, Stone in 1984—for their many contributions to economics.[30]

I conclude this subsection by reminding that underlying these calculations is the concept of money. It is the concept of money that helps us calculate and compare the total output of an economy.

7.2 Factors Affecting Economic Growth

Data show a wide range of income levels—over time as well as among countries. The economist Angus Maddison (1926–2010)[31] compiled data on GDP per capita and other vital economic variables going back to year 1. Yes, 1 AD! A feat that only love of the subject can justify and accomplish. Of course, there weren't any government records of GDP at the time. As we saw earlier, it was only since the early 1930 that governments started collecting data on income in a systematic way. Indeed, the countries that exist today did not even exist. It is more accurate to state that these data represent the regions that are now called by various country names. Maddison compiled estimates of these data using various sources ranging from archeology to biology.

Table 7.3 shows per capita GDP data for 30 countries for the year 1 AD for which these estimates are available in the Maddison database. Table 7.3 also shows data for the year 2008 AD for the same set of countries. This helps us compare how GDP per capita has changed over the past two thousand plus years.

[29] Simon Kuznets' and Richard Stone's work on measuring GDP. https://www.bea.gov/sites/default/files/methodologies/jep_spring2008.pdf. See also, https://www.nber.org/chapters/c9338.pdf (Accessed: November 7, 2019).

[30] Simon Kuznets and Richard Stone, Nobel Prize in Economic Sciences. https://www.nobelprize.org/prizes/economic-sciences/1971/kuznets/facts/; https://www.nobelprize.org/prizes/economic-sciences/1984/stone/facts/ (Accessed: November 7, 2019).

[31] Angus Maddison. http://www.ggdc.net/maddison/oriindex.htm (Accessed: November 14, 2019).

Table 7.3 Per capita GDP (1990 International Geary-Khamis dollars), 1 AD and 2008 AD

[1] Country	*[2] 1 AD*	*[3] 2008 AD*	*[4] Country*	*[5] 1 AD*	*[6] 2008 AD*	*[7] Country*	*[8] 1 AD*	*[9] 2008 AD*
Austria	425	24,131	Switzerland	425	25,104	India	450	2975
Belgium	450	23,655	United Kingdom	400	23,742	Japan	400	22,816
Denmark	400	24,621	Greece	550	16,362	Iran	500	6944
Finland	400	24,344	Portugal	450	14,436	Iraq	500	1049
France	473	22,223	Spain	498	19,706	Turkey	550	8066
Germany	408	20,801	Australia	400	25,301	Algeria	450	3520
Italy	809	19,909	Canada	400	25,267	Egypt	600	3725
Netherlands	425	24,695	United States	400	31,178	Libya	550	2994
Norway	400	28,500	Mexico	400	7979	Morocco	450	3465
Sweden	400	24,409	China	450	6725	Tunisia	550	6103

Table prepared by the author. *Data Source* Angus Maddison database. http://www.ggdc.net/maddison/oriindex.htm (Accessed: November 14, 2019)

The data in Table 7.3 are in 1990 International Geary-Khamis dollars.[32] This is a method of converting currencies of various countries into a comparable measure. It uses not only the exchange rate data but also, what is called the "Purchasing Power Parity." I will go into more detail in the next chapter where I talk about the role that money has played on the international stage. For now, suffice it to say that this measure converts the currencies of various countries into an international measure such that comparisons can be made.

A few points stand out. First, during 1 AD, the region now called Italy had the highest GDP per capita—809 International Geary-Khamis dollars—and the regions now called the United States, Canada, the United Kingdom, among others had the lowest GDP per capita—400 International Geary-Khamis dollars. In fact, Italy was an outlier. Twenty-two of the 30 countries for which data are presented here were clustered at the lower end of the distribution with per capita GDPs between 400

[32] For the Geary-Khamis method, see, for instance, D. S. Prasada Rao and E. A. Selvanathan. "Computation of Standard Errors for Geary-Khamis Parities and International Prices: A Stochastic Approach." *Journal of Business & Economic Statistics* 10.1 (1992): 109–15. *JSTOR*. Web.

and 498 International Geary-Khamis dollars. The mean GDP per capita for these 30 countries was 465.5 with a standard deviation of 84.28.

If we were to divide these 30 countries into five groups, from the poorest to the richest, we see that 22 countries fall into the poorest bin. For the ease of exposition, I will call these countries "very poor" in the discussion that follows in this subsection. Figure 7.1 plots the distribution of GDP per capita for the year 1 AD.

Now let us look at the 2008 data in Table 7.3. Not surprisingly, a lot has changed over the past two thousand plus years. First note that GDP per capita of the countries in the data has increased significantly. Most of the countries during 1 AD were very poor in absolute as well as in relative terms. We can make these statements because the GDPs are measured in the same unit for both years—1990 International Geary-Khamis dollars. Another point worth making is that some countries that had the lowest GDP per capita in 1 AD now have the highest GDP per capita. These include, most notably, the United States. In 1 AD, the region now called the United States had the lowest GDP per capita—400—and now has

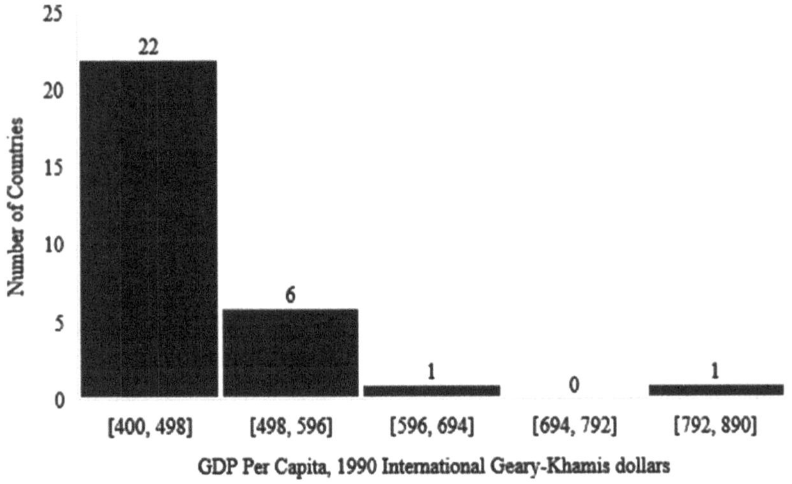

Fig. 7.1 Per capita GDP (1990 International Geary-Khamis dollars), 1 AD (Figure prepared by the author. *Data Source* Angus Maddison database. http://www.ggdc.net/maddison/oriindex.htm [Accessed: November 14, 2019])

the highest GDP per capita—31,178—both values in 1990 International Geary-Khamis dollars.

Again, if we were to divide these 30 countries into five bins, from the poorest to the richest, we find that only nine countries fall in the poorest bin. Figure 7.2 plots these data.

Note that the distribution of GDP per capita in 2008 in Fig. 7.2 is not left-skewed as that of GDP per capita in 1 AD in Fig. 7.1. There were 22 countries that fell into the left-most bin of the histogram graph during 1 AD. Their GDP per capita ranged between 400 and 498. In 2008, there were nine countries that fell in the left-most bin of the histogram graph. Their GDP per capita ranged between 1049 and 7075. Most countries fell in the right-hand side of the distribution. Thirteen countries fell in the fourth bin with GDP per capita ranging between 19,126 and 25,152. Four countries fell in the fifth bin on the right-hand side of the distribution. Their GDP per capita ranged between 25,152.1 and 31,178. The mean GDP per capita for these 30 countries during 2008 was 19,491.47 with a standard deviation of 9,592.62. These figures show that the residents of all the regions of the world are far better off than they were in

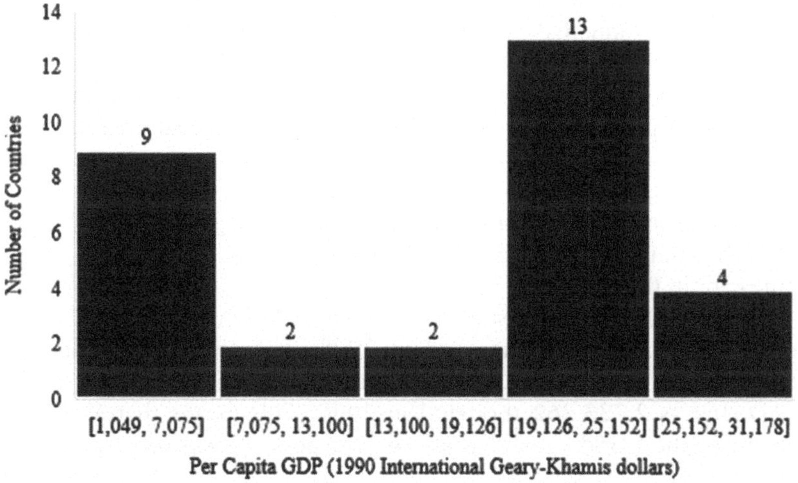

Fig. 7.2 Per capita GDP (1990 International Geary-Khamis dollars), 2008 AD (Figure prepared by the author. Data Source: Angus Maddison database. http://www.ggdc.net/maddison/oriindex.htm [Accessed: November 14, 2019])

Table 7.4 Populations (in 000) of the very poor countries in 1 AD and 2008 AD

[1]	[2]	[3]	[4]	[5]	[6]
Poorest Countries in 1 AD				*Poorest Countries in 2008 AD*	
Country	*Population*	*Country*	*Population*	*Country*	*Population*
Austria	500	Portugal	400	China	1,324,786
Belgium	300	Spain	3750	India	1,147,996
Denmark	180	Australia	360	Iran	65,875
Finland	20	Canada	80	Iraq	28,221
France	5000	United States	680	Algeria	33,770
Germany	3000	Mexico	2200	Egypt	81,714
Netherlands	200	China	59,600	Libya	6174
Norway	100	India	75,000	Morocco	34,343
Sweden	200	Japan	3000	Tunisia	10,384
Switzerland	300	Algeria	2000		
United Kingdom	800	Morocco	1000		

Table prepared by the author. *Data Source* Angus Maddison database. http://www.ggdc.net/maddison/oriindex.htm (Accessed: November 14, 2019)

year 1 AD. Not only that most residents are far better off in relative terms as well. (All values are in 1990 International Geary-Khamis dollars.)

Another way to slice the data is to look at the percentage of population that was very poor in 1 AD versus the percentage of population that was very poor in 2008. Table 7.4 provides population estimates of various countries in 1 AD as well as in 2008 AD that were very poor. These countries fell in the left-most bin of the histogram diagrams (Figs. 7.1 and 7.2). The source of these estimates is, again, Angus Maddison.[33] These figures are in 000s.

During 1 AD, the total estimated world population was 225,820 thousand. It was 6,694,832 thousand in 2008. The estimated population of world's poorest countries—22 countries—was 158,670 thousand in 1 AD. It was 2,733,262 thousand in 2008. This means that about 73 percent of the world's population was very poor. The percentage of the

[33] The Angus Maddison database. http://www.ggdc.net/maddison/oriindex.htm (Accessed: November 14, 2019).

very poor in 2008 was about 41 percent. Most of the population has much higher living standards, both in absolute terms and in relative terms.

I would like to mention here that for one to improve one's lot, one has to be able to evaluate where one stands. To measure and compare the GDPs of the 30 countries that we looked at in this subsection, we used the 1990 International Geary-Khamis dollars. We used the 1990 International Geary-Khamis dollars as a yardstick. Without this yardstick, we would not have been able to compare and contrast the lots of these countries. That is, we used money. Remember again what money is. It is a medium of exchange, it is a unit of account, and it is a store of value. Here, the "unit of account" feature came in handy.

What made some poor countries escape poverty? What factors led to some countries that were rich in 1 AD become poor over time? Why have some countries not been able to escape poverty? Is it the people? Is it the geography? Is it the natural resources? Is it the institutions? Ever since the dawn of the subject of economics, starting at least with Adam Smith's *An Inquiry into the Nature and Causes of the Wealth of Nations*,[34] scholars have tried to find out reasons behind the differences in the prosperity levels of countries. Now I turn to this question. In this regard, I will discuss four main factors. These include technology, specialization and trade, human capital, and institutions.

7.2.1 Technology

As we saw in Chapter 4, technology is defined as the pool of knowledge, our formulae, and our recipes of how to combine various inputs so that various outputs can be produced. Technology, then, refers to our understanding of how the universe works. It is true that when we think of technology the images of cellphones, computers, and all things Internet pop up in our minds. At the base of it all, however, is our understanding of combining various inputs to produce output. Take the example of a computer. At its very basic level, it is silicon, petrochemicals, metal, and other minerals. What makes these rather uninteresting ingredients into computers that are used in everything from satellites to Tesla Roadster starting at $200,000 which accelerates from zero to 60 miles per hour

[34] Adam Smith. *An Inquiry into the Nature and Causes of the Wealth of Nations*. Ed. Edwin Cannan. 1994th ed. New York: Random House, Inc., 1776. Print.

in 1.9 seconds,[35] an earlier model of which Elon Musk, the founder of SpaceX,[36] sent to space on a rocket controlled by computers,[37] is our understanding of how to combine these ingredients.

When we talk about technological advancement, what we are referring to is the addition to our pool of knowledge. That is, having a better understanding of how to combine various ingredients such that machines run faster and more efficiently. The study of the effects of technological progress on the economy goes back to at least Adam Smith and David Ricardo,[38] who, in turn, benefited from the ideas of the Enlightenment philosophers who came before them.[39]

A question arises: How is this pool of knowledge created, expanded, and improved upon? Curiosity seems to be the main reason. Yes, financial incentives play a crucial role, but at the heart of it all is the desire to know how the universe works. This curiosity could be driven by just the desire to know how it all works, or it could be guided by the desire to improve the lots of fellow animals—human and non-human. Indeed, this was the view of the sixteenth-century philosopher Francis Bacon (1561–1626).[40] According to Joel Mokyr (2005), Bacon was of the view that "[T]he main purpose of knowledge was to improve mankind's condition rather

[35] Tesla price and acceleration. https://www.tesla.com/roadster (Accessed: November 18, 2019).

[36] Elon Musk, the founder of SpaceX. https://www.spacex.com/about (Accessed: November 18, 2019).

[37] Elon Musk sent his Tesla Roadster to space. https://www.businessinsider.com/elon-musk-tesla-roadster-space-spacex-orbit-2019-2; https://time.com/5136400/spacex-elon-musk-tesla-space/; and https://twitter.com/elonmusk/status/936782477502246912 (Accessed: November 18, 2019).

[38] History of the study of technological progress. Heinz D. Kurz. "Technical Progress, Capital Accumulation and Income Distribution in Classical Economics: Adam Smith, David Ricardo and Karl Marx." *The European Journal of the History of Economic Thought* 17.5 (2010): 1183–222. Web.

[39] The ideas of the Enlightenment philosophers affecting the thinking of Smith and Ricardo. Joel Mokyr. "The Intellectual Origins of Modern Economic Growth." *The Journal of Economic History* 65.2 (2005): 285–351. Web.

[40] Francis Bacon. *The Stanford Encyclopedia of Philosophy* (Winter 2012 Edition), Edward N. Zalta (ed.). https://plato.stanford.edu/archives/win2012/entries/francis-bacon/ (Accessed: November 19, 2019).

Table 7.5 Research and development expenditure as a percent of GDP

[1] *Country/Entity*	*[2]* *Percent of GDP*
People's Republic of China	2.15
European Union (28 countries)	1.97
Germany	3.04
Israel	4.55
OECD Countries	2.37
United Kingdom	1.66
United States	2.79

Table created by the author. *Data Source* OECD (2019), Gross domestic spending on R&D (indicator). https://doi.org/10.1787/d8b068b4-en (Accessed: November 19, 2019)

than the mere satisfaction of that most creative of human characteristics, curiosity" (p. 293).[41]

Often individuals, firms, and governments make concerted efforts to acquire knowledge. These efforts can take the form of research and development. Just as an example in Table 7.5, I present data on expenditure on research and development as percentage of GDP by People's Republic of China, Germany, Israel, the European Union countries, the OECD countries, the United Kingdom, and the United States.

Sometimes these increases in the knowledge pool are more or less serendipitous. You are building widgets and discover a better way to accomplish your task. The economist Kenneth Arrow (1921–2017) called it "learning-by-doing."[42] Whatever the source of knowledge or the motivation behind its acquisition, knowledge has important implications for economic growth: Increases in knowledge increase economic growth.[43]

[41] Joel Mokyr on Francis Bacon. Joel Mokyr. "The Intellectual Origins of Modern Economic Growth." *The Journal of Economic History* 65.2 (2005): 285–351. Web.

[42] Arrow on learning-by-doing. Kenneth J. Arrow. "The Economic Implications of Learning by Doing." *The Review of Economic Studies* 29.3 (1962): 155–73. Web.

[43] Knowledge increases economic growth. N. Gregory Mankiw, David Romer, and David N. Weil. "A Contribution to the Empirics of Economic Growth." *The Quarterly Journal of Economics* 107.2 (1992): 407–37. Web, Ben S. Bernanke and Refet S. Gurkaynak. "Is Growth Exogenous? Taking Mankiw, Romer and Weil Seriously." *NBER Chapters in: NBER Macroeconomics Annual 2001 (Working Paper 8365)* 16.July (2001): 11–72. Print, Arrow: 155–73, Paul M. Romer. "Endogenous Technological Change." *Journal of Political Economy* 98.5, Part 2: The Problem of Development: A Conference

7.2.2 *Specialization and Trade*

We have known at least since the 1700s that specialization increases output,[44] and that when economic agents specialize and trade takes place, all trading parties benefit. David Ricardo (1772–1823) emphasized the benefits of trade. Ricardo's theories are still being hotly debated, a testament to the longevity of his ideas.[45] Ricardo argued that when economic agents specialized and traded with others, all trading parties benefited. Restrictions on trade, Ricardo argued, reduced the overall welfare of countries. But how does an economic agent know in which product to specialize? A deeper understanding of two fundamental concepts—absolute advantage and comparative advantage—is essential to answer this question.

When an economic agent can produce a good or service at a lower opportunity cost than the other economic agent, then the first economic agent is said to have a comparative advantage in the production of that good or service. And opportunity cost is what we give up to get something. It is the next best alternative forgone. On the other hand, when an economic agent is better at producing a good or service at a lower absolute cost, it is said to have absolute advantage. Another way to put this is to say that when an economic agent can produce a good or service at a lower absolute cost, it is said to have an absolute advantage in the production of that product. What matters for specialization and trade to take place is comparative advantage.

An example will help. Suppose there are two countries, say *Country A* and *Country B*. Suppose also that both countries need and produce *Product X* and *Product Y*. When *Country A* uses all its resources in an

of the Institute for the Study of Free Enterprise Systems (1990a): S71–S102. Web, Paul M. Romer. "Growth Based on Increasing Returns Due to Specialization." *The American Economic Review* 77.2, Papers and Proceedings of the Ninety-Ninth Annual Meeting of the American Economic Association (1987): 56–62. Web, Robert J. Barro and Zavier Sala-I-Martin. *Economic Growth*. New York: McGraw-Hill, 1995. Print.

[44] Benefits of specialization. Smith.

[45] Tests of David Ricardo's theories. Timothy Davis. "David Ricardo, Financier and Empirical Economist." *European Journal of the History of Economic Thought* 9.1 (2002): 1–16. Web, Kalim Siddiqui. "David Ricardo's Comparative Advantage and Developing Countries: Myth and Reality." *International Critical Thought* 8.3 (2018): 426–52. Web, Kurz: 1183–222, Heinz D. Kurz. "David Ricardo: On the Art of 'Elucidating Economic Principles' in the Face of a 'Labyrinth of Difficulties'." *European Journal of the History of Economic Thought* 22.5 (2015): 818–51. Web.

efficient manner (i.e., without any wastage) on the production of *Product X*, it can produce 50 units of *Product X*, and when it uses all its resources on the production of *Product Y* in an efficient manner, it can produce 50 units of *Product Y*.

Analogously, when *Country B* uses all its resources in an efficient manner on the production of *Product X*, it can produce 40 units of *Product X*, and when it uses all its resources in an efficient manner on the production of *Product Y*, it can produce 30 units of *Product Y*. Let us put these data in the form of a table, Table 7.6.

Just looking at the data, it seems like that *Country A* is better at producing both products. Should *Country A* even bother to trade with *Country B*?

In this example, *Country A* has an absolute advantage in the production of both *Product X* and *Product Y*. This is because it can produce more quantities of both goods. Which country has ***comparative advantage*** in the production of which product? To answer this question, we need to calculate opportunity cost of each product for both countries.

Calculating opportunity cost is simple. All one has to do is to figure out how much of a good or service one has to give up in order to produce another good or service. We do this kind of calculation several times a day. Suppose you can buy two identical shirts for $100. Then, the opportunity cost of each shirt is $50. Why? Because you had to give up $50 to buy one shirt. In this case, we are calculating the opportunity cost of a shirt in terms of dollars. That is:

$$Opportunity\ cost\ of\ a\ shirt\ in\ terms\ of\ dollars = \frac{Dollars}{Shirts} = \frac{\$100}{2\,shirts} = \$50\ per\ shirt$$

Table 7.6 Production of products X and Y by countries A and B

[1]	[2] Country A	[3] Country B
Product X	50 units	40 units
Product Y	50 units	30 units

Table prepared by the author

We can do similar calculations for each country and each product in our example. Let us start with *Country A*.

Calculating Opportunity Cost for *Country A*

$$Opportunity\ cost\ of\ producing\ one\ unit\ of\ Product\ X\ in terms\ of\ Product\ Y$$

$$= \frac{Units of\ Product Y}{Units\ of\ Product\ X} = \frac{50_Y}{50_X} = 1\ unit\ of\ Product\ Y per\ unit\ of\ Product\ X$$

$$Opportunity\ cost\ of\ producing\ one\ unit\ of\ Product\ Y\ in\ terms\ of\ Product\ X$$

$$= \frac{Units\ of\ Product\ X}{Units\ of\ Product\ Y} = \frac{50_X}{50_Y} = 1\ unit\ of\ Product\ X\ per\ unit\ of\ Product\ Y$$

The subscripts—50_X, 50_Y—refer to the number of units of the *Product X* and *Product Y*, respectively.

What these calculations tell us that when *Country A* uses all of its resources in an efficient manner to produce a unit of *Product X*, it has to give up one unit of *Product Y*. And when *Country A* uses all of its resources in an efficient manner to produce a unit of *Product Y*, it has to give up one unit of *Product X*.

Let us now perform similar calculations for *Country B*.

Calculating Opportunity Cost for *Country B*

$$Opportunity\ cost\ of\ producing\ one\ unit\ of\ Product\ X\ in\ terms\ of\ Product\ Y$$

$$= \frac{Units\ of\ Product\ Y}{Units\ of\ Product\ X}$$

$$= \frac{30_Y}{40_X} = 0.75\ unit\ of\ Product\ Y\ per\ unit\ of\ Product\ X$$

$$Opportunity\ cost\ of\ producing\ one\ unit\ of\ Product\ Y\ in\ terms\ of\ Product\ X$$

$$= \frac{Units\ of\ Product\ X}{Units\ of\ Product\ Y}$$

$$= \frac{40_X}{30_Y} = 1.33\ units\ of\ Product\ X\ per\ unit\ of\ Product\ Y$$

Again, the subscripts—40_X, 30_Y—refer to the number of units of the *Product X* and *Product Y*, respectively.

These calculations tell us that for *Country B* to produce each unit of *Product X*, it has to give up 0.75 units of *Product Y*. On the other hand, it has to give up 1.33 units of *Product X* when it produces one unit of *Product Y*.

Now compare the opportunity costs of producing *Product X* for *Country A* and *Country B*. Notice that *Country A* has to give up one unit of *Product Y* when it produces *Product X*. When *Country B* produces *Product X*, it has to give up only 0.75 units of *Product Y*. That is, it is cheaper for *Country B* to produce *Product X* than it is for *Country A* to produce *Product X*—one unit of *Product Y* for *Country A* versus 0.75 units of *Product Y* for *Country B*. This means that *Country B* has a comparative advantage in the production of *Product X*. The theory of comparative advantage tells us that *Country B* should specialize in the production of *Product X*; *Country B* has a lower opportunity cost of producing *Product X* as compared with *Country A*.

In a two-product two-country example such as this, once we have calculated comparative advantage of one economic agent, the other economic agent has a comparative advantage in the production of the other product. In this example, *Country A* has a comparative advantage in the production of *Product Y*.

We can see this by looking at the opportunity costs of *Country A* versus *Country B* of producing *Product X* as well. Note that when *Country A* produces *Product X*, it has to give up one unit of *Product Y*. Compare this to the opportunity cost of producing *Product X* for *Country B*—*Country B* has to give up 1.33 units of *Product Y* when it produces one unit of *Product X*.

Since both countries want both products and they have different opportunity costs of producing these products, there are opportunities for trade. For *Country A* to produce one unit of *Product X*, it has to give up one unit of *Product Y*. As long as *Country A* can purchase *Product X* for any amount less than one unit of *Product Y*, it is better off. For *Country B* to produce one unit of *Product X*, it has to give up 0.75 units of *Product Y*. As long as *Country B* can sell *Product X* for any amount more than 0.75 units of *Product Y*, it is better off.

Analogously, for *Country A* to produce one unit of *Product Y*, it has to give up one unit of *Product X*. For *Country B* to produce one unit of *Product Y*, it has to give up 1.33 units of *Product X*. As long as *Country B* can purchase *Product Y* for any amount less than 1.33 units of *Product X*, it is better off. And as long as *Country A* can sell *Product Y* for any amount greater than one unit of *Product X*—its opportunity cost of producing *Product X*—it is better off.

At the risk of belaboring this point, what these calculations tell us is that if *Country A* specializes in the production of *Product Y*—it has a comparative advantage in the production of *Product Y*—sells *Product Y* to *Country B* and purchases *Product X* from *Country B*, it will be better off. And if *Country B* specializes in the production of *Product X*—it has a comparative advantage in the production of *Product X*—sells *Product X* to *Country A* and purchases *Product Y* from *Country A*, it will be better off. That is, both countries will be better off if *Country A* purchases *Product X* from *Country B*, and *Country B* purchases *Product Y* from *Country A*. This is as opposed to each country producing both products.

A main lesson from this lengthy, and perhaps brain-twisting, explanation is that trade benefits all trading parties, even those that are absolutely better at producing all goods and services such as *Country A* in our example. For trade to take place what matters is comparative advantage and not absolute advantage. As long as there are differences in opportunity costs of producing various goods and services, and there are (almost) always differences in opportunity costs in the real world, trade is beneficial for all trading parties. Differences in opportunity costs exist because differences in conditions of economic agents exist. Trade promotes economic growth.

7.2.3 Human Capital

By human capital, we mean the skills the workers have. These skills could be occupation specific or they could be general skills. For a pilot, occupation-specific skills include how to fly a plane. For a nurse, these skills include how to check vitals. For a plumber, these skills include how to plumb. For a teacher, these skills include an in-depth knowledge of the subject, and so on.

General skills, on the other hand, are not specific to a given occupation. The ability to perform basic arithmetic is an example of a general skill. The abilities to read and write, the ability to use a word processor, and the ability drive are also examples of general skills. General skills are transferable from occupation to occupation, whereas occupation-specific skills are not. The ability to fly a plane is not transferable to the nursing profession.

General skills are also transferable from firm to firm. Certain occupation-specific skills may not be transferable from firm to firm. An accountant moving from one firm to the next does not need to learn accounting anew. A cashier, say, working at McDonald, will probably need to learn how to use the cash registers used, say, at T. J. Maxx.

Productivity, which is output per worker hour, depends upon the worker's level of human capital, i.e., worker's skills. Suppose a certain amount of earth needs to be moved. One worker knows how to operate an earth-moving equipment. The other worker does not: He only knows how to use a shovel. All else constant, the first worker can move far more earth than the second worker can in a given hour. The productivity of the first worker is much higher than the productivity of the second worker. The higher the level of human capital in an economy, the higher its output level, all else constant. Furthermore, the more the workers of an economy are able to increase their human capital—learn new skills, keep their skills up to date—the faster that economy will grow.

Note that worker's skill is just another term for worker knowledge. The pool of knowledge, we saw earlier, is technology. The pool of knowledge is not something separable from the individuals who have it. Pool of knowledge is embodied in the workers of the economy.[46]

7.2.4 The Role of Institutions

Perhaps the most important factor that shows up in studies of economic growth is the strength of the institutions in a country. Broadly speaking by "institutions" we mean political institutions, independent judiciary, laws protecting property rights, and economic institutions that facilitate buying and selling of goods and services, i.e., markets. Daron Acemoglu and James Robinson are preeminent scholars on the role of institutions in economic growth.[47] In their 2012 book, *The Origins of Power, Prosperity,*

[46]Technology is embodied in humans. Mankiw, Romer, and Weil: 407–37, Bernanke and Gurkaynak: 11–72, Paul M. Romer. "Endogenous Technological Change." *The Journal of Political Economy* 98.5, Part 2: The Problem of Development: A Conference of the Institute for the Study of Free Enterprise Systems (1990b): S71–S102. Web, Philippe Aghion and Peter Howitt. *Endogenous Growth Theory*. Cambridge, MA: The MIT Press, 1998. Print.

[47]Acemoglu and Robinson on the role of institutions in economic growth. Daron Acemoglu and Fabrizio Zilibotti. "Productivity Differences." *The Quarterly Journal of Economics* 116.2 (2001): 563–606. Web, Daron Acemoglu and Melissa Dell. "Productivity Differences Between and Within Countries." *American Economic Journal: Macroeconomics* 2.1 (2010): 169–88. Web, Daron Acemoglu, Simon Johnson, and James Robinson. "The Colonial Origins of Comparative Development: An Empirical Investigation." 91.5 (2001): 1369–401. Print, Daron Acemoglu and Simon Johnson. "Unbundling Institutions." *Journal of Political Economy* 113.5 (2005): 949–95. Web, Daron Acemoglu and James A. Robinson. *Why Nations Fail: The Origins of Power, Prosperity, and Poverty*. New York: Crown Publishers, 2012. Print.

ad Poverty: Why Nations Fail,[48] Acemoglu and Robinson argue that institutions can be extractive or they can be inclusive. Extractive institutions serve only the well-connected few. Be it the formation of the government, engaging in commerce and trade, or acquisition of education, masses are excluded. Inclusive institutions, on the other hand, write Acemoglu and Robinson[49]:

> allow and encourage participation by the great mass of people in economic activities that make best use of their talents and skills and that enable individuals to make choice they wish. To be inclusive, economic institutions must feature secure private property, and unbiased system of law, and a provision of public services that provides a level playing field in which people can exchange and contract; it also must permit entry of new businesses and allow people to choose their careers. (pp. 74–75)

Acemoglu and Robinson use the examples of South Korea and North Korea, and of the United States and Latin America. They argue that this contrast:

> illustrates a general principle. Inclusive economic institutions foster economic activity, productivity growth, and economic prosperity. Secure private property rights are central since only those with such rights will be willing to invest and increase productivity. A businessman who expects his output to be stolen, expropriated, or entirely taxed away will have little incentive to work, let alone any incentive to undertake investments and innovations. But such rights must exist for the majority of people in society. (p. 75)

Note that without property rights protection, there is no reason to make any technological advancements, increase human capital, and be more productive. Why invest in new ideas when you cannot reap the rewards. Why invest in more productive machines and equipment that embody new ideas when you are uncertain about the security of the increased output. Why produce more than what you can consume right away when

[48] *Why Nations Fail*. Daron Acemoglu and James A. Robinson. *Why Nations Fail: The Origins of Power, Prosperity, and Poverty*. New York: Crown Publishers, 2012. Print.

[49] Inclusive versus extractive institutions. Daron Acemoglu and James A. Robinson. *Why Nations Fail: The Origins of Power, Prosperity, and Poverty*. New York: Crown Publishers, 2012. Print.

you are uncertain about the safety of your output and uncertain whether or not you will be able to exchange the surplus. Why save and lend when you are uncertain about your principal and interest. Why make improvements to your house and make it more attractive to vandals. Amartya Sen agrees. He argues that the lack of property rights may even cause famines.[50] Such is the importance of institutions.

7.3 What Does Money Have to Do with All This?

"Sure, technological advancements, trade and specialization, increases in human capital, and strong institutions enhance economic growth, but what do these factors have to do with money?" The reader may be asking. A simple answer is, "everything." Let me explain.

First, note that the very act of measuring the output of an economy requires a yardstick. Money, as a unit of account, serves as a yardstick. As we saw earlier in this chapter (Sect. 7.1.1), a modern economy produces millions and millions of goods and services of numerous verities. Adding all those goods and services is not an option.

Second, when it comes to trading goods and services, one again needs a yardstick so that one can evaluate what one wants to purchase and what one has to sell in terms of that yardstick. Money, as a unit of account, serves this purpose.

Third, what one wants to sell may not be wanted by the seller of what one wants to buy. As we learned in Chapters 1 and 2, it requires double coincidence of wants. Money solves this problem by being accepted by the seller. It is a medium of exchange.

Fourth, by being acceptable to both buyers and sellers, it allows economic agents to specialize. As we saw, when we specialize in the goods and services in which we have a comparative advantage, and trade, all trading parties benefit, and the total output of the economy grows. Yes, in principle, one can calculate opportunity costs in terms of other goods and services. (In fact this is exactly what we do when we calculate opportunity cost. Money, as a numeraire, makes this calculation much easier.) We can then calculate comparative advantage, and specialize. This, however, is (almost) impossible in any modern economy where millions and millions of goods and services are produced and consumed. Indeed, money itself

[50] Sen on the causes of famines. Amartya Sen. *Poverty and Entitlement: An Essay on Entitlement and Deprivation*. Oxford, UK: Oxford University Press, 1981. Print.

a technological advancement, contributed to the solution to the problem of evaluating goods and services. It economized on transaction costs. And with further technological advancement—learning how to calculate present discounted value—economic agents were able to save and lend.

These are some of the ways in which money—serving as a medium of exchange, a unit of account, and a store of value—enhanced economic growth.

Works Cited

Acemoglu, Daron, and Melissa Dell. "Productivity Differences Between and Within Countries." *American Economic Journal: Macroeconomics* 2.1 (2010): 169–88. Web.

Acemoglu, Daron, and Simon Johnson. "Unbundling Institutions." *Journal of Political Economy* 113.5 (2005): 949–95. Web.

Acemoglu, Daron, Simon Johnson, and James Robinson. "The Colonial Origins of Comparative Development: An Empirical Investigation." 91.5 (2001): 1369–401. Print.

Acemoglu, Daron, and James A. Robinson. *Why Nations Fail: The Origins of Power, Prosperity, and Poverty*. New York: Crown Publishers, 2012. Print.

Acemoglu, Daron, and Fabrizio Zilibotti. "Productivity Differences." *The Quarterly Journal of Economics* 116.2 (2001): 563–606. Web.

Aghion, Philippe, and Peter Howitt. *Endogenous Growth Theory*. Cambridge, MA: The MIT Press, 1998. Print.

Arrow, Kenneth J. "The Economic Implications of Learning by Doing." *The Review of Economic Studies* 29.3 (1962): 155–73. Web.

Barro, Robert J., and Zavier Sala-I-Martin. *Economic Growth*. New York: McGraw-Hill, 1995. Print.

Bernanke, Ben S., and Refet S. Gurkaynak. "Is Growth Exogenous? Taking Mankiw, Romer and Weil Seriously." *NBER Chapters in: NBER Macroeconomics Annual 2001 (Working Paper 8365)* 16.July (2001): 11–72. Print.

Davis, Timothy. "David Ricardo, Financier and Empirical Economist." *European Journal of the History of Economic Thought* 9.1 (2002): 1–16. Web.

Kurz, Heinz D. "David Ricardo: On the Art of 'Elucidating Economic Principles' in the Face of a 'Labyrinth of Difficulties'." *European Journal of the History of Economic Thought* 22.5 (2015): 818–51. Web.

———. "Technical Progress, Capital Accumulation and Income Distribution in Classical Economics: Adam Smith, David Ricardo and Karl Marx." *The European Journal of the History of Economic Thought* 17.5 (2010): 1183–222. Web.

Mankiw, N. Gregory, David Romer, and David N. Weil. "A Contribution to the Empirics of Economic Growth." *The Quarterly Journal of Economics* 107.2 (1992): 407–37. Web.

Mokyr, Joel. "The Intellectual Origins of Modern Economic Growth." *The Journal of Economic History* 65.2 (2005): 285–351. Web.

Pinker, Steven. *Enlightenment Now: The Case for Reason, Science, Humanism, and Progress*. New York: Penguin Books, 2018. Print.

Prasada Rao, D. S., and E. A. Selvanathan. "Computation of Standard Errors for Geary-Khamis Parities and International Prices: A Stochastic Approach." *Journal of Business & Economic Statistics* 10.1 (1992): 109–15. *JSTOR*. Web.

Romer, Paul M. "Endogenous Technological Change." *Journal of Political Economy* 98.5, Part 2: The Problem of Development: A Conference of the Institute for the Study of Free Enterprise Systems (1990a): S71–S102. Web.

———. "Endogenous Technological Change." *The Journal of Political Economy* 98.5, Part 2: The Problem of Development: A Conference of the Institute for the Study of Free Enterprise Systems (1990b): S71–S102. Web.

———. "Growth Based on Increasing Returns due to Specialization." *The American Economic Review* 77.2, Papers and Proceedings of the Ninety-Ninth Annual Meeting of the American Economic Association (1987): 56–62. Web.

Sen, Amartya. *Development as Freedom*. Westminster, MD, USA: Alfred A. Knopf Incorporated, 1999. Print.

———. *Poverty and Entitlement: An Essay on Entitlement and Deprivation*. Oxford, UK: Oxford University Press, 1981. Print.

Siddiqui, Kalim. "David Ricardo's Comparative Advantage and Developing Countries: Myth and Reality." *International Critical Thought* 8.3 (2018): 426–52. Web.

Smith, Adam. *An Inquiry into the Nature and Causes of the Wealth of Nations*. Ed. Edwin Cannan. 1994th ed. New York: Random House, Inc., 1776. Print.

Stiglitz, Joseph E., Amartya Sen, and Jean-Paul Fitoussi. *Mismeasuring our Lives: Why GDP Doesn'T Add Up*. New York, NY: The New Press, 2010. Print.

CHAPTER 8

Money in an Interconnected World

In this chapter, after showing how interconnected the world is, I talk about the role that money plays in international trade. I talk about the determinants of trade patterns among countries and how exchange rates are determined. I show how actions of a foreign central bank affect the domestic economy, and vice versa. I end the chapter by talking about common currency areas and the European Monetary Union.

8.1 An Interconnected World

The world is interconnected. It has been for some time. We are all members of the same ancestral village in East Africa. Some of our ancestors left that village in search of greener pastures some 90,000 to 70,000 years ago,[1] perhaps even earlier. According to a recent study, our human ancestors left Africa around 200,000 years ago and then some of them came back.[2] Now, there are 53 ethnic groups as defined by the Human Genome Diversity Project spread across the globe, all members

[1] Out of Africa. Quamrul Ashraf and Oded Galor. "The 'Out of Africa' Hypothesis, Human Genetic Diversity, and Comparative Economic Development." *The American Economic Review* 103.1 (2013): 1–46. Print.

[2] Human ancestors leaving Africa around 200,000 years ago. Lu Chen, et al. "Identifying and Interpreting Apparent Neanderthal Ancestry in African Individuals." *Cell* 180 (2020): 1–11. Web.

M. Ashraf, *Money*,
https://doi.org/10.1007/978-3-030-50378-9_8

of the same ancestral village in East Africa.[3] Differences are deceptive. Evolution's handy work at display.[4]

It is not a stretch of imagination to say that the ones who moved out of their ancestral village stayed in touch with those who decided to stay put. They stayed in touch with each other at least for some time. They stayed in touch until close relatives and acquaintances died off and a newer set of close relatives and acquaintances took the place of the old ones. Some wandered to even distant places and physical distance between them and their kin became a barrier. Geological changes led to some routes being cut off and new ones being formed. The world is connected. While the nature of connections has changed, the connections have stayed intact.

Take the example of unemployment rates across four countries—the United States, Canada, the United Kingdom, and Australia. The United States and Canada share a border, the United Kingdom is separated by an ocean, and Australia is on the other side of the world, literally. Figure 8.1 plots data from the mid-1960s to the middle of the second decade of the twenty-first century.

While there are differences among the countries' unemployment rates due to institutional differences—depth and width of social safety nets, for instance—the unemployment rates move together. See the increase in unemployment rate around 2008. That was the result of the 2007–2009 financial crisis and the Great Recession that spread across the world.

Another example of how we are all connected across the globe is through the spread of viruses. Be it Ebola, H1NI flu virus, or the novel coronavirus (COVID-19). COVID-19, which started in Wuhan, Hubei Province, China, in late 2019, spread around the globe. The World Health Organization (WHO) declared it a "public health emergency of international concern" on January 30, 2020.[5] By March, the COVID-19 had spread to 90 countries including the United States.[6] On March 9,

[3] 53 ethnic groups and Human Genome Diversity Project. Ashraf and Galor: 1–46.

[4] Evolution's handy work. Richard Dawkins. *The Ancestor's Tale: A Pilgrimage to the Dawn of Evolution*. New York, NY: Houghton Mifflin, 2004. Print.

[5] World Health Organization declares COVID-19 emergency. https://www.who.int/news-room/detail/30-01-2020-statement-on-the-second-meeting-of-the-international-health-regulations-%282005%29-emergency-committee-regarding-the-outbreak-of-novel-coronavirus-%282019-ncov%29 (Accessed: March 7, 2020).

[6] Coronavirus locations across the globe. https://www.cdc.gov/coronavirus/2019-ncov/locations-confirmed-cases.html (Accessed: March 8, 2020).

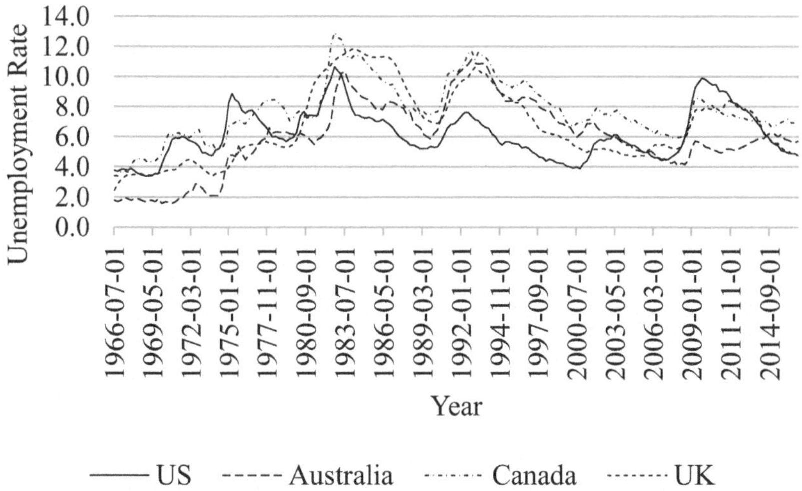

Fig. 8.1 Unemployment rates of the United States, Canada, the United Kingdom, and Australia (*Source* Figure prepared by the author. *Data Source* US Bureau of Labor Statistics, Unemployment Rate [UNRATE], retrieved from FRED, Federal Reserve Bank of St. Louis. https://fred.stlouisfed.org/series/UNRATE; Organization for Economic Co-operation and Development, Unemployment Rate: Aged 15 and Over: All Persons for Canada [LRUNTTTTCAM156S], retrieved from FRED, Federal Reserve Bank of St. Louis. https://fred.stlouisfed.org/series/LRUNTTTTCAM156S; Bank of England, Unemployment Rate in the United Kingdom [AURUKM], retrieved from FRED, Federal Reserve Bank of St. Louis. https://fred.stlouisfed.org/series/AURUKM; Organization for Economic Co-operation and Development, Unemployment Rate: Aged 15 and Over: All Persons for Australia [LRUNTTTTAUQ156S], retrieved from FRED, Federal Reserve Bank of St. Louis. https://fred.stlouisfed.org/series/LRUNTTTTAUQ156S [Accessed: March 8, 2020])

2020, the World Health Organization announced that the COVID-19 epidemic was close to becoming a pandemic.[7] China implemented a complete lockdown in the affected regions to control the virus. As the virus spread to Europe, Italy was the first European country to adopt the

[7] WHO announcement. https://www.wsj.com/articles/confirmed-coronavirus-cases-outside-china-tripled-in-past-week-11583748569?mod=hp_lead_pos1 (Accessed: March 9, 2020).

measure. The Italian government banned public gatherings and all travel except for work or emergencies. All schools and universities were closed. By March 9, 2020, Italy had recorded over 9000 cases of infections and 463 deaths due to the COVID-19 coronavirus. Pictures of empty streets and airports started appearing in the news media.[8] On March 11, 2020, as the number of infected individuals hit 121,564 and the number of dead reached over 4370 across 118 countries, the WHO declared COVID-19 a pandemic. "We're deeply concerned, both by the alarming levels of spread and severity, and by the alarming levels of inaction. We have never before seen a pandemic sparked by a coronavirus," the WHO Director-General, Tedros Adhanom Ghebreyesus, said in a statement.[9] By May 26, 2020, COVID-19 had spread to 188 countries and regions, with 5,589,932 confirmed cases and 350,456 deaths worldwide, according to the Johns Hopkins University's Coronavirus Resource Center.[10] With new cases of infections and deaths being reported on an hourly basis if not sooner, the situation was evolving so rapidly that it was hard to keep up.

Sensing recession on the horizon due to decreased economic activity stock markets in the United States, the United Kingdom, Canada, Japan, France, Germany, and Australia, among other countries, plunged. In order to allay fears of the stock market participants, on March 3, 2020, the Federal Open Market Committee (FOMC) had an emergency meeting in between their regularly scheduled meetings. Later that day, the Federal Reserve Chair, Jerome H. Powell, announced in a press conference that the FOMC had decided to lower the target federal funds rate by 0.5 percent. This rather unusual action by the FOMC did not soothe the concerns of the stock market participants. According to the *Wall Street Journal*, for the year starting from January 2, 2020, by the closing time on March 9, 2020, various stock market indices were down by over 15 percent—United States (Dow Jones Industrial Average: –16.5 percent), United Kingdom (FTSE 100: –20.9 percent), Canada (S&P/TSX: –14.94 percent), Japan (Nikkei 225: –19.82 percent),

[8] Italy bans travel and public gatherings. https://www.nytimes.com/2020/03/09/world/coronavirus-news.html?action=click&module=Spotlight&pgtype=Homepage (Accessed: March 9, 2020).

[9] COVID-19 declared a pandemic. https://www.wsj.com/articles/u-s-coronavirus-cases-top-1-000-11583917794?mod=hp_lead_pos1 (Accessed: March 11, 2020).

[10] Spread of COVID-19 according to Johns Hopkins University. https://coronavirus.jhu.edu/map.html (Accessed: May 26, 2020).

France (CAC40: −21.25 percent), Germany (DAX: 19.84 percent), and Australia (S&P/ASX 200: −14.7 percent). By the close of the trading day on March 11, 2020, the losses had worsened. The headline on the *Wall Street Journal*'s Webpage read, "Dow Jones Industrial Average's 11-Year Bull Run Ends."[11] The index had dropped more than 20 percent from its February 12, 2020, peak. The *Wall Street Journal*'s Liz Hoffman in an article on Saturday, March 14, 2020, recalled the week from March 8, 2020, through March 13, 2020. The article's title "Diary of a Crazy Week in the Markets" captures the essence well.[12]

We are all connected. No country is an island, not even an island.

8.2 Money and International Trade

Subaru is a Japanese car company with plants in Japan, the United States, and Canada, among other countries. It produces a midsize sedan called Subaru Legacy. The window sticker on the car says that it was assembled in a Subaru plant in Lafayette, Indiana, from parts made in the United States and Canada (50 percent), and Japan (40 percent). According to Subaru's Website, its main businesses are automotive and aerospace. It has over 15,274 employees as of March 31, 2019. Established in 1953, Subaru has a global footprint—Americas (18 countries), Asia (17 countries), Europe (35 countries), Middle East and Africa (13 countries), and Oceania (4 countries). As far as companies with international footprints are concerned, Subaru is a relatively small company. Even in the car manufacturing world, it's not a large firm. It is not even among the top 20 car manufacturers in the world according to the International Organization of Motor Vehicle Manufacturers. In 2017, Subaru ranked 21st in the world as measured by the number of cars produced.[13]

There are about 30,000 parts in a typical car with an internal combustion engine according to Toyota's Website.[14] These include the smallest

[11] DOW ends its bull run. https://www.wsj.com/articles/global-markets-calmer-after-two-hectic-days-11583899913 (Accessed: March 11, 2020).

[12] "Diary of a Crazy Week in the Markets." https://www.wsj.com/articles/diary-of-a-crazy-week-in-the-markets-11584143715 (Accessed: March 15, 2020).

[13] Rank of Subaru as a car manufacturer. http://www.oica.net/wp-content/uploads/World-Ranking-of-Manufacturers-1.pdf (Accessed: February 12, 2020).

[14] Number of parts in a car. https://www.toyota.co.jp/en/kids/faq/d/01/04/ (Accessed: February 12, 2020).

screw to a sophisticated computer that runs a complicated engine. Each of these parts has to be priced so that its value can be compared across parts and across manufacturers who often reside in different countries. We saw a glimpse of the detail with which various goods and services are categorized in Chapter 7.

According to the United Nations database, there are 193 member countries and two non-member countries (Holly Sea, also known as the Vatican City, and the State of Palestine) in the world as of this writing,[15] and there are 164 currencies used in the world.[16]

A trivia question: Just looking at the UN members, with which alphabet do the most country names start? Answer: Letter "S" is the most fecund; 25 country names start with the letter "S." Letters "W" and "X" are issueless. Poor things.

When we include all the various countries and territories (UN members and non-members) with which the United States has trade relations, the number rises to 233, according to the United States Bureau of Census.[17] In 2019, the total world trade—the sum of imports and exports of all countries—was $38,028,788 million US dollars. Out of that, according to the US Census Bureau, the total value of the US trade in goods and services in 2019 was $5,616,278 million US dollars. In case you are wondering, China is the biggest trading partner of the United States, as measured by trade value, followed by Mexico and Canada, respectively.

Imagine trading billions and billions of various goods and services with over 7.6 billion individuals[18] spread across 233 countries and territories: a practical impossibility without a numeraire, i.e., money.

[15] Number of countries in the world. https://www.un.org/en/member-states/index.html (Accessed: February 17, 2020).

[16] Number of currencies used in the world. https://www.countries-ofthe-world.com/ (Accessed: February 12, 2020).

[17] Number of countries and territories with which the United States trades. https://www.census.gov/foreign-trade/Press-Release/2019pr/12/index.html. See also https://ec.europa.eu/info/european-union-and-united-kingdom-forging-new-partnership/eu-uk-withdrawal-agreement_en (Accessed: March 2, 2020).

[18] World population. https://www.census.gov/ (Accessed: March 2, 2020).

8.3 The Determinants of Trade Patterns

What determines the volume of trade between two countries? One factor is an economy's size as measured by its output. The larger an economy's output, the larger its purchases and sales, including purchases from other countries (i.e., imports) and its sales to other countries (i.e., exports), holding everything else constant. Another factor that determines trade between two countries is the geographical distance. The farther apart the two countries are, the lower the volume of trade between the two countries. It makes sense. Holding all else constant, transportation costs increase with the increase in distance, which, in turn, raises the costs of goods and services. This model, called the Gravity Model in the economics literature, gives us a *rough* estimate.[19] In Table 8.1, I provide trade in goods data, as a percentage of total US trade in goods, and GDP data, as a percentage of US GDP, for Canada, Mexico, Germany, Australia, and Ireland. (These data exclude trade in services.)

Looking at the data in Table 8.1, a few points stand out. One, even though the economies of Canada and Mexico, as measured by GDP as a percentage of the US GDP, are about the same size as Australia, their trade with the United States is a lot larger. Each country has about 15 percent of the US total trade in goods. Two, Germany has a lot larger economy as compared with Canada, Mexico, and Australia. Its share of trade in goods with the United States, however, is relatively small. Three, given the size of the Irish economy, its share of trade in goods with the United States is large. How do we explain these statistics?

The relatively low share of the US trade in goods with Australia may be explained by the physical distance between the two countries. As mentioned earlier, all else constant, the farther apart the two countries are, the higher the transportation costs, and the lower the volume of trade. Canada, Mexico, and the United States not only have common borders, they also have a free trade agreement—North American Free Trade Agreement (NAFTA).[20] Singed in 1992, NAFTA took effect on

[19] Gravity Model. *Gravity Equations: Workhorse, Toolkit, and Cookbook*, April 2013. http://blogs.ubc.ca/khead/files/2016/07/headmayer_revised.pdf (Accessed: March 10, 2020). See also Michael E. Waugh. *International Trade and Income Differences*. 100 Vols., 2010. Web, Pauline Grosjean. *The Weight of History on European Cultural Integration: A Gravity Approach*. 101 Vols., 2011. Web.

[20] NAFTA. https://www.cbp.gov/trade/nafta (Accessed: March 10, 2020).

Table 8.1 Trade and GDP percentages—Canada, Mexico, Germany, Australia, and Ireland

[1] *Country*	*[2]* *GDP as a percentage of US GDP*	*[3]* *Trade in goods as a percentage of total US trade in goods*
Canada	8.33	14.78
Mexico	5.93	14.83
Germany	19.18	4.53
Australia	6.97	0.89
Ireland	1.86	1.71

Source Table prepared by the author. *Note* Data are in current US dollars. *Data Source* https://www.census.gov/foreign-trade/balance/index.html (Accessed: March 2, 2020)

January 1, 1994. Its expressed purpose is to gradually remove all trade barriers between the three countries.

If one were to fly from Washington, DC, to Berlin, Germany, depending upon the airline and stops along the way, it would take about 10 hours. It would take about the same flight time from Washington, DC, to Dublin, Ireland. Why does Ireland trade a lot with the United States given the size of the Irish economy? One reason is cultural ties.[21] The United States has a large population of Irish descent. According to the 2000 United States Census data, there are 30,524,799 individuals of Irish ancestry in the United States. As is usually the case, immigrants bring with them their cultures and cultural ties, which help promote trade. Studies show that cultural familiarity promotes trust, one of the main currencies of any relationship, commercial or otherwise.[22] Trust helps promote trade.

As a comparison, according to the 2000 Census data, there are 42,839,711 individuals of German descent, 14,443,629 are of Mexican descent, 4,890,581 are of Scottish descent, and 74,544 are of Australian descent. Given the high number of individuals of German ancestry, why does Germany not have closer trade ties with the United States? One reason may be the circumstances in which individuals of German descent

[21] Cultural ties and trade. Paul R. Krugman, Maurice Obstfeld, and Marc J. Melitz. *International Economics: Theory and Policy*. 11th ed. New York, NY: Pearson, 2018. Print.

[22] Familiarity and trust. Grosjean.

left Germany after the rise of Hitler. It is quite likely that those who left Germany for the United States did not have friendly ties with those who stayed even when they were in Germany. This is certainly true for at least a part of those who migrated to the United States from Germany. Who would want to maintain any relationship with one's oppressor after having achieved freedom?

So geographic proximity, as espoused by the Gravity Model, does not provide an accurate estimate of trade patterns. It provides only a rough estimate. There are certainly other factors, including randomness, that affect trade patterns keeping trade economists busy. Further exploration of this topic, however, will take us too far afield.

Furthermore, it will be a mistake to think that just because a group of individuals happens to live in geographic proximity will have the same cultural mores. It may take hundreds of years for cultural integration to take place. Europe and the European Union provide vivid examples. Pauline Grosjean (2011) uses a modified Gravity Model to estimate social trust.[23] She uses the historical divisions of 21 countries of the "central, eastern, and southeastern Europe" that belonged to "the Ottoman, Habsburg, Russian, or Prussian empires" (p. 504). Discussing her study's empirical results, she writes:

> Having belonged to the same former empire for more than 100 years has the consistent and robust effect of diminishing dissimilarities in social trust, even when physical distance between locations, sociodemographic, economic, and geopolitical conditions are taken into account. Such a persistent effect of past historical events, which are quite distant in time, is notable and sizeable and, strikingly, far outweighs the influence of current geopolitical factors, in particular nation states' borders. (p. 506)

Trade agreements play a large role, and countries try very hard to form such agreements. Negotiations take years, if not decades. Even after that, all the hard work may not reach fruition. A recent example of such a failed effort is Trans-Pacific Partnership Agreement between Australia, Brunei, Canada, Chile, Japan, Malaysia, Mexico, New Zealand, Peru, Singapore, Vietnam, and the United States. After the Obama administration signed the agreement in February 2016, it was not ratified; the

[23] History and social trust. Pauline Grosjean. *The Weight of History on European Cultural Integration: A Gravity Approach.* 101 Vols., 2011. Web.

Trump administration withdrew the US signature in January 2017.[24] Even the agreements that have been ratified and have been successful for decades are not really safe. The United Kingdom had been a part of the European Union for nearly half a century. On January 31, 2020, the United Kingdom left the Union following a referendum in 2016 in which the British people voted to leave.[25] The exit of the United Kingdom from the European Union, commonly known as "Brexit," continues to be a topic of impassioned debate.

The point to be made here is that whatever the determinants of trade patterns, the fact remains that trade is mutually beneficial, and that money facilitates trade.

8.4 What Are Exchange Rates and Why Do We Need Them?

Exchange rates are the prices of one currency in terms of other currencies. These prices are determined in the foreign exchange markets in major financial centers of the world (New York, London, Tokyo, Frankfurt, and Singapore) with forces of demand for and supply of a currency. For instance, on March 12, 2020, at 5:05 p.m., the price of one pound sterling, the currency used in the United Kingdom, in terms of US dollars was $1.2583. That is, for each pound sterling, one could get 1.2583 US dollars. Note that I am quoting the price of pounds sterling in US dollars by the minute. The purpose is not to sensationalize. The reason for providing the hour and the minute is that prices of currencies in terms of other currencies change very rapidly. Why does this happen? Why do prices change so rapidly? I will address this point shortly.

In Fig. 8.2, I plot daily data for the US dollar and pound sterling exchange rate from February 28, 2019, to February 28, 2020.

Note the fluctuations.

Why do we need to know about exchange rates? This is because for us to compare the value of two or more goods and services we have to evaluate these goods and services in the same unit. This is why we need

[24] Trump administration withdraws from TPP. https://money.cnn.com/2017/01/23/news/economy/tpp-trump-china/ (Accessed: March 27, 2020).

[25] UK leaves the EU. https://www.wsj.com/articles/brexit-brings-slow-change-in-uk-and-an-overhaul-in-brussels-11580399915?mod=article_inline. See also https://europa.eu/european-union/about-eu/easy-to-read_en (Accessed: March 27, 2020).

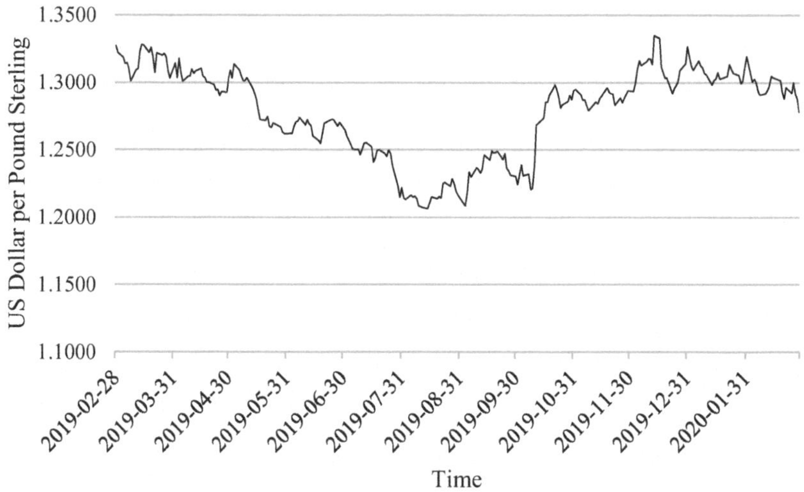

Fig. 8.2 US dollar and pound Sterling exchange rate (*Source* Figure prepared by the author. *Data Source* Board of Governors of the Federal Reserve System [US], US/UK Foreign Exchange Rate [DEXUSUK], retrieved from FRED, Federal Reserve Bank of St. Louis. https://fred.stlouisfed.org/series/DEXUSUK [Accessed: March 15, 2020])

exchange rates. Take another look at Table 8.1. These data are reported in terms of US dollars. Had these figures been given in local currencies, one would first have to convert those figures into a common currency to be able to compare the values of goods and services. One would need exchange rates.

For the price of a good or service to exist, there has to be demand for and supply of the good or service. Currencies are no different. There has to be demand for and the supply of a given currency. From where do the demand for and the supply of a currency come? Take, again, the example of the price of the US dollar in terms of pound sterling—the US dollar and the pound sterling exchange rate. Why do the UK residents demand the US dollar and why do the US residents supply US dollars, and vice versa?

To keep things simple for now, assume that the source of demand by the UK residents is trade in goods and services. Same goes for the US residents. (There are other sources of demand for a currency, as we will see later.) Suppose EasyJet, a British airline company, wants to purchase a Boeing 777-8 jet from Boeing, a US company that manufactures airplanes among other sophisticated machines. Its list price is 410.2 million US dollars.[26] Boeing accepts US dollars for its planes. EasyJet charges its customers in pounds sterling. EasyJet must convert pounds sterling into US dollars. EasyJet has created a demand for 410.2 million US dollars. When EasyJet wants to buy 410.2 million US dollars in exchange for $1.2583 per pound sterling, the exchange rate that prevailed on March 12, 2020, at 5:05 p.m., EasyJet has simultaneously created a supply of about 326 million pounds sterling.

From where does the supply of the US dollars come? Suppose that Bristol Myers Squibb, a biopharmaceutical firm headquartered in the United States with offices across the globe, buys iron, zinc, and platinum.[27] These are some of the metals used in modern medicines. AngloAmerican is a British mining company which sells these metals for £400 million to Bristol Myers Squibb.[28] Bristol Myers Squibb is an American company and uses US dollars to buy and sell goods and services. AngloAmerican is a British company which buys and sells goods and services using pounds sterling. For the exchange to take place either Bristol Myers Squibb will have to convert US dollars into pounds sterling or AngloAmerican will have to accept US dollars equivalent to £400 million and then convert those dollars into pounds sterling.

Why can't AngloAmerican just buy and sell goods and services using US dollars? The answer: AngloAmerican's employees and suppliers who live in the United Kingdom only accept pounds sterling. Unless everyone in the United Kingdom starts accepting US dollars, at some point someone will have to convert US dollars into pounds sterling.

Suppose then that Bristol Myers Squibb converts US dollars into pounds sterling. At the exchange rate of $1.2583 per pound sterling, the exchange rate that prevailed on March 12, 2020, at 5:05 p.m., Bristol Myers Squibb buys 400 million pounds sterling for 503.32 million US

[26] List price of a Boeing 777-8. https://www.boeing.com/commercial/777x/#/technical-specs (Accessed: March 15, 2020).

[27] Three commonly used metals in medicine. https://www.angloamerican.com/futuresmart/our-industry/our-products/metals-in-medicine (Accessed: March 16, 2020).

[28] AngloAmerican. https://www.angloamerican.com/ (Accessed: March 16, 2020).

dollars. When Bristol Myers Squibb purchased 400 million pounds sterling for 503.32 million US dollars, it simultaneously created demand for £400 million and supply of $503.32 million.

In a similar fashion when someone from the US travels to the United Kingdom and they convert US dollars into pounds sterling, they supply US dollars and demand pounds sterling. And when someone from the United Kingdom travels to the United States and they convert pounds sterling into US dollars, they supply pounds sterling and demand US dollars.

Another example of the demand for and supply of a currency may be foreign students coming to the United States. Suppose that a Chinese student is admitted to a US university. Suppose also that annual room, board, tuition, and fees are $50,000. The Chinese student would have to convert Chinese Yuan into US dollars. On March 12, 2020, at 6:05 p.m., the price of each US dollar in terms of Chinese Yuan was 7.0296 Yuan.[29] This means that 50,000 US dollars were worth 351,480 Chinese Yuan. This Chinese student created the demand for 50,000 US dollars and the supply of 351,480 Chinese Yuan.

As every student who has taken a principles-level economics course knows, when the price of a product increases, holding all else constant, its quantity demanded decreases, and when the price of a product decreases, its quantity demanded increases. This is the so-called law of demand. Let us revisit the example of EasyJet buying a Boeing 777-8. Suppose the exchange rate changes; the price of US dollars in terms of pounds sterling increases. Earlier each pound sterling could fetch 1.2583 US dollars, now each pound sterling is worth only 1.1 US dollars. That is, the US dollar appreciates (or strengthens) in terms of pound sterling. What does this imply for EasyJet? Assuming that price of a Boeing 777-8 stays the same in terms of US dollars ($410,200,000), in terms of pounds sterling the price has increased from £325,995,390.61 to £372,909,090.91. As a result, EasyJet buys fewer Boeing 777-8s.

What about Bristol Myers Squibb? How does this appreciation of the US dollar affect their purchase of iron, zinc, and platinum from AngloAmerican? Assuming that the price of iron, zinc, and platinum does not change in terms of pound sterling, after the appreciation of the US dollar, it has become cheaper for Bristol Myers Squibb to purchase the

[29] US dollar Yuan exchange rate. https://www.wsj.com/market-data/quotes/fx/USDCNY?mod=md_curr_overview_quote (Accessed: March 18, 2020).

same amount of the three metals. It now only has to pay $440,000,000 as opposed to $503,320,000. Holding all else constant, it is likely that Bristol Myers Squibb will now purchase higher quantities of these metals. AngloAmerican's sales to the United States will increase.

An appreciation of the US dollar makes imports cheaper for the domestic buyers and exports more expensive for the foreign buyers. As a result, an appreciation of a currency hurts exporters and helps importers, and a depreciation of a currency helps exporters and hurts importers.

8.4.1 Spots, Forwards, Swaps, Futures, and Options

As we saw, in our example, when the exchange rate was $1.1 per pound sterling and Bristol Myers Squibb needed £400 million to purchase iron, zinc, and platinum, the company needed $440 million. On the other hand, had the exchange rate been $1.2583 per pound sterling, Bristol Myers Squibb would have needed $503.32 million. Quite a bit of risk is associated with this transaction.

When someone buys a currency right when it is needed, the rate one pays is called spot rate—two parties agree to make the transaction (exchange bank deposits) "on-the-spot." The data shown in Fig. 8.2 are spot exchange rate data. As we can see, there is quite a bit of fluctuation and hence risk associated with such transactions. Is there any way to avoid the uncertainty of exchange rate changes? The answer is "yes." Financial markets offer several avenues of mitigating risks associated with exchange rate changes. These include currency forwards, currency swaps, currency futures, and currency options.

In a currency forward contract, two parties agree to exchange currencies at a given exchange rate at a particular date in the future. These dates may range from 30 days to several years in the future. In our example, suppose that Bristol Myers Squibb knew the date on which the said metals would be delivered. To avoid uncertainty, it could have agreed to purchase £400 million on the delivery date (or any other date in the future) at an agreed upon price. In this way, Bristol Myers Squibb would have had no concerns about fluctuations in the exchange rate and hence in the price of the metals. Roughly speaking, the forward exchange rate would be equal to the spot exchange rate expected to prevail when £400 million will be exchanged for US dollars.

In a currency swap, two parties agree to the sale of a currency now along with a repurchase agreement in the same amount at a future date.

"Why can't someone in the US who needs, say pounds sterling, in the future sell US dollars now (in a spot market) and buy pounds sterling in a forwards market? Why have a different mechanism for this type of transaction?" you may ask. A reason may be that brokerage fees may be lower when you are making this one transaction as compared with two transactions, first to sell US dollars in the spot market and then to buy pounds sterling in currency forward market.

In a currency future, the buyer of the contract buys the right to purchase a given amount of foreign currency at a predetermined date in the future. The holder of the contract then can sell the contract—the right to purchase a given amount of foreign currency—in the futures market should they deem it a better choice as opposed to purchasing the currency at the said date. A currency future contract is different from a currency forward contract. In the latter case, the purchaser must fulfill their end of the deal.

Then, we have currency options. In a currency option, the purchaser of the contract can buy or sell the said amount of foreign currency at an agreed upon exchange rate any time up to the expiration date of the contract, and the seller of the contract must oblige. We can further divide currency option into "put option" and "call option." In a put option, the buyer of the option has the right to sell foreign currency at an agreed upon exchange rate at any time up to the expiration date of the contract. A call option, on the other hand, gives the buyer of the option the right to purchase foreign currency at an agreed upon exchange rate any time up to the expiration of the contract date. Note that currency forwards, currency swaps, currency futures, and currency options are examples of financial derivatives. They are designed to hedge the risk in the foreign exchange market.

The curious reader may be wondering about the lack of detail provided in discussing the ways to hedge the exchange rate risks—currency forwards, currency swaps, currency futures, and currency options. I have avoided the details here because, in my opinion, these discussions, while certainly extremely valuable, will take too far afield from the topic at hand—the understanding of the concept of money. I refer the reader to the literature in the field.[30]

[30] Studies on the various ways to hedge the exchange rate risk. Frank McCormick. *Covered Interest Arbitrage: Unexploited Profits? Comment*. 87 Vols., 1979. Web. See also Krugman, Obstfeld, and Melitz, Chapter 14.

8.4.2 *Foreign Currency as a Store of Value*

Buying and selling goods and services, of course, is not the only reason for the demand for and supply of foreign currencies. Individuals, firms (e.g., commercial banks, corporations, non-bank entities, etc.), and governments hold currencies as a store of value as well.

At this point, a reminder that money is something that serves as a medium of exchange, a unit of account, and a store of value, may be in order. Recall that as a store of value, money, as an asset, helps transfer purchasing power from present to the future. Recall also that currency is part of the M1 monetary aggregate. Since we are talking about currencies of different countries, I will focus on the currency component of M1.

8.4.2.1 Liquidity

Economic agents (individuals, firms, governments, etc.) hold currency as a store of value. But why currency? Why not a house or a piece of land or a piece of precious metal such as gold? Isn't currency in danger of losing value in times of high inflation when price level is rising rapidly? True, if the rate of inflation is high, currency will lose its value rapidly. But currency, you may recall, is the most liquid asset. That is, it can be transferred into another asset the quickest. A house, on the other hand, may take some time to sell. And, depending upon the market conditions, if you want to sell a house quickly you may have to reduce the price significantly. Liquidity is a desirable quality in an asset. Holding all else constant, economic agents may keep currency as an asset because it is the most liquid asset.

8.4.2.2 The Expected Rate of Return

Savers look for the rate of return. As we saw in earlier chapters when one rents a house or an apartment, the owner of the dwelling charges rent. In the same fashion when someone borrows, one is renting purchasing power, and the lender charges interest. In the case of money, interest is the counterpart of rent of a dwelling. Interest rate is just the interest payment as a percentage of the principal. Holding all else constant, the higher the interest rate a borrower is paying, the more attractive the opportunity it is for the lender.

When it comes to holding foreign currency as a store of value, the picture is a bit more complicated. Take the example of holding US dollars versus pounds sterling as a store of value. Simply comparing interest rates on pound sterling deposits with the interest rates on US dollar deposits will not do. We have to get the exchange rate. Including exchange rate between US dollar and pound sterling into the equation will give us a better understanding. It will give us total rate of return on US dollar deposits versus the total rate of return on pound sterling deposits.

Suppose that you want to compare the US dollar rate of return on pound sterling deposits with the rate of return on US dollar deposits. We have to convert pounds sterling and the US dollars into the same measure—either pounds sterling into US dollars or the US dollars into pounds sterling—so that they can be compared. Since, in this example, we want the US dollar rate of return, we need to convert pounds sterling into US dollars. Holding the interest rates offered on both currency deposits constant, if one currency's price in terms of the other currency is expected to change, it will certainly affect the rate of return.

The example of Celsius and Fahrenheit may be helpful. While both Celsius and Fahrenheit are measures of temperature, a zero degree Celsius is not the same as zero degree Fahrenheit. A given value represents different temperatures under Celsius versus Fahrenheit. (Except, of course at −40 degrees: −40 degrees Celsius is equal to −40 degrees Fahrenheit.) And a one degree increase in Celsius is not the same as a one degree increase in Fahrenheit. In essence, converting one currency into another currency is no different than converting Celsius into Fahrenheit or Fahrenheit into Celsius so the change in temperature can be measured.

Let us continue the example of comparing the rate of return on US dollar deposits with the rate of return on pound sterling deposits. Suppose that the US dollar is expected to depreciate against the pound sterling. That is, the price of a pound sterling in terms of US dollars is expected to increase. A simple rule, which takes the exchange rate changes into consideration, is as follows: The US dollar rate of return on pound sterling deposits, in US dollar terms, is approximately equal to pound sterling interest rate plus the expected US dollar rate of depreciation against pound sterling.[31]

Why do we add the US dollar rate of depreciation to the pound sterling interest rate on deposits? We do this to capture the changes in exchange rate. We want to look at the rate of return on pound sterling deposits

[31] Simple rule for calculating one currency's rate of return on deposits in another currency. Paul R. Krugman, Maurice Obstfeld, and Marc J. Melitz. *International Economics: Theory and Policy*. 11th ed. New York, NY: Pearson, 2018. Print.

in terms of the US dollars. If the US dollar rate of depreciation against pound sterling is high, the US dollar rate of return on pound sterling deposits, in terms of US dollars, will be high. The reverse will be the case if the expected US dollar rate of depreciation is low. Keep also in mind that we are talking about real rates of return, not nominal rates of return. That is, rates of return after having the effects of changes in price levels taken out.

By way of summing up, we can say that the demand for a currency is positively related to the expected rate of return, positively related to its liquidity, and negatively related to its riskiness, all else equal. I must mention here that when it comes to the demand for a currency, economists primarily focus on the expected rate of return of the currency relative to the expected rates of return of other currencies.

8.4.3 The Exchange Rate Equilibrium

(Readers who are not interested in the underlying details of the exchange rate equilibrium mechanism may skip this subsection.)

As you may have guessed, an equilibrium in the foreign exchange market takes place when the quantity demanded of a currency is equal to the quantity supplied of a currency. At this point, the expected rates of return on both domestic and foreign currencies, when measured in the same currency, are the same. This condition is referred to as the Interest Parity Condition.

Figure 8.3 and Eq. 8.1, which are based on the framework presented in Krugman et al. (2018),[32] provide a detailed explanation of the exchange rate equilibrium.

We may write the expression $\$r_{£}^{e}$ as follows:

$$\$r_{£}^{e} = r_{£} + \frac{\left(\frac{\$}{£}\right)^{e} - \left(\frac{\$}{£}\right)}{\left(\frac{\$}{£}\right)} \tag{8.1}$$

where, as defined above, $\$r_{£}^{e}$ is the expected real rate of return, in terms of US dollars, on pound sterling deposits; $r_{£}$ is the real interest rate on

[32] Source of the framework in Fig. 8.3. Paul R. Krugman, Maurice Obstfeld, and Marc J. Melitz. *International Economics: Theory and Policy*. 11th ed. New York, NY: Pearson, 2018. Print, Chapter 14.

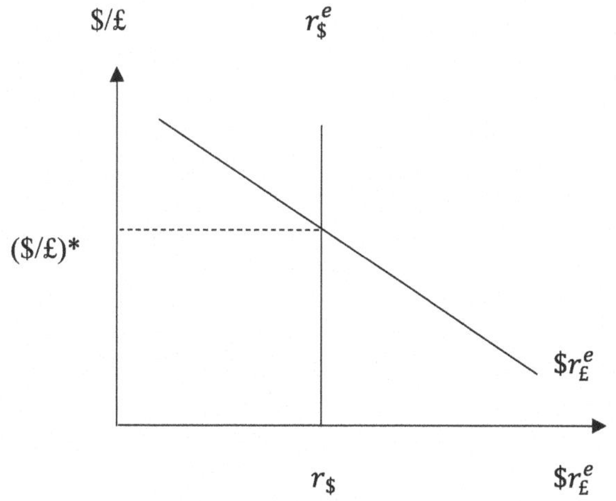

Fig. 8.3 Equilibrium in the exchange rate market (*Source* Figure prepared by the author. $\$/£$ is the US dollar-pound sterling exchange rate. $\$r^e_£$ is the expected real rate of return on pound sterling deposits in US dollars. The curve $r^e_\$$ is the real expected rate of return on US dollar deposits which is vertical at $r_\$$, the real rate of return on US dollar deposits, set by the Fed)

pound sterling deposits; and $\frac{\left(\frac{\$}{£}\right)^e-\left(\frac{\$}{£}\right)}{\left(\frac{\$}{£}\right)}$ is the expected rate of depreciation of the US dollar against pound sterling.

Why does the expected real rate of return on pound sterling deposits in US dollars curve slope downward? Suppose that the quantity $(\$/£)$ increases. That is, the price of a pound sterling in terms of US dollars increases—US dollar depreciates against pound sterling now. Given the real interest rate on pound sterling deposits, $r_£$, and the expected price of a pound sterling in terms of US dollars, $\left(\frac{\$}{£}\right)^e$, i.e., expected exchange rate, say, a year from now, when the quantity $\left(\frac{\$}{£}\right)$ increases now, the quantity $\frac{\left(\frac{\$}{£}\right)^e-\left(\frac{\$}{£}\right)}{\left(\frac{\$}{£}\right)}$ decreases. This means that the expected real rate of return on pound sterling deposits in US dollars, $\$r^e_£$, decreases. In terms of Eq. 8.1, we are adding a smaller quantity to $r_£$ after the depreciation of the US dollar against pound sterling.

Why is the expected real rate of return on US dollar deposits, $r^e_\$$, is vertical at $r_\$$? Recall from Chapter 5 that the Fed sets the target for the federal funds rate—the interest rate that banks charge each other for overnight loans. The Fed then changes money supply such that the target is met. Furthermore, while there are differences between the various interest rates that prevail in an economy at any given time, they tend to move together. And while the federal funds rate is in nominal terms, real interest rate moves accordingly for given inflation rate. As we saw in Chapter 7, when we want to convert a nominal variable into a real variable, we take the effects of prices out. Using the same underlying reasoning, one may get real interest rate, r, by deducting inflation rate, π,—the percentage increase in price level—from the nominal interest rate, i. Real interest rate may be expressed as follows:

$$r = i - \pi \tag{8.2}$$

In Eq. (8.2), π represents inflation rate.

How do we arrive at $(\$/£)^*$, the equilibrium exchange rate? Suppose now that the exchange rate is above $(\$/£)^*$. The rate of return on US dollar deposits is higher than the expected real rate of return on pound sterling deposits, in terms of US dollars. Savers will convert pounds sterling into US dollars. As a result, price of the US dollar in terms of pound sterling will increase—the US dollar will appreciate—leading to a decline in the quantity $(\$/£)$. The reverse will happen when the exchange rate is below $(\$/£)^*$.

8.5 The Effects of the Foreign Central Bank Action on the Domestic Economy

We saw in Chapter 5 that a central bank may change money supply to affect interest rates in the economy. Take, again, the example of the central bank of the United States, the Federal Reserve System, or the Fed, for short. When the Fed wants to decrease interest rates in the economy, it lowers the target of the federal funds rate. The Fed then decreases money supply, using the monetary policy tools at its disposal (Chapter 5, Sect. 5.3.1), such that the target is met. Since various interest rates that prevail in the economy move together, these interest rates also decrease. A decrease in interest rates makes borrowing cheaper which leads firms to borrow more and build more factories or expand the existing ones, and so on. A lowered interest rate also makes borrowing cheaper for households as well, which affords them to build new houses or add a room or two, or buy big-ticket items like cars and appliances. The demand for these items increases. Firms increase production to meet the demand. As a result, output increases. The reverse happens when the Fed increases interest rates.

Do the actions of a central bank affect other economies as well? A short answer is "yes." Let me go into a bit more detail.

8.5.1 Changes in Money Supply, Interest Rates, and Exchange Rates

Recall, again, that a change in the federal funds rate triggers changes in other interest rates that prevail in the economy, including interest rate on US dollar deposits and other financial assets. One can modify Fig. 5.6, which shows money demand, M_d, money supply, M_s, and interest rate, i, in nominal terms, to show money demand, money supply, and interest rate in real terms. Recall, again, that in order to convert nominal variables into real variables one has to take the effect of prices out. We have already seen how to convert nominal interest rate into real interest rate using Eq. (8.2). We can convert nominal money demand, M_d, and nominal money supply, M_s, by dividing both variables by price level, P, $\frac{M_d}{P}$ and $\frac{M_s}{P}$, respectively. Figure 8.4 shows this modified version. Figure 8.4 also shows how a decrease in real money supply, where price level is held constant, will affect the real interest rate.

Suppose that the Fed increases the federal funds rate target and decreases money supply in order to meet the new target. In terms of Fig. 8.4, with a given price level, real money supply curve, $\frac{M_s^1}{P}$, shifts to the left to $\frac{M_s^2}{P}$. This, in turn, leads to an increase in equilibrium real interest rate from r_1^* to r_2^*.

Link this chain of events to Fig. 8.3 to see how this action by the Fed will affect US dollar and pound sterling exchange rate. In terms of Fig. 8.3, the curve $r_\$^e$, which represents the expected real rate of return on US dollar deposits, shifts to the right. Since now the expected real rate of return on US dollar deposits is higher than the expected real rate of return on pound sterling deposits, in terms of US dollars, savers exchange their pounds sterling for US dollars. The US dollar exchange rate against

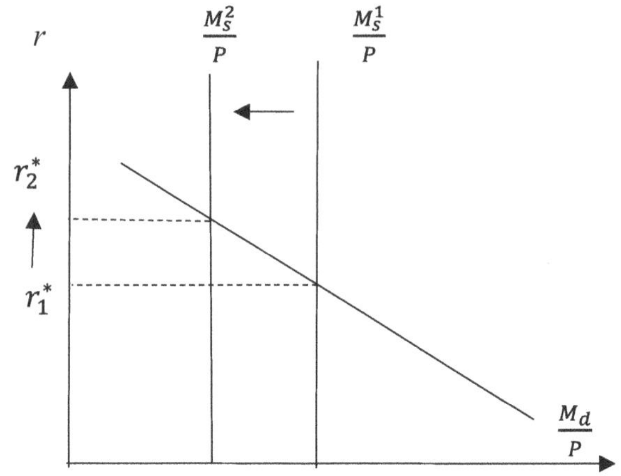

Fig. 8.4 Interaction of real money demand and real money supply (*Source* Figure prepared by the author. r is the real interest rate, $\frac{M_s}{P}$, is the real money supply, and $\frac{M_d}{P}$, is the real money demand)

pound sterling improves—the price of US dollars in terms of pounds sterling increases. In terms of Fig. 8.3, the quantity $\left(\frac{\$}{£}\right)$ decreases. Now a given number of pounds sterling can purchase fewer US dollars.

8.5.2 *Changes in Money Supply, Price Level, and Exchange Rates*

In the previous subsection, we held the price level constant. This assumption is closer to reality in the short run, but not in the long run. Note that short run, as economists define it, is a situation where at least one cost of production—wages, prices of raw materials, rents, etc.—is fixed. In the long run, on the other hand, all costs of production are variable. Prices of inputs are able to adjust. This means that the impact of money supply changes in the short run may be different from that in the long run.

While some input prices adjust on a daily basis, most input prices are set for a significant amount of time throughout the year. Examples of prices that change daily, if not hourly, include prices of crude oil, gas, various metals, exchange rates, etc. Indeed, as we saw earlier in this chapter, exchange rates are reported on a minute-by-minute basis. On the other hand, take the example of wages of labor, the major cost of production in most manufacturing jobs.[33] Usually, salaried workers get the same pay throughout the year, and salary changes, if any, are made on an annual basis. Similarly, suppliers of raw materials and intermediate goods prefer not to change prices that often. One important reason is that renegotiating contracts is costly. It would not be optimal for suppliers to renegotiate contracts as long as the marginal cost of renegotiation is higher than the marginal benefit. This means that prices are relatively stable.

Suppose now that the Fed increases money supply to spur aggregate demand. Producers increase output to meet the increased demand. Demand for raw materials increases and workers are asked to work longer hours. Employers will have to pay overtime even if there is not any renegotiation of contracts right away. Over the course of the year, however, when contracts become due, workers demand higher wages and salaries, and raw materials and intermediate goods suppliers demand higher prices. The overall price level increases, so does the price of foreign currency in terms of domestic currency, i.e., the exchange rate. After all, exchange rate is the price of foreign currency in terms of domestic currency. The country whose money supply increases has a depreciated currency, and the country whose money supply decreases sees an appreciation in its currency, all else constant. A takeaway is that in the long run, changes in price level and exchange rate are proportionate to the changes in money supply.

8.6 Common Currency Areas

Robert Mundell wrote the following in an article[34]:

> Two thousand years ago, in the days of Caesar Augustus, there was the Roman aureus. A thousand years ago, there was a successor of the aureus, the bezant, which was still a unit of account through most of Europe. Five aurei or bezants were always equal to one libra, the unit of account of the Roman Empire, and that was the link through the ages to the currency of

[33] Share of labor wages in cost of production. Michael D. Giandrea and Shawn A. Sprague. "Estimating the U.S. Labor Share." *Monthly Labor Review* (2017): A1. *ProQuest Business Collection (Alumni Edition)*. Web.

[34] Historical records of single currency. Robert Mundell. "The Case for a World Currency." *Journal of Policy Modeling* 34.4 (2012): 568–78. Web.

> Charlemagne to those of Queen Victoria. A hundred years ago, the pound sterling could pass for a universal unit of account. Even as recently as forty years ago, there was the "1944 gold dollar" that was the universal unit of account for most of the world. (p. 569)

In fact, in the initial plans of Bretton Woods Agreement, there was a suggestion of having a world currency. "The American Plan named it *unitas*; the British plan named it *bancor*" (p. 571, italics original), Mundell continues.

One can avoid all the complications that arise from having different currencies. There would not be any issues involving exchange rates if there were only one currency. After all, in the United States, we do not have any exchange rate issues: There are 50 states and all use the same US dollar. There have been concerted efforts to do just that starting in the second-half of the twentieth century.

Centuries of wars among various European countries and city-states had cost countless lives and immeasurable treasure. European intellectuals and politicians alike had been thinking about formulating a cohesive union to avoid a repeat ever since the end of World War II. In 1951, Belgium, Germany, France, Italy, Luxembourg, and the Netherlands decided to cooperate economically. At the end of 2018, there were 28 members of the European Union (EU) with a combined GDP of $18.8 trillion (current US dollars),[35] rivaling that of the United State—$20.6 trillion (current US dollars). At the time of this writing, after the United Kingdom had decided to leave the EU, there are now 27 countries that are members of this Union. In January 1999, 11 member countries of the EU joined the European Monetary Union (EMU), and by 2002 fully adopted a single currency, the euro. The United Kingdom and Denmark did not adopt the euro. Over time, the number of countries that adopted the euro grew. There are now 19 member countries that use the euro.[36]

[35] GDP of EU at the end of 2018. World Bank, Gross Domestic Product for the European Union [NYGDPMKTPCDEUU], retrieved from FRED, Federal Reserve Bank of St. Louis. https://fred.stlouisfed.org/series/NYGDPMKTPCDEUU (Accessed: March 28, 2020).

[36] The European Union member countries and the euro. https://europa.eu/european-union/about-eu_en (Accessed: March 28, 2020).

While the estimates may differ, economists agree that the benefits of having a single currency are numerous.[37] For starters, information and transaction cost associated with converting one currency into another go away. For instance, the European Commission estimated that the gains from carrying out transactions in a single currency could be as high as 0.5 percent of the EU GDP per year.[38]

There are, however, four conditions that have to be met for these benefits to arise. As Michael Kouparitsas (1999) put it:

> 1) countries should be exposed to similar sources of disturbances (common shocks); 2) the relative importance of these common shocks should be similar (symmetric shocks); 3) countries should have similar responses to common shocks (symmetric responses); 4) if countries are affected by country-specific sources of disturbances (idiosyncratic shocks), they need to be able to adjust quickly. (p. 2)

The reason is that when countries join a single currency they give up their freedom to conduct monetary policy. When the economic shocks are asymmetric, this inflexibility may lead to low economic growth rates and high unemployment rates.

In an empirical analysis to test the long-term viability of EMU, Kouparitsas (1999) combined countries on the basis of similarity of disturbances and responses to these disturbances. He considered Austria, Belgium and Luxembourg (treated as one country due to data limitations), France, Italy, the Netherlands, Portugal, and Spain as the "center," while Finland and Ireland as the "periphery." The results of this study led Kouparitsas to conclude that "the EMU will be a viable currency union for the center countries" (p. 3). Based on the results of his study, he questioned the long-run viability of countries in the periphery.

The 2007–2009 financial crisis and the following Great Recession that engulfed the developed world presented another test of the feasibility of the euro. While the euro survived, there was unnecessary hardship

[37] Benefits of single currency. Robert A. Mundell. "Currency Areas, Common Currencies, and EMU." *American Economic Review* 87.2 (1997): 214–16. Web, Mundell: 568–78.

[38] Gains from carrying out transactions in a single currency. Michael A. Kouparitsas. "Is the EMU a Viable Common Currency Area? A VAR Analysis of Regional Business Cycles." *Federal Reserve Bank of Chicago Economic Perspectives* 23.4 (1999): 2–20. Web.

imposed on countries like Greece, Ireland, and Spain. As the Great Recession hit and output declined, tax revenues in these countries declined as well. As a result, these countries' debt-to-GDP ratios soared. To meet the mandates of the EMU regarding budget deficit limits, member countries adopted austerity measures. Governments decreased their expenditure and raised taxes. Not surprisingly, this fiscal contraction further decreased output and increased unemployment. A downward spiral began leading to even lower government revenues and higher deficits as a percentage of GDP. Spain, for instance, had a budget surplus on the eve of the Great Recession. Spain's *surplus* in 2007 was 20,739 million euros. Soon after this budget, surplus turned into budget deficit. By 2009, Spain's *deficit* reached 116,429 million euros. (Data in current euros.)[39] Paul Krugman, in his 2012 book, *End This Depression Now!*, presents a detailed analysis.[40]

What can make a single currency work? An oft-used apt analogy is that of a three-legged stool. Economic theory and empirical evidence suggest that for a single currency to function properly, having monetary union is not enough. Along with monetary union, we have to have a political union and a fiscal union. If either of them is missing the other two will not work either; the stool will not be a stool.

Optimists, however, remain undeterred. Robert Mundell (2012) suggested going even further. He suggested creating a world currency that would combine "dollar–euro–yen or dollar–euro–yuan" and called it "DEY."[41]

The next chapter, Chapter 9, provides some concluding remarks. I present some questions that have not yet been answered in the literature.

Works Cited

Ashraf, Quamrul, and Oded Galor. "The 'Out of Africa' Hypothesis, Human Genetic Diversity, and Comparative Economic Development." *The American Economic Review* 103.1 (2013): 1–46. Print.

Chen, Lu, et al. "Identifying and Interpreting Apparent Neanderthal Ancestry in African Individuals." *Cell* 180 (2020): 1–11. Web.

[39] Spain's surplus turns into deficit. "Government deficit/surplus, revenue, expenditure and main aggregates, SNA93" https://stats.oecd.org/ (Accessed: March 29, 2020).

[40] *End This Depression Now!* Paul Krugman. *End This Depression Now!* New York, NY: W. W. Norton, 2012. Print.

[41] "DEY" Mundell: 568–78.

Dawkins, Richard. *The Ancestor's Tale: A Pilgrimage to the Dawn of Evolution*. New York, NY: Houghton Mifflin, 2004. Print.

Giandrea, Michael D., and Shawn A. Sprague. "Estimating the U.S. Labor Share." *Monthly Labor Review* (2017): A1. *ProQuest Business Collection (Alumni Edition)*. Web.

Grosjean, Pauline. *The Weight of History on European Cultural Integration: A Gravity Approach*. 101 Vols., 2011. Web.

Head, Keith, and Thierry Mayer. *Gravity Equations: Workhorse, Toolkit, and Cookbook*, April 2013. Web. http://blogs.ubc.ca/khead/files/2016/07/headmayer_revised.pdf.

Kouparitsas, Michael A. "Is the EMU a Viable Common Currency Area? A VAR Analysis of Regional Business Cycles." *Federal Reserve Bank of Chicago Economic Perspectives* 23.4 (1999): 2–20. Web.

Krugman, Paul. *End This Depression Now!* New York, NY: W. W. Norton, 2012. Print.

Krugman, Paul R., Maurice Obstfeld, and Marc J. Melitz. *International Economics: Theory and Policy*. 11th ed. New York, NY: Pearson, 2018. Print.

McCormick, Frank. *Covered Interest Arbitrage: Unexploited Profits? Comment*. 87 Vols., 1979. Web.

Mundell, Robert. "The Case for a World Currency." *Journal of Policy Modeling* 34.4 (2012): 568–78. Web.

Mundell, Robert A. "Currency Areas, Common Currencies, and EMU." *American Economic Review* 87.2 (1997): 214–16. Web.

Waugh, Michael E. *International Trade and Income Differences*. 100 Vols., 2010. Web.

CHAPTER 9

Some Concluding Thoughts

This is the final chapter of this book. In the preceding chapters, I have tried to explain the concept of money. I presented a brief history of money. I went over the various forms of money that humans have used over thousands of years of recorded history. In the preceding chapters, I have also shown how money affects the economy. In this chapter, I will make concluding remarks and present questions for future research.

9.1 A Longing for Gold

Gold holds a special place.[1] While our knowledge of the functioning of economy along with our understanding of the relationship between money and the economy has improved, this knowledge does not seem to have spread widely. We now know that changes in money supply are necessary for the smooth functioning of a modern economy. Experts in this field have presented a convincing case against having a fixed amount of money in a dynamic economy. Yet anytime a central bank changes money supply the motives of central bankers are considered sinister. This is so even in the developed world where central banks remain largely independent of political pressures. And this is especially so in the age of newfound appeal of populism across the globe. As we saw it in the

[1] Gold holds a special place. James Ledbetter. *One Nation Under Gold: How One Precious Metal Has Dominated the American Imagination for Four Centuries*. London: W. W. Norton, 2017. Print.

M. Ashraf, *Money*,
https://doi.org/10.1007/978-3-030-50378-9_9

dialog between the former Fed chair, Ben Bernanke, and the former Congressman, Ron Paul in Chapter 1, there seems almost an aching longing for having gold as the monetary standard.

The realization of the spread of COVID-19 was a shock to the world. In the United States, along with some people hoarding basic necessities from toilet paper to canned food, the demand for gold also increased.

Why do people want to hold gold? Some argue that since the value of gold is stable, the prices of goods and services will also be stable. An article in the *Wall Street Journal* put it this way[2]:

> Gold is popular with survivalists and conspiracy theorists but it is also a sensible addition to investment portfolios because its price tends to be relatively stable. It is especially in-demand during economic crises as a shield against inflation. When the Federal Reserve floods the economy with cash, like it is doing now, dollars can get less valuable.

The beliefs that gold holds its value and that prices would be stable if we were to either use gold as currency, or back currency by gold, do not pass the evidence test, however. In Fig. 9.1, I plot data that show the value of gold in terms of goods and services. As a comparison, the figure also plots data for personal consumption expenditure, chain-type index.

Note the fluctuations in the series representing "Value of Gold in Terms of Goods and Services." This series is represented by thicker of the two lines. The mean of this series is 270.44 with a standard deviation of 122.69. Compare this with the "Personal Consumption Expenditure Index." represented by the thinner of the two lines. The mean of this series is 88.51 with a standard deviation of 9.15. It is not hard to see that had gold, or gold-backed currency, been used as money, price fluctuations would have been much larger. The reason is that the supply of gold and the demand of gold is outside the control of the Fed. With the fixed quantity of gold, when economic activity changes (economy goes through business cycles, Chapter 6), prices of goods and services change along with it. The supply of fiat money, however, is in the control of the Fed. In order to maintain price stability, the Fed changes money supply accordingly. As we saw in Chapters 3 and 5, in the case of the Fed,

[2] COVID-19 and gold rush. https://www.wsj.com/articles/coronavirus-sparks-a-global-gold-rush-11585332624?mod=hp_featst_pos2 (Accessed: March 28, 2020).

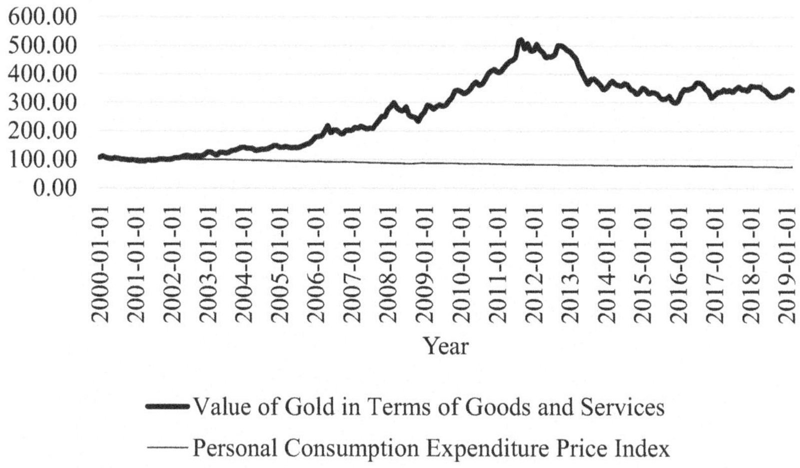

Fig. 9.1 Value of gold in terms of goods and services (*Source* Figure prepared by the author. *Data Source* ICE Benchmark Administration Limited [IBA], Gold Fixing Price 10:30 a.m. [London time] in London Bullion Market, based in US Dollars [GOLDAMGBD228NLBM], retrieved from FRED, Federal Reserve Bank of St. Louis. https://fred.stlouisfed.org/series/GOLDAMGBD228NLBM; US Bureau of Economic Analysis, Personal Consumption Expenditures: Chain-type Price Index [PCEPI], retrieved from FRED, Federal Reserve Bank of St. Louis. https://fred.stlouisfed.org/series/PCEPI [Accessed: April 22, 2020]. The series "Value of Gold in Terms of Goods and Services" is calculated as: (100/3.46276) × (GOLDAMGBD228NLBM/PCEPI), (100/3.46276) × (US $ per Troy Ounce/Index 2012 = 100), Monthly, and the series [PCEPI] is calculated as: (100/.01217) × (1/PCEPI), (100/.01217) × (1/Index 2012 = 100). See Stephen Williamson [2018] for calculation details)

price stability is one of its dual mandates. The other mandate is maintaining high employment. So the stability of the second series (Personal Consumption Expenditure Index) in Fig. 9.1 is not an accident. Any responsible central bank would do this.

Note that one can also construct similar series in terms for silver. One would find that the fluctuations in series would be similar to that of the first series in Fig. 9.1 (Value of Gold in Terms of Goods and Services). How about Bitcoin and other similar cryptocurrencies? One would, again, find that the fluctuations in series would be similar to that of the series labeled "Value of Gold in Terms of Goods and Services."

The reason is the fixed quantity of such mediums. While there are skeptics (Chapter 3), Bitcoin and its cousins, for instance, advertise a fixed quantity so that prices would not change much. However, since the economy goes through business cycles, having a fixed quantity of money is not a virtue when the objective is to have stable prices.

As we saw in Chapter 3, military ventures may be another reason that people want to have currency backed by gold or silver. People fear that unbacked currency may turn into a "Continental." If the reason for advocating specie-backed currency is price stability then, as we just saw, data do not support this contention.

9.2 A Longing for the Tangible

But what explains the increase in cash holdings during perceived and actual crises. After all, cash as it stands as it stands now, is not backed by gold or silver. For instance, on the eve of the twenty-first century, when people thought that ATMs would stop working due to computer glitches, the amount of dollars bills held increased significantly. In Fig. 9.2, I plot data for the total value of twenty-dollar bills in circulation.

The data plotted in Fig. 9.2 are in billions of US dollars. These are annual average data so the daily fluctuations have been smoothed out. Still note the jump in the value right before 2000. The total value in circulation jumped by about 27.7 percent. Similar trends are found in the five-, ten, and fifty-dollar denomination bills. The twenty-dollar bill, however, seems to be the most popular. Once the threat subsided and cooler heads prevailed, the value of hard cash held outside banks dropped to the trend level.

I mentioned that people want to hold on to something solid especially in times of crises, actual or perceived. Be it a dollar bill, a comfort blanket, or a loved one, the actual object is irrelevant. I wonder whether this desire is rooted in our evolutionary past. Our brains evolved in an environment where everything familiar was tangible. And even those tangibles have to have certain dimensional qualities.

Indeed, phenomenon that did not make sense was assigned to some entity that was tangible. Various cultures called it by various names—gods, God, Krishna, Yahweh, Allah, and many more. Readers may find

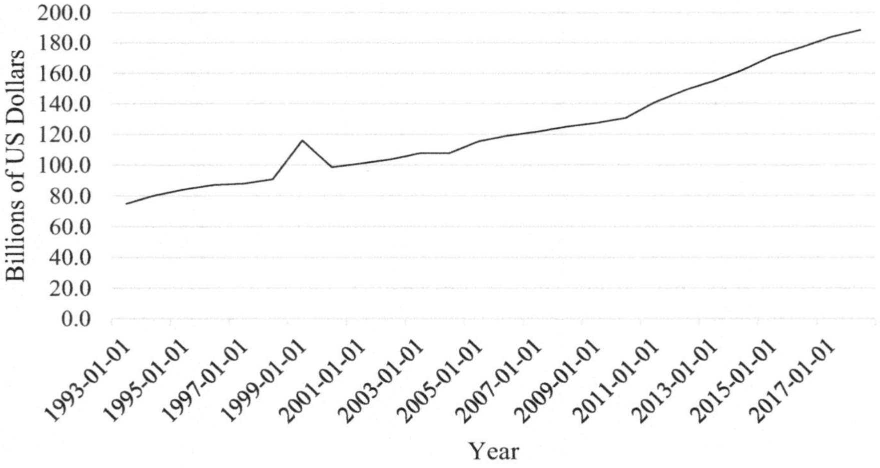

Fig. 9.2 Value of twenty-dollar bills in circulation (*Source* Figure prepared by the author. *Data Source* Board of Governors of the Federal Reserve System [US], Value of Currency in Circulation: $20 [CURRVAL20], retrieved from FRED, Federal Reserve Bank of St. Louis. https://fred.stlouisfed.org/series/CURRVAL20 [Accessed: April 23, 2020])

Robert Wright's book, *The Evolution of God*, useful.[3] Numerous qualities were assigned to various entities. (I wish Wright had titled his book "*The Evolution of the Concept of God*." This way he would have avoided the so-called use-mention error where one confuses the concept with the phenomenon.[4])

What explains the desire to hold gold or silver, or for that matter, the desire to hold cash. What this behavior may imply for the future of electronic forms of currencies. I leave these questions for future research. Evolutionary psychology is not my area of expertise. I leave this to the experts—the evolutionary psychologists.

And expertise matters. There aren't any authorities when it comes to knowledge. But there are certainly experts. When we need a blocked artery re-plumbed we go to a heart surgeon. When we need our hearts mended we go to a therapist. And when we want to give voice to our heartache we go to an artist—a poet, a musician, a painter, a sculptor. We confuse one with the other at our own peril. We confuse authority with expertise at our own peril.

Works Cited

Block, Ned. "What Is Dennett's Theory a Theory of?" *Philosophical Topics* 22.1 (1994): 23–40. *JSTOR*. Web.

Ledbetter, James. *One Nation Under Gold: How One Precious Metal Has Dominated the American Imagination for Four Centuries*. London: W. W. Norton, 2017. Print.

Williamson, Stephen. "Is Bitcoin a Waste of Resources?" *Federal Reserve Bank of St. Louis Review* 100.2 (2018): 107–15. Print.

Wright, Robert. *The Evolution of God*. New York, NY: Little, Brown, 2009. Print.

[3] Various names of gods. Robert Wright. *The Evolution of God*. New York, NY: Little, Brown, 2009. Print.

[4] Use-mention error. Ned Block. "What Is Dennett's Theory a Theory of?" *Philosophical Topics* 22.1 (1994): 23–40. *JSTOR*. Web. See also https://www.logicallyfallacious.com/logicalfallacies/Use-Mention-Error (Accessed: April 23, 2020).

Index

M. Ashraf, *Money*,
https://doi.org/10.1007/978-3-030-50378-9

The manufacturer's authorised representative in the EU is Springer Nature Customer Service Centre GmbH, Europaplatz 3, 69115 Heidelberg, Germany. If you have any concerns regarding our products, please contact ProductSafety@springernature.com

Printed and bound by CPI Group (UK) Ltd, Croydon, CR0 4YY

05/10/2026

02228121-0003